Global Development Finance

The Role of International Banking

I: Review, Analysis, and Outlook

Global Development Finance

The Role of International Banking

I: REVIEW, ANALYSIS, AND OUTLOOK

2008

THE WORLD BANK

This volume is a product of the staff of the International Bank for Reconstruction and Development / The World Bank. The findings, interpretations, and conclusions expressed in this paper do not necessarily reflect the views of the Executive Directors of The World Bank or the governments they represent.

The World Bank does not guarantee the accuracy of the data included in this work. The boundaries, colors, denominations, and other information shown on any map in this work do not imply any judgement on the part of The World Bank concerning the legal status of any territory or the endorsement or acceptance of such boundaries.

Cover art: Charles Arnoldi, "Jumbo," 2000 (detail).
Cover design: Drew Fasick.

ISBN: 978-0-8213-7388-0
eISBN: 978-0-8213-7389-7
DOI: 10.1596/978-0-8213-7388-0

The cutoff date for data used in this report was May 15, 2008. Dollars are current U.S. dollars unless otherwise specified.

Table of Contents

Tables

Figures

Boxes

Foreword

THE WORLD ECONOMY HAS ENTERED a period of financial market turmoil, slowing growth, and heightened inflationary pressures, a reality that poses complex policy challenges for the international community. Although developing countries have weathered the storm well thus far, they cannot afford to be complacent, particularly with unusually high uncertainty in the global macroeconomic outlook and with their growing trade and investment linkages with high-income countries. It is imperative that policy makers in both developing and high-income countries take firm actions to alleviate the impact of soaring food and energy prices on the poor while they address the longer-term challenges of financial globalization and economic interdependence.

An important consequence of this growing interdependence is that developing countries are now a locomotive of world economic growth, serving to cushion the impact of the slowdown in the United States. Global growth is projected to drop to 2.7 percent in 2008, from 3.7 percent in 2007, with much of the weakness originating in high-income countries. Developing-country growth is projected to decline—from 7.8 percent in 2007 to 6.5 percent in 2008—but remain well above the average of the 1980s, 1990s, and even the recent period of 2000–05, indicating that improved underlying structural factors are influencing overall economic performance.

The emerging-market asset class has moved into the mainstream in the wake of deepening financial integration across high-income and developing countries and much improved macroeconomic management in many developing countries. Private capital inflows to developing countries surged to an all-time high of $1 trillion in 2007, the fifth consecutive year of strong gains. It is important to keep in mind, however, that the bulk of private capital flows go to relatively few of the largest economies. Although some developing countries have recently gained access to the international bond market, many will continue to depend heavily on concessional loans and grants

from official sources to meet their financing needs. Thus, in the lead-up to the implementation review conference on the Monterrey Consensus of 2002 in Doha late this year, it is essential that donor countries reaffirm their commitment to fulfill the goals laid out in that consensus and make concrete progress to honor their commitments over the balance of the decade.

Concurrent with the ongoing globalization of financial markets, the world is confronting dramatic increases in commodity prices. Indeed, no other issue captures the complexity of the current policy agenda facing the international community than rapid inflation in food prices, particularly for such basic items as wheat and rice. For both food and agricultural commodities, the dominant drivers of higher prices are increased demand for biofuels in the United States and Europe, the weak dollar, and increased prices of fertilizer and energy inputs. Low inventories of grains and export restrictions by a number of countries have exacerbated the problem and contributed to the price increases. Additionally, weather patterns have reduced agricultural output in some countries, and speculation by commodity market investors has also pushed up prices. The increases have been largest for grains, which during the first months of 2008, were twice as expensive as a year earlier. High food prices are now the major force behind increased inflation across developing countries—and worryingly, they are hitting the poorest people the hardest.

Demand for international banking services in developing countries has evolved over time in response to their changing position on the global economic and financial stage. Attracted by the prospects of asset growth and risk diversification, foreign banks have expanded their business in developing countries through both cross-border and local market activity. The benefits of a growing international bank presence—enhanced sources of credit to firms and households, greater provision of sophisticated financial services, knock-on efficiency improvements in domestic banks, and in the long run, contributions to economic growth—are significant. Efforts to reap these benefits, though, require greater attention to bank soundness at entry through closer coordination with home-country regulators, and improved safeguards against the risk of financial contagion in the international banking system. A high premium should also be placed on parent banks' compliance with international standards and regulations regarding capital adequacy, corporate governance, and transparency. There is no room for complacency, as today's increasingly globalized financial system has the potential to speed the transmission of negative financial shocks throughout the world; in recent months, this potential has played out primarily through troubles in the banking industry.

Tackling these challenges requires collective resolve and clear thinking. That the magnitude of the credit turmoil was not on financial regulators' radar screens, however, reveals a critical shortcoming in the current framework of financial market supervision and regulation. In developing countries, it is vital that policy makers maintain their commitment to the sound macroeconomic and financial policies of the recent past while recognizing changes in the international financial climate and differences in their monetary framework, exchange-rate regime, regulatory and supervisory capability, level of financial sector development, and nature of exposure to foreign capital. In high-income countries, recent collaboration between major central banks on the provision of liquidity has been a positive step in calming market volatility. And reworking financial market supervision and regulation in several major financial centers could help avert another credit crisis, as could enforcing more transparency in complex financial instruments and institutions' exposure to them. In general, greater coordination between high-income and developing countries will contribute to greater international financial stability in the long run.

Global Development Finance is the World Bank's annual review of global financial conditions facing developing countries. The current volume provides analysis of key trends and prospects, including coverage of the role of international banking in developing countries. A separate volume contains detailed standardized external debt statistics for 134 countries, as well as summary data for regions and income groups. Additional material and sources, background papers, and a platform for interactive dialogue on the key issues can be found at www.worldbank.org/prospects. A companion online publication, "Prospects for the Global Economy," is available in English, French, and Spanish at www.worldbank.org/ globaloutlook.

Justin Yifu Lin
Chief Economist and Senior Vice President
The World Bank

Acknowledgments

THIS REPORT WAS PREPARED BY THE International Finance Team of the World Bank's Development Prospects Group (DECPG). Substantial support was also provided by staff from other parts of the Development Economics Vice Presidency, World Bank operational regions and networks, the International Finance Corporation, and the Multilateral Investment Guarantee Agency.

The principal author was Mansoor Dailami, with direction by Uri Dadush. The report was prepared under the general guidance of Alan Gelb, Acting World Bank Chief Economist and Senior Vice President. The principal authors of each chapter were:

Overview	Mansoor Dailami, with contributions from the International Finance Team
Chapter 1	Mick Riordan and Hans Timmer
Chapter 2	Douglas Hostland, Dilek Aykut, and Eung Ju Kim,
Chapter 3	Mansoor Dailami, Dilek Aykut, Robert Hauswald, and Haocong Ren

Preparation of the commercial and official debt restructuring appendixes was managed by Eung Ju Kim. Research assistance on chapter 3 was provided by Joaquin Mercado Sapiain; and the database on foreign banking ownership was developed by Stijn Claessens, Neeltje van Horen, Joaquin Mercado Sapiain, and Tugba Gurcanlar under a World Bank Research Support Budget. The financial flow and debt estimates were developed in a collaborative effort between DECPG and the Financial Data Team of the Development Data Group (DECDG), led by Ibrahim Levent and including Nevin Fahmy, Shelley Lai Fu, and Gloria R. Moreno. The main macroeconomic forecasts were prepared by the Global Trends Team of DECPG, led by Hans Timmer and including John Baffes, Maurizio Bussolo, Betty Dow, Teng Jiang, Annette de Kleine, Denis Medvedev, Don Mitchell,

Mick Riordan, Cristina Savescu, and Shane Streifel, with advice from Andrew Burns. Gauresh Rajadhyaksha managed and maintained the modeling and data systems.

Contributors to the regional outlooks include, among many others, Milan Brahmbhatt (East Asia and Pacific), Ivailo Izvorski (Europe and Central Asia), Augusto de la Torre (Latin America and the Caribbean), Jennifer Keller (Middle East and North Africa), Ernesto May (South Asia), and Shantayanan Devarajan and Sudhir Shetty (Sub-Saharan Africa).

Background notes and papers were prepared by Valentina Bruno (American University); Haluk Unal (University of Maryland); and from the World Bank, Constantino Hevia, Olga Sulla (ODA), William Shaw, and Dilip Ratha (workers' remittances). Paul Masson (University of Toronto) provided a background note and served as an adviser to chapter 3. The online companion publication, "Prospects for the Global Economy," was prepared by Andrew Burns, Sarah Crow, Cristina Savescu, Maria Amparo Gamboa with the assistance of the Global Trends Team. Technical help in the production of that Web site was provided by Reza Farivari, Saurabh Gupta, David Hobbs, Shahin Outadi, Raja Reddy Komati Reddy, Malarvizhi Veerappan, Cherin Verghese, and Kavita Watsa.

The report also benefited from the comments of the Bank's Executive Directors, made at an informal board meeting on May 15, 2008.

Many others provided inputs, comments, guidance, and support at various stages of the report's preparation. Marilou Uy, Barbara Mierau–Klein, Milan Brahmbhatt, Stijn Claessens (IMF), Charles Blitzer (IMF), Augusto de la Torre, and Michael Fuchs were discussants at the Bankwide review. In addition, within the Bank, comments and help were provided by Alan Gelb, Jeff Lewis, Doris Herrera-Pol, Pradeep Mitra, Willem van Eeghen, Ivailo V. Izvorski, Luis Serven, Maria Soledad Martínez Peria, Penelope Brook, Jacqueline Irving, and Alessandro Magnoli Bocchi.

Outside the Bank, several people contributed through meetings and correspondence on issues addressed in the report. Presentation of various parts of the report during late 2007 and early 2008 at several international conferences and seminars helped the authors better monitor and form views on the evolving financial market conditions and prospects. In this respect, special thanks are due to Christian Deseglise (HSBC), Marc Uzan, (Reinventing Bretton Woods Committee), Ricardo Espina (United Nations, Financing for Development Office), Joyce Chang (JP Morgan Chase Bank), and Aviva Werner (EMTA).

Dana Vorisek edited the report. Maria Amparo Gamboa provided assistance to the team. Araceli Jimeno and Merrell Tuck-Primdahl managed production and dissemination activities by DECPG. Book design and editorial production were coordinated by Janet Sasser of the World Bank Office of the Publisher.

Selected Abbreviations

ADB	Asian Development Bank	IDA	International Development Association
ATM	automated teller machine	IFC	International Finance Corporation
BIS	Bank for International Settlements	IFS	International Financial Statistics
BRICs	Brazil, Russia, India, and China		database (IMF)
CDOs	collateralized debt obligations	IMF	International Monetary Fund
CIS	Commonwealth of Independent States	IPO	initial public offering
DAC	Development Assistance Committee	IRAI	IDA Resource Allocation Index
EC	European Commission	LDC	least developed country
ECB	European Central Bank	LIBOR	London interbank offered rate
EU	European Union	M&A	mergers and acquisitions
FDI	foreign direct investment	M2	broad money
GDP	gross domestic product	NAFTA	North American Free Trade Agreement
Gemloc	Global Emerging Markets Local Currency Bond Program	OECD	Organisation for Economic Co-operation and Development
GNI	gross national income	OPEC	Orgaization of Peteroleum Exporting Countries
HIPC	heavily indebted poor country		
IBRD	International Bank for Reconstruction and Development	saar	seasonally adjusted annual rate
		WGI	*Worldwide Global Indicators*
ICRG	International Country Risk Guide	WTO	World Trade Organization

Overview

THE WORLD ECONOMY HAS EN-
dured a period of financial turmoil and slowing growth since mid-2007. As these events
have unfolded, financing conditions facing developing countries have shifted from the benign environment of 2002–06 to the current state of heightened
market volatility and tight credit conditions. With
these tensions setting the stage, 2008 is shaping up
to be a challenging year for development finance.

Strong fundamentals underpinned most developing countries' initial resilience to deteriorating
economic and financial conditions. As of mid-
2007, total developing-country foreign exchange
reserves amounted to $3.2 trillion (23.6 percent of
their combined GDP, with the top five countries
accounting for 68 percent of the total figure),
many countries were posting strong economic
growth, emerging equity markets were rallying
(outperforming mature markets by a wide margin
for the fourth consecutive year), and spreads on
emerging-market sovereign bonds had reached
record low levels. The balance of risks, however,
has now plainly tilted to the downside. Various indicators signal that economic growth in the United
States and Europe is slowing more than previously
expected. Across the developing world, inflationary pressures, stemming from dramatic increases
in energy and food prices in many cases, compli-
cate the role that monetary and fiscal policy can
play in maintaining macroeconomic stability over
the medium term. Meanwhile, as financial services
have become increasingly globalized, the reconcili-
ation of national autonomy with the demands of
international banking has become more difficult.

The international financial community has a
complex burden to shoulder in ensuring that the
turmoil does not undermine long-term global
growth and stability. In mature markets, governments have responded with a series of unprecedented policy measures aimed at preserving
orderly conditions in certain financial market
segments and instilling confidence in the financial
system as a whole. Yet developing and high-
income countries alike face the challenge of balancing short-term and long-term policy goals.
Striking the appropriate balance will vary from
country to country, but in general policy makers
need to recognize the limitations of activist measures. Countries that undertake prudent fiscal
planning and use monetary policy instruments to
effectively maintain price stability will be better
placed to sustain growth over the long term.

Global growth is slowing

The slowdown in high-income countries has
become more apparent since the end of 2007.
GDP growth in the United States is expected to decline from 2.2 percent in 2007 to 1.1 percent in
2008, significantly weaker than the World Bank's
December 2007 projection of 1.9 percent. Although to a lesser extent, growth projections for
Japan and the Euro Area for 2008 have also been
revised downward, to 1.4 percent and 1.7 percent,
respectively. The incipient downshift in high-
income countries is expected to be relatively short
lived, however—growth rates are expected to pick
up in 2009 and to fully recover by 2010.

Growth in developing countries will also decline in 2008. Working together, factors including
the slowdown in high-income countries, financial

market turmoil, and overheating in several developing countries are expected to curtail growth in developing countries as a whole from 7.8 percent in 2007 to 6.5 percent in 2008, considerably below the projection of 7.1 percent made in December 2007. The deceleration is expected to be broadly based across most developing regions, with the largest declines in East Asia and the Pacific (1.9 percentage points) and Latin America and the Caribbean (1.2 percentage points). The decline in the East Asia and Pacific region will be concentrated in China, where growth is expected to fall by 2.5 percentage points. Growth in Sub-Saharan Africa, in contrast, is expected to pick up moderately in 2008, reaching 6.3 percent, the highest rate in 38 years, but then decline to 5.9 percent by 2010, a rate slightly above the average over the past five years. In general, the slowdown in developing countries is expected to be more moderate but longer lasting than that in developed countries, reflecting an adjustment to a more sustainable growth rate. Despite the adjustment, the projected developing-country growth rate of 6.4 percent in 2009–10 is above the average over the first half of this decade (5.6 percent) and well above the average of the 1980s and 1990s (3.4 percent), illustrating the acceleration of the underlying growth potential.

The striking rise in goods and services trade between developing and high-income countries and among developing countries (South-South trade) over the past few years and the increase in flows of labor and capital across borders imply that economic and financial links are now stronger than ever. These tighter links will tend to accentuate the transmission of cyclical fluctuations across countries, in contradistinction to the notion that the business cycle in developing countries has become decoupled from that in high-income countries. Although developing and developed countries have become more closely integrated, trend growth rates in developing countries will continue to be significantly higher, indicating that underlying structural factors are playing an important role in overall economic performance. While the current slowdown in high-income countries is expected to curb the cyclical element of growth in developing countries, it is unlikely to affect the underlying trend component, implying that improved policies, higher investments, and technological progress in developing countries will support robust growth over the longer term.

Tighter financing conditions are curbing private capital flows

Net private capital flows to developing countries increased by $269 billion in 2007, reaching a record $1 trillion. This marks five consecutive years of strong gains in both private debt and equity components. Net bank lending and bond flows have increased from virtually zero in 2002 to 3 percent of developing countries' GDP in 2007, while net foreign direct and portfolio equity flows have increased from 2.7 percent of GDP to 4.5 percent. The regional composition of private debt and equity flows became more broadly based in 2007, as shares shifted away from the East Asia and Pacific and Europe and Central Asia regions toward Latin America and the Caribbean and South Asia. Gains were especially strong in Latin America and the Caribbean, where the share of total private debt and equity doubled from 10 to 20 percent, while the share going to Europe and Central Asia declined from 48 to 40 percent.

Although financial institutions in developing countries are believed to have little direct exposure to U.S. subprime mortgage securities or related assets, large write-downs on mortgages and other assets incurred by major banks and securities firms that operate worldwide have forced these institutions to reduce lending activity in order to restore their balance sheets. The manner in which such credit retrenchment will affect the financing of corporate borrowers in developing countries depends on the nature of international credit intermediation—cross-border versus locally funded credit, foreign banks' internal capital market operations, and the maturity structure of credit extended. Both experience and research indicate that home-country conditions matter for foreign banks' credit supply behavior and reaction to financial shocks.

The practical impacts of ongoing credit turmoil in mature markets have been particularly visible in markets for emerging-market corporate borrowers, who have seen their access to syndicated bank lending affected in terms of cost and volume of deals transacted. Currently available evidence indicates that both the number of loans signed and the total deal value declined in the fourth quarter of 2007 and the first quarter of 2008.

Developing countries have become more vulnerable to external shocks

Most developing countries were on a strong footing when economic and financial conditions began to deteriorate in mid-2007, although the external financial position of many countries has weakened in the interim. Current account balances, for example, have worsened in two-thirds of developing countries. (China and major oil exporters such as Algeria, the Islamic Republic of Iran, Nigeria, República Bolivariana de Venezuela, and the Russian Federation are exceptions; their current account balances improved significantly in 2007.) Half of developing countries ran current account deficits in excess of 5 percent of GDP in 2007. But alongside this trend, developing countries have continued to cumulate foreign exchange reserves, providing a substantial buffer should they encounter trouble meeting their external financing needs. Foreign exchange reserve holdings by developing countries increased from 100 percent of the value of their short-term debt in 2000 to almost 320 percent in 2007. Three-quarters of the increase, however, was held by the BRICs (Brazil, Russia, India, and China).

Separately, the dramatic rise in global food and other commodity prices has worsened the external position of some developing countries over the past few years. For example, in Lesotho, an extreme case, commodity price increases worsened the trade balance by an estimated $550 million over 2003–07 as the country's current account deficit widened from 12.6 to 27.4 percent of GDP. Lesotho received only $315 million in foreign aid over 2002–06, enough to cover slightly more than half of the external financing gap caused by the rise in commodity prices. However, most other developing countries have seen higher food import costs offset by increased export earnings from other commodities, such as metals or oil.

The deterioration in external positions over the past year has left many developing countries more vulnerable to external shocks. Countries with heavy external financing needs are most vulnerable, particularly in cases where private debt inflows into the banking sector have fueled rapid expansion in domestic credit and raised inflationary pressures. The surge in energy and food prices has intensified such pressures, making a timely monetary policy response all the more important for maintaining macroeconomic stability and protecting the hard-fought-for gains in credibility achieved over the past several years. Moreover, the sharp rise in oil prices over the past six months may threaten growth in a way that the increases between 2003 and 2006 did not. These earlier increases occurred in a context of strong growth, low and stable inflation, and healthy current account positions that facilitated developing countries' absorption of the oil price rise. With inflation intensifying, growth slowing, and current account deficits worsening in many developing countries, the recent hikes may adversely affect growth and domestic demand more strongly than currently projected.

Soaring food and energy prices pose daunting challenges

Prices of food staples have soared more than 100 percent since 2005 in nominal dollar terms, though the rise is much less when domestic inflation and exchange rates in developing countries are considered. Nevertheless, the increase in food prices is a cause for great concern. The real price of rice hit a 19-year high in March 2008; almost simultaneously, the real price of wheat reached a 28-year high that was almost twice the average price over the past 25 years. In some countries, escalating food and energy prices have more than offset the benefits of robust economic growth, reducing the purchasing power of the poorest people, many of whom have no margin for survival. These increases have serious implications for developing countries' abilities to reduce poverty and make progress on the other Millennium Development Goals. Countries hardest hit are in dire need of foreign aid. Donors, however, have made slow progress in scaling up development assistance in recent years.

Even though more low-income countries have accessed the international bond market in recent years (Ghana, Mongolia, Nigeria, and Vietnam have all issued first-time external bonds since 2005), most private capital flows to developing countries go to just a few large economies. Low-income developing countries still depend heavily on grants and concessional loans from official sources to meet their financing needs. In 2006, net disbursements of official development assistance (ODA) exceeded net private debt flows in almost two-thirds of developing countries. Although these countries are less vulnerable than other developing countries to an abrupt downturn in the credit cycle, many of them are battling a much more fundamental challenge: the dramatic rise in food and energy prices.

At the United Nations Conference on Financing for Development in Monterrey in 2002, participants agreed to take steps to correct dramatic shortfalls in the resources required to achieve internationally agreed-upon development goals. The United Nations urged donor countries to make concrete efforts to increase ODA toward its target of 0.7 percent of their gross national income (GNI). Although debt relief continues to play an important role in the development agenda, especially for the poorest countries burdened by heavy debt service payments, donors pledged that debt relief would not displace other components of ODA. Five years on, little progress has been made. Net ODA disbursements by the 22 member countries of the Development Assistance Committee (DAC) of the Organisation for Economic Co-operation and Development totaled $103.7 billion in 2007, down from a record $107.1 billion in 2005. The decrease in ODA over the past two years largely reflects the return of debt relief to more normal levels following two extraordinary Paris Club agreements in 2005, under which Iraq and Nigeria received a total of $19.5 billion in debt relief from their Paris Club creditors, followed by another $13 billion in 2006. Excluding debt relief, ODA increased from 0.23 percent of the GNI of donor countries to 0.25 percent between 2002 and 2007, still well below the 0.33 percent attained in the early 1990s. Donors would have to increase ODA by an annual rate of more than 14 percent, three times that observed in the years since the Monterrey Consensus, over the balance of the decade just to meet existing commitments. Even with that rate of growth, ODA net of debt relief would be only 0.35 percent of GNI in DAC countries by 2010, half the U.N. target. This year will be a critical one for development finance as donors meet to address progress made and to reaffirm goals and commitments at the United Nations' Follow-up

International Conference on Financing for Development to Review the Implementation of the Monterrey Consensus.

Internationalization of banking offers distinct economic benefits

While the current weakness in international banks' balance sheets will adversely affect some borrowers in developing countries, the positive implications of changes in the nature and character of international credit intermediation are likely to be more enduring. Foreign bank presence today constitutes an important structural feature of the banking industry in many developing countries, particularly countries in Europe and Central Asia, Latin America and the Caribbean, and Sub-Saharan Africa. Driven by technological advances, easing regulatory constraints, and global economic integration, foreign banks have dramatically increased their cross-border lending to, and investment in, developing countries. As a result, developing countries have reaped substantial gains through the increased availability of finance to credit-constrained firms and households, the provision of sophisticated financial services, and incentives for improved efficiency as domestic banks compete with foreign entrants. Such benefits, which can make critical contributions to growth and development, deserve to be protected.

The process, however, needs to be carefully managed because the presence of international banks also presents some potential risks. First, as has been seen recently, international banks can transmit adverse financial shocks around the globe: pressure on major banks' capital positions, deteriorating liquidity positions in interbank markets, and tightening of credit standards can lead international banks to sharply reduce credit to developing countries. Second, the ability of foreign-owned banks to raise funding from their parent banks abroad can fuel a domestic credit boom, potentially offsetting efforts by central banks to contain domestic inflationary pressures or restrict capital inflows. Efforts to reap the benefits of foreign bank presence while controlling risks could focus on vetting the soundness of entering banks, in part by soliciting information from home-country financial authorities and by ensuring effective coordination between host- and home-country supervisors.

Current challenges require an enlightened international policy response

Rarely has the international community been called upon to respond to so many complex policy challenges at once—from immediate actions to address soaring global food and energy prices and the taming of volatility in private global finance to the needs for mitigating the effects of high-income-country slowdown and sustaining economic momentum without jeopardizing long-term growth and stability. Tackling such challenges requires collective resolve and clear thinking. It is crucial that developing-country policy makers renew their commitment to the sound policies of the recent past while recognizing the implications of changes in the financial climate currently under way. Priorities should include sustaining the structural changes and institution-building efforts that have allowed developing countries' continued integration into global capital markets, strengthening regulation and supervision aimed at limiting currency and maturity mismatches, and in countries that hold a large share of their foreign debt in short-term instruments, intensifying efforts to monitor foreign borrowing by banks and risk management strategies by corporations with access to external debt markets.

Recent events in financial markets have illustrated once again that policy coordination among the world's major central banks is necessary at times of stress to prevent global instability. To date, coordination has mainly taken the form of joint liquidity provision, and that has been critically successful in preventing a liquidity squeeze in global interbank markets developing into broader systemic risk. Given the extent of cross-border exposures, coordination of financial regulation is also necessary in the current environment, as inadequate regulation in one country can have major repercussions in others. In this context, recent recommendations by the Financial Stability Forum to raise capital requirements for certain structured credit products, to increase oversight of banks' risk management practices, and to improve credit rating agencies' safeguards against conflicts of interest are welcome. As for interest-rate policy, synchronized moves among central banks are limited because of the nature of the current global payment imbalances, which dictate differentiated policy responses and approaches.

Helping developing countries adjust to soaring food prices represents a major policy challenge and the most critical in terms of its impact on the poor. In the short term, donors are urged to augment financing to the United Nations World Food Programme to help address this emergency in a timely manner. In addition, providing more aid in the form of budgetary support would enable developing countries to extend safety net programs, such as targeted cash transfers, to the most vulnerable groups and to expand risk management instruments to protect the poor. Over the longer term, assistance aimed at developing domestic agricultural sectors would help alleviate the impact of high food prices on the poor and would promote sustainable employment and growth.

These are the themes and concerns of this year's edition of *Global Development Finance*.

1

Prospects for Developing Countries

TURMOIL IN FINANCIAL MARKETS, slower growth in high-income countries, and rising inflation have all adversely affected growth prospects for developing countries over the near term. Most countries have shown impressive resilience in this turbulent environment, and growth for developing countries as a group is expected to moderate from 7.8 percent in 2007 to a still strong 6.5 percent in 2008 (table 1.1). However, vulnerable countries that depend on foreign capital flows are likely to experience a sharper slowdown. Moreover, despite strong production growth at the aggregate level, higher food and energy prices have caused real incomes to decline, significantly increasing the hardships faced by the very poor, particularly in urban centers.

Not all of the news is gloomy. In some respects, the slowing of the global economy is welcome, coming as it does on the heels of several years of very fast growth and increasing signs of overheating, as illustrated by a dramatic increase in international commodity prices and by excessive inflationary pressures in a number of countries. And the slowdown in U.S. domestic demand, along with the depreciation of the dollar, is helping to resolve long-standing global imbalances. The U.S. current account deficit narrowed from 6.2 percent of GDP in 2006 to 4.9 percent during the final quarter of 2007. These factors bode well for longer-term prospects, once the current cyclical adjustment—heightened by continuing financial turbulence—comes to closure.

But now, more than at any other time in recent years, the uncertainty surrounding the outlook is quite pronounced and tilted to the downside. The turmoil in financial markets has deepened since late 2007. Major banks, securities firms, and financial guarantors have announced sizable valuation losses on mortgages and other assets, which have strained their balance sheets. The ensuing tightening of credit conditions, and the disruption to the financial system more generally, have been felt most directly by high-income economies, particularly the United States, where the housing sector has borne the brunt of the fallout from the subprime crisis. The slowdown in the United States and in much of Europe appears to have intensified since the end of 2007, and GDP for the high-income members of the Organisation for Economic Co-operation and Development (OECD) is now projected to grow 1.5 percent in 2008, down a full percentage point from 2007. Growth in developing countries is projected to slow by 1.3 percentage points in 2008, but at an expected 6.5 percent, growth will remain well above the average gains of the 1980s (2.9 percent), the 1990s (3.8 percent), and even the more recent period 2000–05 (5.3 percent) (figure 1.1).

Moreover, the continued strength of domestic demand and imports in developing countries is helping to cushion the global effects of the slowdown in high-income countries. Developing-country imports have become an increasingly important driver of global growth. More than half of the growth in global import demand is now originating in developing countries. Partly as a result, U.S. and, to a lesser extent, European exports have been booming—helping to moderate the extent of decline in their GDP growth.

The continued strong growth of developing countries despite the financial turmoil and slowdown among OECD countries demonstrates their increased resilience to external shocks. Compared with earlier episodes of global financial turbulence, far fewer developing countries are currently

Table 1.1 The global outlook in summary
(percentage change from previous year unless noted)

Indicator	2006	2007e	2008f	2009f	2010f
Global conditions					
World trade volume	9.7	7.5	4.5	7.2	8.4
Consumer prices					
G-7 countries[a,b]	2.0	1.9	2.6	1.8	2.0
United States	3.2	2.9	3.9	2.3	2.5
Commodity prices (US$ terms)					
Non-oil commodities	29.1	17.0	24.1	−8.2	−9.0
Oil price (US$ per barrel)[c]	64.3	71.1	108.1	105.5	98.5
Oil price (percentage change)	20.4	10.6	52.1	−2.4	−6.7
Manufactures unit export value[d]	1.6	3.9	6.8	0.7	1.4
Interest rates					
$, 6-month (percent)	5.2	5.2	3.0	3.8	4.5
€, 6-month (percent)	3.1	4.4	4.5	4.0	4.5
Real GDP growth[e]					
World	4.0	3.7	2.7	3.0	3.4
Memo item: World (PPP weights)[f]	5.4	5.4	4.3	4.5	4.8
High-income countries	**3.0**	**2.6**	**1.6**	**2.0**	**2.5**
OECD countries	2.9	2.5	1.5	1.8	2.3
Euro Area	2.8	2.6	1.7	1.5	1.9
Japan	2.4	2.0	1.4	1.6	2.1
United States	2.9	2.2	1.1	1.9	2.5
Non-OECD countries	5.7	5.5	4.8	4.8	5.0
Developing countries	**7.6**	**7.8**	**6.5**	**6.4**	**6.4**
East Asia and Pacific	9.7	10.5	8.6	8.5	8.4
China	11.1	11.9	9.4	9.2	9.0
Indonesia	5.5	6.3	6.0	6.4	6.5
Thailand	5.1	4.8	5.0	5.4	5.5
Europe and Central Asia	7.3	6.8	5.8	5.4	5.4
Russian Federation	7.4	8.1	7.1	6.3	6.0
Turkey	6.9	4.5	4.0	4.3	5.0
Poland	6.1	6.5	5.7	5.1	5.0
Latin America and the Caribbean	5.6	5.7	4.5	4.3	4.2
Brazil	3.8	5.4	4.6	4.4	4.5
Mexico	4.8	3.3	2.7	3.5	3.6
Argentina	8.5	8.7	6.9	5.0	4.5
Middle East and North Africa	5.4	5.7	5.5	5.3	5.1
Egypt, Arab Rep. of	6.8	7.1	7.0	6.8	6.5
Iran, Islamic Rep. of	5.9	7.6	5.7	5.2	4.5
Algeria	1.8	3.0	3.5	3.5	4.0
South Asia	9.0	8.2	6.6	7.2	7.6
India	9.7	8.7	7.0	7.5	8.0
Pakistan	6.9	6.4	5.0	5.5	6.0
Bangladesh	6.6	6.4	5.0	5.5	6.0
Sub-Saharan Africa	5.8	6.1	6.3	5.6	5.9
South Africa	5.4	5.1	4.2	4.4	4.8
Nigeria	6.0	6.1	7.9	7.2	6.6
Kenya	6.1	6.3	5.0	5.7	5.9
Memorandum items					
Developing countries					
excluding transition countries	7.6	7.9	6.5	6.5	6.5
excluding China and India	6.0	6.1	5.2	5.0	5.0

Source: World Bank.
Note: PPP = purchasing power parity; e = estimate; f = forecast.
a. Canada, France, Germany, Italy, Japan, the United Kingdom, and the United States.
b. In local currency, aggregated using 2000 GDP weights.
c. Simple average of Dubai, Brent, and West Texas Intermediate.
d. Unit value index of manufactured exports from major economies, expressed in US$.
e. GDP in 2000 constant dollars; 2000 prices and market exchange rates.
f. GDP measured at 2000 PPP weights.

Figure 1.1 Real GDP growth, 1980–2010

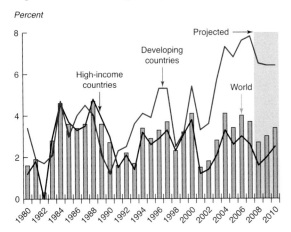

Source: World Bank data and forecasts.

burdened by large external imbalances or heavy external financing requirements. Many countries have accumulated ample foreign reserves and have reduced their external debt burdens significantly. Unlike high-yield corporate bonds in the United States, where spreads now stand 400 basis points above the levels of summer 2007, emerging-market sovereign spreads increased just 120 basis points, to stand now at 310 points. Because the yield on U.S. Treasury bonds fell by about the same amount, yields on developing-country sovereign bonds have remained relatively stable. And most countries have expanded and diversified their export base, a move that facilitates external adjustment.

Notwithstanding this strong performance among developing countries, the volume of world trade tends to show more pronounced cyclical swings than GDP does and is projected to slow to 4.5 percent in 2008, substantially less than the 10 percent expansion of trade just two years ago. At the same time, there are signs that capital flows to developing countries are slowing (see chapter 2). That combination may place particular stress and force significant adjustment on several developing countries with large current account deficits. In particular, the resilience of private corporate balance sheets in these countries will be tested, as the private sector was in many cases the main beneficiary of the surge in international lending in recent years. An additional challenge for the oil-importing developing countries is the further rise in energy prices, which has again increased import bills and financing requirements.

The sharp rise in food and energy prices of the past few years has cut into the real incomes of the very poor and raised inflation in a growing number of countries. Moreover, stocks of several major foodstuffs are at record low levels, raising the specter of an even sharper rise in food prices should a major crop failure occur in 2008. In this context, governments face a daunting challenge of protecting the most vulnerable of their citizens in a fiscally responsible and sustainable manner. As much as possible governments should use or expand social safety nets to provide targeted income support instead of subsidizing prices generally, which can be extremely expensive, and without reverting to export bans or price controls, which can jeopardize incentives to expand agricultural production and aggravate shortages in other countries.

Policy makers in developing and high-income countries alike face the difficult challenge of managing the short-term slowing of their economies and potential financial stress on one hand and the risks associated with rising inflation on the other. While a rapid and substantial slowdown would be unwelcome, some easing in activity for most developing countries is probably desirable. As a result, automatic stabilizers should be allowed to function, but given the inherent difficulties in fine-tuning an economy, in most countries a strongly stimulative policy stance would be a mistake. With very few exceptions, most countries should follow a fiscal and monetary policy approach that emphasizes medium-term fiscal sustainability and price stability. Moreover, a strengthening of financial sector supervision and review of risk management capabilities of financial institutions take on increased importance at the present juncture.

Global growth
High-income OECD countries

The U.S. economic slowdown intensified in 2007, dominated by a substantial contraction in residential investment (home construction). Falling home prices and mounting foreclosures tied to subprime mortgages helped to set the stage for turmoil in financial markets, though the roots of the housing crisis go deeper, into the loose monetary policy following the recession in 2000–01, surging home prices, and a search for yield among investors. Financial turbulence and the consequent freeze-up of lending, in conjunction with rising fuel and other import prices (due in part to the falling dollar), began to weigh on other components of domestic spending. Overall, U.S. GDP growth eased from 2.9 percent during 2006 to 2.2 percent in 2007, but increased only at a 0.6 percent annual pace in the final quarter of the year. The falloff of U.S. domestic demand continued in the first quarter of 2008.

Although GDP registered another small gain of 0.6 percent during the first quarter (in large measure due to a 0.8 point contribution to growth from stock building), consumption eased to 1 percent growth (seasonally adjusted annual rate [saar]), and business investment dropped 2.5 percent in the quarter from an increase of 6 percent in the previous period. Net exports added a strong 0.6 points to growth. This profile—stagnation in domestic absorption, offset by positive impetus from trade—is likely to continue, keeping U.S. GDP growth soft over the coming quarters.

In Europe and Japan, the second half of the year is expected to be weaker than the first, as leading indicators point to weakness in activity over the period three to six months ahead (figure 1.2). Based on these indicators, the strong outcomes for GDP growth in the first quarter, Euro Area (3 percent, saar) and Japan (3.3 percent), are unlikely to be repeated.

Figure 1.2 Leading indicators of growth in high-income OECD countries

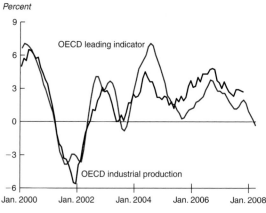

Percent

Sources: World Bank and OECD.

Figure 1.3 Trends in U.S. home sales

Index, Oct. 2005 = 100

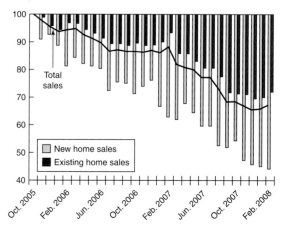

Sources: National Association of Realtors and U.S. Department of Commerce.

United States

The slowdown in U.S. GDP reflects a sharp weakening of domestic demand, which has been partially offset by strong gains in net exports. Growth in domestic demand eased from 2.8 percent in 2006 to 1.5 percent in 2007, growing at less than half the pace of GDP; domestic demand actually declined in the final quarter of the year. Much of the slowdown can be explained by the recession in the housing sector, which is the worst since 1982. Overall, residential investment fell by 17 percent in 2007, sales of new homes were down a whopping 56 percent, and sales of existing homes dropped 28 percent (figure 1.3). Housing construction was off 25 percent in the final quarter of 2007 (saar) and U.S. home prices fell between 7 and 11 percent over the past 12 months.[1] The weakness in domestic demand also reflects an end to housing price–induced dissaving on the part of consumers, weaker real-income growth, and rising fuel, food, and import prices. Taken together, these factors help explain why high-frequency data on consumer sentiment and retail sales are much closer to recession levels than data on industrial orders and production might suggest (figure 1.4).

The U.S. traded sector has performed much better. The sharp depreciation of the dollar against the major currencies (and a large number of developing-country units), together with still-strong

Figure 1.4 U.S. employment growth and retail sales volume

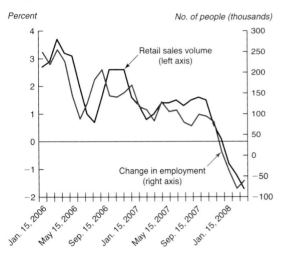

Source: U.S. Departments of Commerce and Labor.

Note: Change in employment is expressed as a three-month moving average. Growth of retail sales is expressed as percentage change of a three-month moving average year over year.

Figure 1.5 Cuts in main U.S. interest rate

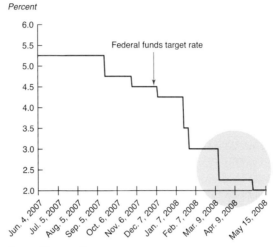

Source: Thomson/Datastream.

growth in export markets, supported U.S. export volumes at a 6.5 percent pace during the fourth quarter of 2007, in the wake of a robust 19 percent gain during the third quarter (saar). At the same time, weak domestic demand meant that imports declined 1.4 percent. As a result, net exports contributed more than 1.6 and 1 percent to GDP growth in the third and fourth quarters. And the U.S. current account deficit declined from 6.2 percent of GDP in 2006 to 4.9 percent by the fourth quarter of 2007.

As noted, the 0.6 percent growth of the first quarter of 2008 reflected continued positive contributions of net-exports to growth, and weakening of key segments of domestic demand. The falloff in residential investment accelerated to a 27 percent pace (saar); and the decline in home prices intensified. Manufacturing output dropped sharply in response to the ongoing difficulties in housing as well as in autos. And retail volumes for goods slipped to negative ground, as soaring food and fuel prices took a toll on household purchasing power.

Since August 2007 the Federal Reserve has cut its main policy interest rate 7 times for a total of 325 basis points, bringing the federal funds rate to 2.0 percent as of April 2008 (figure 1.5). Interest

rates faced by business and consumers have fallen by much less. Thirty-year mortgage rates stand at 5.75 percent—about 25 basis points lower than a year ago, while adjustable rate mortgages are available at about 5 percent. Interest rates facing prime borrowers remain low in historical perspective, but borrowing criteria have tightened. Expectations of deteriorating consumer servicing of debt and rolling-credit obligations have maintained rates on credit card and auto loans at high levels. And counterparty risk (banks not knowing the underlying financial condition of their transaction partner) plays an important role for business finance. Moreover, given uncertainty in interbank trades and the need to accommodate balance sheet losses, banks have been quite leery to lend.

Policy easing has not been confined to interest rates but also includes measures to shore up financial markets, addressing the waning of confidence in the banking system. The Federal Reserve, in concert with central banks in Europe, has made large amounts of liquidity available to both the traditional banking and investment banking systems; that has included giving nonbank financial institutions access to its discount window for a limited time following the dramatic collapse of Bear Sterns in late March 2008. Notwithstanding these steps, deep uncertainties continue to characterize financial markets, suggesting that significant time will be required before they return to normalcy. At the same time the long-term consequences of the substantial monetary policy easing of the past few months will not be visible for some time, but there is a risk that the extent of the policy easing could contribute to future inflationary pressures.

In addition to the steps taken by the Federal Reserve, the U.S. Congress enacted a fiscal stimulus package worth some $168 billion, which is expected to provide a fillip to consumer demand in the third quarter.[2] Overall, GDP is expected to grow 1.1 percent in 2008, about half as quickly as in 2007, although financial uncertainties tilt risks well to the downside. On the back of further reductions in home prices that help restore affordability to newcomers in the market, continued gains in exports, and moderation in energy prices accompanying slowing U.S. and global demand for petroleum, a rebound in U.S. activity should be taking shape by late 2008. Notably, as current housing starts fall well short of new household formation, the decline in residential investment is expected to bottom out later in 2008. Growth anticipated for 2009, at 1.9 percent, reflects these developments, and recovery is expected to come to fuller fruition by 2010, with GDP gains registering 2.5 percent. The U.S. current account deficit is expected to narrow to 5.1 percent of GDP by 2010 from 5.4 percent in 2007.

Euro Area

Economic activity in the Euro Area peaked in 2006 at 2.9 percent. Output slowed in 2007, expanding only 1.4 percent (saar) in the fourth quarter, but registered a strong 2.6 percent for the year as a whole. Despite falling unemployment, consumer confidence waned and household consumption increased by only 1.5 percent. Investment demand held up better, increasing 4.1 percent, but capital outlays faded over the course of the year, from 7 percent in the first quarter to 2 percent in the last quarter (saar). Weaker export growth (attributable in part to the 10.7 percent appreciation of the euro vis-à-vis the dollar over the year) also contributed to the easing pace of GDP growth. Overall, European exports slowed from 8.4 percent in 2006 to 5.5 percent in 2007, with German export volumes declining rapidly toward the end of the year (figure 1.6).

During the first months of 2008, the euro appreciated an additional 7.2 percent against the dollar, sending exports destined for the U.S.

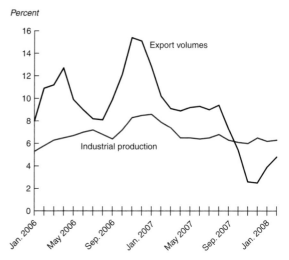

Figure 1.6 Trends in German exports and industrial production

Percent

Source: Eurostat through Thomson/DataStream.

Note: Export volumes and industrial production are expressed as percentage change for a three-month moving average year over year.

market into decline. Yet for European exporters, as well as for those in East Asia, the potential remains for growing sales by targeting markets outside of the dollar zone. Asian (including Japanese) exports to Europe have been considerable in the past months, while European exports outside of the United States have been robust. German exports to countries outside Europe gained 12 percent in January 2008 (year-on-year), while exports to EU partners advanced 7.7 percent. Similar developments in France are under way. These advances have been a key factor in buoying business sentiment in the Euro Area, underpinning a degree of confidence among executives that Europe can weather the U.S. downturn.

Following the disappointing 1.4 percent GDP advance (saar) of the final quarter of 2007, preliminary figures for European growth in the first quarter of 2008 (3 percent) were quite strong. However, the picture is becoming more diverse, with apparent robust growth in Germany (6.3 percent), which benefits from export opportunities for investment goods in developing countries, and further waning of momentum in southern Europe and the United Kingdom. Moreover, high-frequency numbers suggest softer GDP outturns for the coming quarters.

On balance, GDP in high-income Europe is expected to slow further in 2008, coming in at 1.7 percent. Although exports to the developing world appear to be maintaining momentum, domestic demand is expected to respond to weaker real-income growth (due to high inflation) and relatively tight monetary policy. As the inflationary effects of increased food and energy prices ease in 2009, demand conditions are expected to improve, setting the stage for recovery in activity beginning in mid-2009, with growth reaching 1.9 percent by 2010. Given the importance of Central and Eastern Europe and the Middle East for high-income European exports, a weaker-than-expected outturn for these countries (notably among those Central and Eastern European countries exposed to the impact of financial turmoil; see below) would be experienced as slower export growth and weaker economic activity in the Euro Area.

Japan

Developments over the course of 2007 underscored the fragility of Japan's foundations for growth, and GDP in 2007 dipped to 2 percent from the 2.4 percent advance of 2006. Quarterly patterns of growth were quite volatile, ranging from an advance of 4.6 percent during the first quarter to a decline of 2.5 percent in the second (saar), reflecting variability in domestic segments of demand and the vagaries of trade. More than half of overall growth came from net exports in 2007 (figure 1.7), highlighting the weakness of domestic demand and the sensitivity of future outcomes to the projected slowing of U.S. imports and world trade more broadly. Although conditions

Figure 1.7 Contributions to real GDP growth in Japan

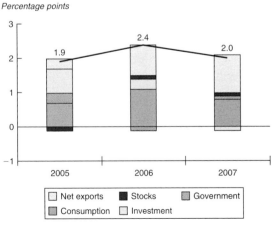

Sources: Japan Cabinet Office and World Bank calculations.

for stronger gains in household spending were widespread over 2006–07 (declining unemployment, rising job offers), real consumer spending grew just 2 percent and 1.5 percent, respectively, in 2006 and 2007, well short of levels able to sustain economywide growth. At the same time, business investment softened from gains of 9.2 percent in 2005 to 1.9 percent by 2007.

Recently consumer sentiment has waned on a string of rising inflation reports and a dramatic 22 percent falloff in Japan's equity markets during the first quarter of 2008. Moreover, weak end-of-year bonuses meant that wages declined 2.4 percent in January 2008 (year over year). At the same time, the yen has appreciated 14 percent against the dollar since the start of 2008. These developments appear to bode ill for rekindling momentum in Japan's household demand. On the other hand, emerging economies are now the destination for more than half of Japan's overseas shipments, a development that should make the economy less sensitive than in the past to changes in U.S. import demand. Although export momentum is fading at present, demand growth in China, other East Asian countries, western Europe and the world's oil exporters is expected to more than compensate for declining shipments to the United States over the coming two years.

Indeed, preliminary first-quarter GDP outturns for Japan reveal a surge in exports from 10 percent in the final quarter of 2007 to 20 percent (saar), such that net exports accounted for 2.4 points of 3.4 percent growth during the quarter. At the same time, household spending revived, advancing 3.4 percent, more than double the 1.6 percent gains of the last quarter of 2007 (a number of respected analysts attribute the outsized gain to a leap year effect, and without such distortion, consumption growth may have registered 1.8 percent). Business investment dropped 3.4 percent on expectations of weaker growth ahead and on steep declines in consumer confidence. *Tankan* surveys point to retrenchment in corporate capital spending, suggesting that growth is likely to soften from the favorable results of the first months of 2008.

Financial contagion from difficulties in the United States and European markets appears to be limited to co-movements in equity prices, with little evidence to date of large-scale losses tied to holdings of troubled U.S.-structured assets by

Japanese institutions. Nonetheless, Japanese commercial and investment banking institutions are well integrated into international flows of interbank lending, funding of hedge funds, private investment entities and similar groups, such that second-order risks are of concern. Moreover, the use of low-interest yen funds by international investors as a conduit for investment in higher-yielding assets in a number of mature, as well as emerging, markets (the so-called carry trade) places the yen at risk of rapid change should such flows escalate or unwind.

With little momentum from the consumer (growth of 1–1.5 percent through 2010) or business investment, Japan's prospects will continue to be shaped by trade developments. Japanese exports are projected to grow 2.2 percent during 2008 (down from 8.6 percent in 2007), before rebounding toward longer-term average growth of 6.5 percent by 2010. With subdued import demand, and in the absence of financial market difficulties, GDP growth is projected to ease to 1.4 percent in 2008 before picking up to grow by 2.1 percent in 2010.

Outlook for developing regions

In contrast with the high-income countries where GDP growth eased from 3 percent in 2006 to 2.6 percent in 2007, gains for developing countries as a group picked up modestly to 7.8 percent from 7.6 percent in the year. Improved macroeconomic fundamentals, diminished sovereign exposures to international financial markets, largely favorable terms-of-trade developments, and buildup of large international reserve positions helped to insulate many countries from financial spillovers. And as figure 1.8 shows, robust momentum in domestic demand, driven in many countries by investment outlays, was sufficient to buffer the initial shocks stemming from the financial turmoil in mature markets. Indeed, growth stepped up across all developing regions during 2007, with the exceptions of Europe and Central Asia and South Asia.

In looking forward, developing countries will be faced with exceptional weakness in their traditional export markets, as import demand falters among the high-income OECD countries. This will exact a toll on aggregate growth, with GDP gains slipping to 6.5 percent in 2008 and easing further to 6.4 percent in 2009–10. GDP outturns are likely to differ substantially across regions.

Figure 1.8 Developing-country GDP growth, 2005–07

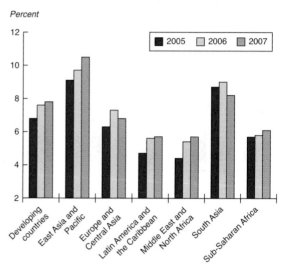

Source: World Bank.

During 2007, the *East Asia and Pacific* region recorded its highest growth rate in over a decade (10.5 percent), capping more than 10 years of improvements following its home-grown financial crisis in 1998. Even more important, the region's investment in sound macroeconomic policies and structural reforms since that crisis has added economic resilience and flexibility that will help deal with the rapidly deteriorating global environment. Foreign exchange reserves are at all-time highs, nonperforming bank loans have been steadily lowered, external and public debt burdens are at acceptable levels, most governments have unused fiscal space, and diversification of trade and financial flows provides some flexibility in adjusting to the impending global slowdown. In most of the developing countries of the region, corporate financing to a large extent occurs through retained earnings or domestic bank borrowing, so exposure to international markets may be less extensive than in other developing regions.

East Asian growth is expected to diminish to 8.6 percent in 2008, which is still considerably higher than growth in other regions. Growth is as much constrained by insufficient production capacity and bottlenecks in infrastructure as by lack of effective demand. Hence, investment is likely to remain robust, and with continued prudent economic management, East Asia, and especially China, can continue to emerge as a

Figure 1.9 Real GDP growth in East Asia and Pacific, 2005–10

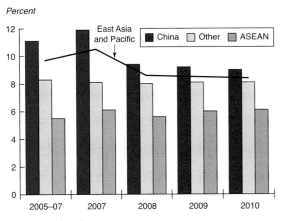

Percent

Source: World Bank.

Note: ASEAN = Association of Southeast Asian Nations.

growth pole for the world economy, providing a potential counterweight to the slowing high-income economies. To absorb in part the decline in U.S. import demand, export flows are shifting to markets in Europe and developing countries, encouraged by the strong euro and by continued strong momentum in the developing world, including in East Asia itself. Looking further ahead, GDP gains are anticipated to ease moderately to 8.4 percent by 2010 (figure 1.9).

The main risks for East Asia and Pacific do not necessarily stem from the global slowdown but from volatility in financial markets, which could manifest in steep declines in securities markets across East Asia—especially in equities and to a lesser degree, offshore bond markets. The decline has been driven not just by uncertainty and the liquidation of portfolio holdings by foreign financial institutions but also by a more realistic evaluation of risk in global financial markets. A potential risk that requires attention is that a falloff in stock prices may have a contagion effect through the balance sheets of corporations or banks. Dealing with high food and fuel prices also constitutes a challenge to governments. In the medium term, the answer lies in greater fuel efficiency and stronger and more productive agriculture. But in the short term, the bigger concern is to alleviate the harsh burden rising prices impose on the poor. East Asia has faced these problems before and adopted a variety of solutions in the past to fit different circumstances, ranging from targeted subsidies to conditional cash

transfers to school lunch programs. These programs now need to be reconsidered and reintroduced before the problem becomes more acute.

GDP growth during 2007 in *Europe and Central Asia* exceeded earlier expectations, easing moderately from 7.3 percent in 2006 to 6.8 percent, largely on the back of continued high oil prices and robust growth among oil exporters in the region. Members of the Commonwealth of Independent States (CIS)—led by key hydrocarbon exporters the Russian Federation, Kazakhstan, Uzbekistan, and Azerbaijan—benefited from surging energy prices, and the CIS achieved growth of 8.6 percent, the second strongest in a decade. And in both central and eastern Europe and the CIS, GDP gains were underpinned by strong domestic demand, with investment and imports registering double-digit advances in a number of countries.

The slowdown in growth during 2007 may be attributable in large measure to fiscal consolidation in Hungary, the effects of financial market turmoil on capital inflows to countries such as the Baltics, Kazakhstan, and Romania and an easing of activity in Turkey. Accession to the European Union has also played an important role in generally strong growth outturns for central and eastern Europe, promoting capital inflows and in turn, yielding wider current account deficits. For the smaller countries of the CIS, demand has been financed by substantial inflows of remittances (which in 2006 accounted for 18 percent of GDP in Armenia, 6.5 percent in Georgia, 27 percent in the Kyrgyz Republic, and 36 percent in Moldova).

These favorable outturns are being clouded by increasing uncertainties. The region showed little improvement over the past years in its traditional exposures and vulnerabilities. Save for oil exporters, almost all economies witnessed a deterioration in current account position during 2007 (figure 1.10). This was most pronounced for the Baltic states, Bulgaria, and Romania, raising concerns about the sustainability of growth in these countries. Inflows of foreign direct investment (FDI) to the region achieved record highs in 2007 ($162 billion), but in light of the global credit crunch, flows are expected to fall off in 2008, covering a diminishing portion of current account deficits. An increasing reliance on foreign bank borrowing suggests that economic activity could suffer if the external financial environment deteriorates suddenly.

Figure 1.10 Current account as a share of GDP in Europe and Central Asia, 2006–07

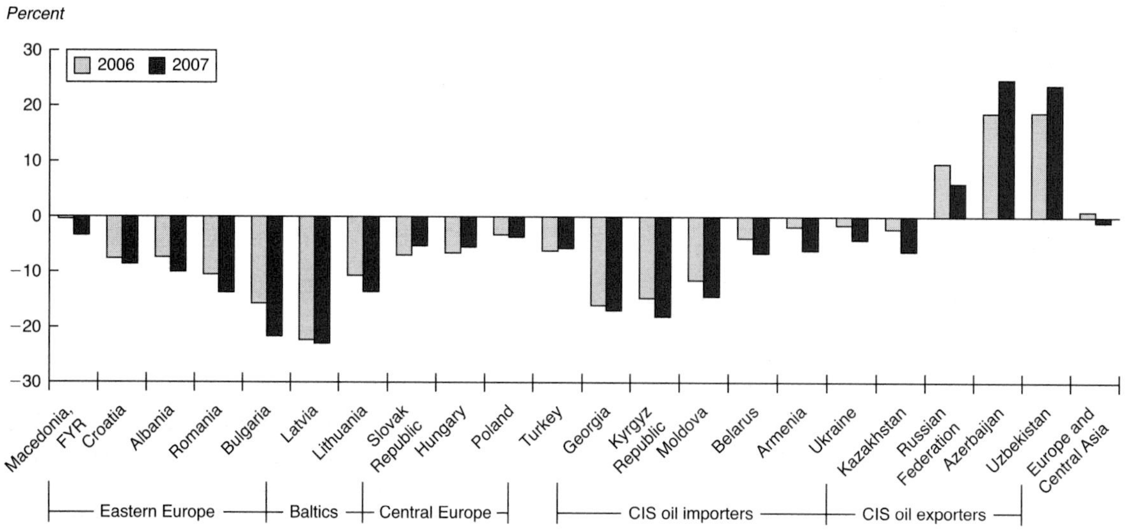

Percent

Source: World Bank.

Note: CIS = Commonwealth of Independent States.

The region has exhibited surprising resilience to tremors stemming from the financial turmoil in high-income financial markets. But risk appetites of international investors will be tested during 2008. Sovereign spreads have been widening since the start of the turbulence in August 2007, but increases have differed across countries. Spreads for Turkey, Hungary, Bulgaria, Ukraine, and Kazakhstan have increased by 93 to 270 basis points moving across the four countries, compared with Russia (63) and Poland (42). Investor sentiment has also been reflected in currency movements: the National Bank of Kazakhstan used reserves to stabilize its currency in the second half of 2007; and the Turkish lira dropped 16 percent against the euro in the first quarter of 2008.

The region's prospects display a gradual slowing of growth to 5.4 percent by 2010, but performance will become more diverse across countries. Central and Eastern European countries will see a downturn in export growth, as demand conditions in the Euro Area fade during 2008. That slowdown will be partly offset by increased demand from neighboring oil exporters as oil prices are likely to persist at high levels through 2008. The Baltic economies have shown signs of cooling, partly because of more prudent lending by banks, but there is risk of a hard landing. An abrupt slowing of growth

in Latvia in the previous two quarters underscores the downside risks.

An increasingly serious risk facing the region is inflation, which jumped to nearly double digits in a number of countries, including Bulgaria, Latvia, Russia, and Ukraine in recent months. Although a global phenomenon, the inflation situation in the Europe and Central Asia region is more complicated. Unlike other regions where inflation is being stoked by surging food and energy prices, with unclear second-round effects, this region has seen strong real wage growth (from tightening labor markets) much earlier than others. Regulated prices and indirect tax increases among the central and eastern European economies, currency board systems in the Baltics and Balkans, large capital inflows into CIS oil exporters (and these countries' spending of expansive oil revenues), and high energy prices for oil importers all bode unfavorably for the region's near-term inflation outlook.

GDP growth in *Latin America and the Caribbean* registered 5.7 percent in 2007, up modestly from 5.6 percent in 2006. This marks the first time in nearly three decades that growth has exceeded 5 percent for two years in succession, and the first time since the early 1970s that GDP gains have registered more than 4 percent for four consecutive years. Growth in the region has become

Figure 1.11 Contributions to GDP growth in Latin America and the Caribbean, 1985–2007

Percentage points

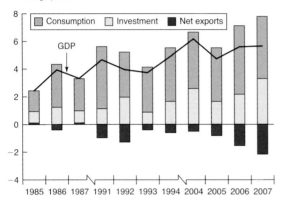

Source: World Bank.

more resilient, and countries are likely better positioned to weather the unfolding slowdown in the United States. Although a favorable external environment has played a key role in the region's improved performance, stronger domestic fundamentals have been just as important. Capital formation has made a stronger contribution to GDP growth during the recent growth spell than during two previous growth episodes in the early 1980s and 1990s (figure 1.11). Financial stability across a large number of countries in the region also played a role in supporting growth, and this environment is anticipated to buffer what is likely to be continued turbulence stemming from U.S. financial markets over 2008–09.

In contrast with previous episodes of market instability in high-income economies, the increase in risk premiums in Latin America has been fairly contained in the current credit crisis. Similarly, capital inflows remain strong, suggesting the region's financial markets may be providing diversification benefits for international investors. International reserve levels are large and foreign debt stocks continue to decline, limiting the region's vulnerability to terms-of-trade shocks or to a sudden withdrawal of capital.

Despite improved resilience, deterioration in the global environment is considered likely to weigh down regional growth in 2008. GDP gains are projected to ease to 4.5 percent in 2008, with further moderation to 4.2 percent by 2010. A key factor in the continued step-down in growth is a marked

slowing in Argentina, from 8.7 percent in 2007 to 4.5 percent by 2010, and an even sharper decline in República Bolivariana de Venezuela, from 8.4 percent in 2007 to 3 percent. Excluding these countries, regional GDP is likely to slow from 4.9 percent in 2007 to 4.3 percent in 2010, with a dip to 4 percent in 2008 due to weak conditions in the United States.

Many countries in the region have been riding a wave of high commodity prices that have buttressed current account surpluses. As commodity prices ease over 2009–10, the surpluses of oil, metals, and agricultural exporters are likely to diminish substantially, although many energy importers in Central America and the Caribbean will experience much-needed relief. While many exporters have capitalized on the benefits of high commodity prices, the region has been less successful in exploiting the opportunities produced by the changing global trade landscape. Latin America has not taken advantage of the rising share of China in global imports, which keeps growth of export volumes subdued, especially during the current period. For several countries the damage is not coming from the external environment, but from internal stimulus and resulting overheating, leading to open or suppressed inflation.

GDP growth in the developing *Middle East and North Africa* region fared well during 2007, supported by record-high crude oil prices, stronger growth in key export markets (particularly in western Europe), and continued flows of remittances and tourism earnings. Regional growth stepped up to 5.7 percent in 2007, a 12-year high, from 5.4 percent in 2006 on the back of improved activity among the developing oil exporters of the region, as well as by a majority of diversified exporters. Foreign direct investment continued to play an important role in shaping growth outturns, registering some $30.5 billion in 2007, up from a record $27.5 billion in 2006. Three countries are attracting the bulk of flows: Saudi Arabia, the Arab Republic of Egypt, and the United Arab Emirates, which now account for more than half of inward FDI into the broader geographic region (figure 1.12).

Among the economically diversified countries, GDP gains eased from 6.2 percent in 2006 to 5.5 percent in 2007, although a severe drought suffered by Morocco (the second in three years) reduced output there from a record 8 percent in 2006 to 2.3 percent.[3]

Figure 1.12 Growth of FDI in selected countries of the Middle East and North Africa

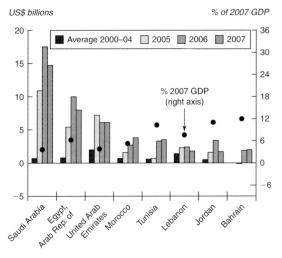

Source: World Bank.

This decline tends to mask improvements across a wider range of countries. Growth in Egypt, which reached a record 7.1 percent in the year, is broadly based, with non-oil manufacturing and retail trade accounting for half of overall output growth. Although deficits continue on merchandise trade, for Egypt and other countries of the group, tourism and other services receipts and burgeoning remittances tend to outweigh these shortfalls and help maintain current account surplus positions. Growth among the developing oil exporters increased to 5.8 percent from 4.7 percent in 2006. Output gains in Algeria have been constrained by a fall in hydrocarbon output, with GDP advancing just 1.8 percent in 2006 and 3 percent in 2007. Non-hydrocarbon activity expanded by a strong 6 percent in 2007. A major government investment initiative there has belatedly started and is slated to expend more than $22 billion over the next years on housing, transport, and agriculture. In the Islamic Republic of Iran, major fiscal expansion over the past two years has pushed growth up smartly to 7.6 percent in 2007 from 5.9 percent in 2006.

Rising food prices represent a growing vulnerability and risk for the developing Middle East and North Africa region, a net importer of food, especially in the context of poorly targeted safety nets. Large food and energy subsidies are quite unique to this region, ranging from 3 percent to 15 percent of GDP. Rising food prices have made reforming these programs even more difficult. At the aggregate, the region suffers from low levels of poverty, with less than 2 percent of the population living on less than $1 a day. However, there is tremendous disparity across countries and within countries in the region, and large numbers of people live above (but close to) the poverty line. Overall, some 20 percent of the population lives on less than $2 a day. With heavy clustering of large proportions of the population around the poverty line, rising global food prices represent a serious risk to wider-scale poverty.

The keys to the 2008 outlook for the diversified economies are rebounds in Morocco, to 5.5 percent growth from the depths of drought, and in Lebanon, to 3.5 percent, which would offset a modest easing across the remainder of the group tied to conditions in the external environment—and support a return to growth of 6.2 percent in the year. Beyond 2008 GDP growth is anticipated to average 6 percent. Investment-led growth appears increasingly well established in Egypt, and activity there should remain within a 6.5–7 percent range. Sustained growth near 6 percent is also likely in Jordan and Tunisia, grounded in services exports and increasingly in investment and construction funded by FDI. Growth among the oil-dominant economies is anticipated to ease by almost a full percentage point to 4.9 percent in 2008, largely attributable to a sharp slowdown in Iran. Continued work to supplement hydrocarbon output in Algeria, with implementation of the government's public works plan, should underpin investment and consumption, carrying GDP growth back to a 4 percent range. For the region overall, growth is expected to ease from a high of 5.7 percent in 2007 to 5.1 percent by 2010.

GDP growth in *South Asia* registered 8.2 percent in 2007, moderating from a 25-year-high 9 percent in 2006. Output gains reflected continued dynamic—albeit softening—domestic activity, while slowing external demand also contributed to the regional moderation. All South Asian countries experienced a slowing, to varying degrees, save Afghanistan and Bhutan, where GDP accelerated. Restrictive monetary policies in a number of countries, combined with a degree of fiscal consolidation, helped to dampen the robust pace of domestic demand; and the momentum of growth in South Asia's export market diminished, exacting a toll on the region's outbound shipments. Inflation accelerated, evidenced by a buildup in the median GDP deflator to 7 percent in 2007 from 6.6 percent the previous year. Inflation pressures are reflecting sharp increases in international food and fuel prices as well as limits to domestic output linked to capacity constraints. Despite sustained worker remittance inflows, high commodity prices and weaker external demand combined to yield a worsening in the region's current account deficit in 2007.

The turmoil in U.S. and international financial markets has affected South Asia primarily through a falloff in portfolio inflows and weakness in local equity markets, with the latter most pronounced in India. Further effects on the real side of the economy are likely to be muted compared with other regions. The decline in share of the United States and the European Union in South Asia's export market in recent years has been offset by a concomitant increase in China and oil-exporting countries' shares, so effects on export volumes should be less severe than in other regions. Moreover, although South Asia's integration with the global economy advanced rapidly in recent years, it remains the least integrated among developing regions. Trade openness as a share of GDP is twice as high in East Asia and the Pacific and in Europe and Central Asia as in South Asia.

For South Asia's poor, one of the more direct effects of the deterioration in the external environment could come through international remittances. A falloff in growth in the countries where migrants are employed—combined with the sharp depreciation of the dollar—could lead to substantially lower remittance flows in local currency terms. For the poor whose incomes are being squeezed by higher food and fuel prices, lower remittances would make a difficult situation still worse. For most South Asian countries, remittances represent a major source of hard currency, and in some countries, inflows significantly boost the current account position. In Nepal, remittance inflows were equivalent to 15.1 percent of GDP in 2006, and in Sri Lanka and Bangladesh, they represented close to 9 percent and 7.3 percent, respectively (figure 1.13).

South Asia is poised for a further easing of GDP growth to 6.6 percent in 2008. Private consumption and investment will likely ease, due to tighter domestic and international credit conditions and to lower purchasing power for consumers due to higher food and fuel prices. High prices for grain, oilseed, and energy in particular

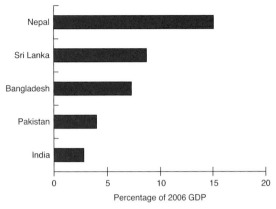

Figure 1.13 Worker remittances as a share of GDP in South Asian countries, 2006

Source: World Bank.

are expected to continue to exert upward pressures on inflation, representing perhaps the largest challenge for regional policy makers. The prices for these staples would strike the poor directly, since food and fuel represent a significant share of household consumption. Continuing volatility in international financial markets and a decreased appetite for risk among international investors may lead to still-lower capital inflows over the next years.

Growth outturns in 2007 for *Sub-Saharan Africa* were stronger than estimated in *Global Economic Prospects 2008* (World Bank 2008), with GDP gains picking up to 6.1 percent, from 5.8 percent in 2006, as South African output was revised up to 5.1 percent, and growth in oil importers outside South Africa was more robust than earlier anticipated. Regional growth appears to be increasingly broad based, with one in three countries growing by more than 6 percent during 2007 (figure 1.14). Moreover, growth has accelerated in resource-poor economies as well as in resource-rich countries, in landlocked as well as coastal countries. Per capita GDP has increased markedly in most countries in the region. Domestic demand (investment and private consumption) continues to supply the driving force for activity, a profile that, barring a collapse in commodity prices, stands to help the region weather the anticipated slowdown among the high-income countries. Indeed, many of the ingredients that contributed to robust expansion in Sub-Saharan Africa over the past years are still present, including high commodity prices,

Figure 1.14 GDP growth in Sub-Saharan Africa, 1994–2007

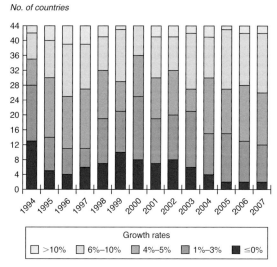

No. of countries

Growth rates

☐ >10% ☐ 6%–10% ☐ 4%–5% ▨ 1%–3% ■ ≤0%

Source: World Bank.

increased trade openness, and improved macroeconomic stability. But risks are significantly tilted to the downside, as weaker global expansion could translate into a downshift in export growth and deterioration in current account positions.

Economic expansion in Sub-Saharan Africa should remain strong, with growth picking up to 6.3 percent in 2008 on the back of gains in oil-producing countries, notably Cameroon, Nigeria, and the Republic of Congo. GDP growth among the oil-exporting countries of the region is likely to register 9.8 percent in the year. In South Africa, growth is projected to ease to 4.2 percent because of weaker private consumption and lower export growth; and capacity constraints in the electricity sector will limit output growth in mining and manufacturing. Slower growth in the regional powerhouse may spill over to other countries in the region (especially in southern Africa) that trade heavily with South Africa. Growth in East Africa is expected to ease on weaker agricultural output in 2008. Drought conditions and high inflationary pressures caused by surging food and energy prices will erode real incomes throughout the region, undermining private consumption. The risks for regional growth are mainly to the downside and include a sharper-than-expected slowdown in the global economy with negative consequences for export growth and investment

on the real side and weaker commodity prices on the nominal side.

Increased volatility in the international financial system and increased risk aversion among international investors create risks for South Africa in particular, which runs a significant current account deficit. In recent years on average 84 percent of South Africa's current account deficit was financed by portfolio investment, but this share plunged to 38 percent in the final quarter of 2007. Unwillingness to continue to provide such short-term flows could put pressure on the rand, which in turn would fuel inflationary pressure and add impetus for the country's Reserve Bank to hike interest rates.

International trade links

The slowing of domestic demand in the United States and the relative strength of its exports reflects a more general rotation of global demand away from dissaving fueled by the collapse of the U.S. housing sector toward a more balanced profile where demand in developing countries is increasingly driving the global expansion. The rotation in demand is helping to rebalance both the U.S. and the global economies. The effects are already visible in the U.S. balance of payments. Despite rising oil prices, the U.S. trade deficit narrowed by 0.6 percent of GDP during 2007. Although a scaling back in household spending is painful in the short run and is likely to amplify the distress in financial markets, rebalancing of growth is crucial for long-term stability, because it will reduce the potential for future financial turmoil.

While the improvement in the U.S. trade balance is positive news from a global perspective, it has been accompanied by a sharp decline in U.S. imports, which prompts the question of whether domestic demand in the rest of the world can expand quickly enough to support strong growth for developing countries while at the same time cushioning the slowdown in the United States (and potentially in Europe and Japan) by providing sufficient demand for its exports.

Since the early 1990s, developing countries have become increasingly integrated in global markets. Paradoxically, their overall growth has become less dependent on their external environment or more specifically, on imports of the high-income

Figure 1.15 Share of developing countries in
world exports, 1992–2008

Percent

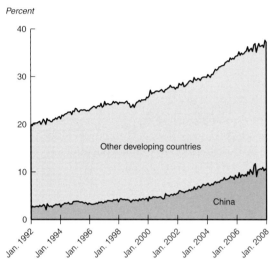

Source: World Bank.
Note: Nominal dollar exports were used in the calculation.

Figure 1.16 Comparison of trend GDP growth

Percent

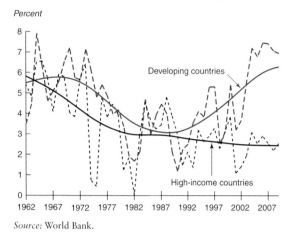

Source: World Bank.

countries. Over the past 15 years, developing countries opened up their economies, increased exports, and quickly gained market share in global trade. Exports as a share of developing economies' GDP increased from 22 percent in 1992 to 29 percent in 2000 and to 39 percent in 2007. Over the same period their share in world exports increased gradually from 20 percent to 37 percent, with China responsible for fully one-half of the increase in market share (figure 1.15).

On first sight, the more dominant role of exports in developing countries suggests that their economies depend now—more than 15 years ago—on import demand in the high-income countries and on the global trade cycle. However, this is not the case for two reasons. First, the remarkable export performance of developing countries has been driven by increased production capacity, not by acceleration of foreign demand. Production capacity is currently constrained by a lack of adequate infrastructure (including power), not a lack of effective demand in world markets. Second, South-South trade is growing more than twice as fast as North-South trade, which reduces the impact of import demand in high-income countries.

The shifts toward domestic drivers of growth in the developing world can be illustrated by decomposing GDP growth into trend and cyclical

components. Since the 1960s growth rates of developing countries and their high-income counterparts were remarkably similar. But during the 1990s structural growth rates diverged rapidly (figure 1.16). In the meantime, the cyclical components of growth remained strongly correlated. If anything, the correlation coefficient for cyclical growth between developing and high-income countries increased over time, consistent with the penetration of developing countries into global markets (figure 1.17). However, overall growth in the developing world was increasingly dominated by quite strong trend growth, and cyclical fluctuations became a smaller percentage of growth. And even with a cyclical downturn, growth rates exceeded previous peak rates.

Figure 1.17 Comparison of cyclical GDP growth

Percent

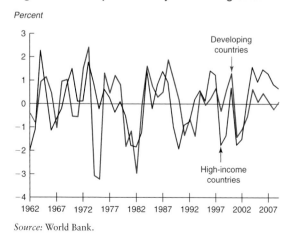

Source: World Bank.

The acceleration in developing-country growth that set in after 2002 corresponds with the period of increasing commodity prices (lasting through today). Could the current upturn in growth be simply a function of favorable terms of trade for developing commodity exporters (a boom, potentially "bust," cycle), rather than a reflection of shifts in fundamentals? This is unlikely, in that the initial surge in oil, metals, and agricultural prices was initiated by the onset of faster output growth and strong materials demand in large emerging-market countries, such as the BRICs, or Brazil, Russia, India, and China.

The divergence in trend growth is also clearly visible in trade performance. During the 1980s growth of export and import volumes in high-income countries exceeded the corresponding growth rates in developing countries, where imports (in particular) were hindered by debt burdens and macroeconomic instability. During the 1990s circumstances were quite similar across the two country groups, but since 2000, developing countries' trade growth has accelerated to an annual pace of 10 percent, almost double that of the high-income countries.

The rapid increase in developing-country market share over the past 15 years means that developing countries themselves have become a driving force underlying the global trade cycle, reducing (but certainly not eliminating) the influence of high-income countries. During the 1980s the contribution of high-income countries to growth in global import volumes was nine times as large as the contribution of developing countries. High-income imports grew three times as fast as developing countries' imports, and the share of high-income countries in world trade was three times as large. During the 1990s the relative contribution of high-income countries was reduced from ninefold to threefold, already a major shift, increasing the relevance of developing countries. But the breakthrough occurred in the current decade as developing countries became larger contributors to global imports than high-income countries. The size in value of developing countries' imports has risen to two-thirds that of OECD imports, and annual import growth exceeds OECD import growth by 60 percent. Relative to the United States, where import growth has slowed sharply, the increased contribution of developing countries to global import demand is even more impressive (figure 1.18).

Figure 1.18 Nominal import growth, developing countries and the United States, 1991–2007

Source: World Bank.

This dramatic reversal in relative importance means that the direct effects of a drop in OECD import growth are still important, but smaller, than in earlier decades, even taking into account the now larger ratio of developing-country exports to GDP. More and more, export opportunities for developing countries are shaped by import demand in other developing countries.

The combination of a pronounced slowing of imports in high-income countries and strong trends in developing countries provides a mixed picture at the global level. Global industrial production, strongly correlated with global GDP, is slowing. This has been confirmed by other cyclical indicators such as metal prices (figure 1.19), though these prices rose sharply during the first quarter of 2008. And because industrial production remains so strongly correlated with GDP at the global level (figure 1.20), high-frequency indicators can provide a reliable proxy for global growth. Indeed, the coming slowdown in the developing world is likely to reflect to a greater degree the direct and indirect effects of global credit tightening rather than the direct impact of slowing import demand in high-income countries.

The impact of higher commodity prices

Commodity prices have shown spectacular increases since the summer of 2007. Most of the increases were directly or indirectly linked to higher oil prices and increased demand for

Figure 1.19 Global industrial production and metal prices

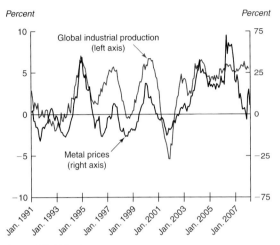

Source: World Bank.

Figure 1.20 Global industrial production and GDP

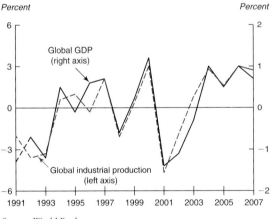

Source: World Bank.

Note: Industrial production and GDP are expressed in percentage points as deviations from period average growth.

Figure 1.21 Metal prices rebound in 2008

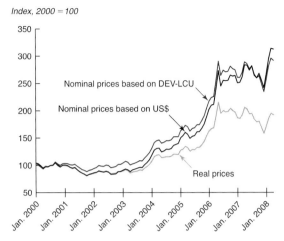

Source: World Bank.

Note: DEV-LCU = developing-country local currency units.

biofuels. Oil prices approached $130 per barrel in May 2008, almost double the price a year earlier. Fertilizer prices caught up with the oil price increases of the last several years and almost tripled over the year to May 2008. Grain prices doubled over the past year. The run-up in grain prices started in the summer of 2006 when maize prices jumped, largely as a result of increased use of maize for ethanol. In the summer of 2007, wheat prices followed, largely because cropland for wheat had been diverted to feedstock for biofuels (maize and soybeans in the United States, and rapeseed and sunflowers in wheat exporters such

as Argentina, Canada, and Europe). Rice prices remained low in 2007 compared with other grains. However, that changed dramatically in the first quarter of 2008, when rice prices almost tripled, partly because of substitution on the demand side between wheat and rice and partly because of policy responses that included export restrictions and import increases to build reserves.

Increases in other commodity prices have been more moderate, and more mixed. The average price of metals actually declined in late 2007 before rising to new highs in early 2008 (figure 1.21). Expressed in dollars, metals prices dropped 15 percent over the second half of 2007, but then jumped almost 30 percent through April 2008, leaving them 10 percent above the levels of a year earlier. At the same time, currencies of commodity-importing developing countries appreciated 9 percent against the dollar on average over the past 12 months, such that metals prices expressed in local currencies of those countries have basically not changed from a year ago. And relative to domestic consumption prices, that is, corrected for overall inflation, metals prices declined 7 percent over the previous year.

Oil markets. Oil prices moved sharply higher during the final months of 2007, surpassing $130 a barrel in May 2008 (figure 1.22). The recent jump in oil prices mainly reflects stagnant supply conditions due to sluggish non-OPEC production

Figure 1.22 Energy prices spiked on supply concerns

Index, 2000 = 100

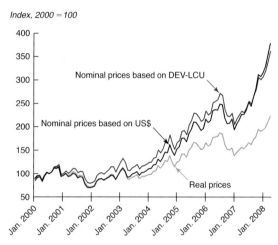

Source: World Bank.

Note: DEV-LCU = developing-country local currency units.

growth, and OPEC output restraint, rather than strong growth in demand. Growth in global oil demand has slowed substantially, from 3.6 percent in 2004 to near 1 percent in both 2006 and 2007, as OECD oil demand has fallen slightly the past two years and was down in the first quarter of 2008. Non-OECD oil demand has continued at a brisk pace, particularly in Asia and in oil-exporting countries. In China, oil demand is estimated to have jumped 8 percent in the first quarter, as the country resumed using diesel in backup generators because of power shortages. Nevertheless, global demand has eased as the effects of high oil prices of the last several years are now being felt, triggering increases in energy efficiency and substitution to non-hydrocarbon energy sources.

Global oil supply stagnated in 2007. Production by members of the Organization of Petroleum Exporting Countries (OPEC) declined due to large cuts of 1.7 million barrels a day in late-2006/early-2007. This contributed to the large decline in stocks in the second half of 2007 and to sharply higher prices. More recently, production has gradually increased to meet market demand, including increases from Iraq and new member Angola. But non-OPEC supply gains outside the former Soviet Union have been disappointing, as large declines in the North Sea and the United States—and more recently Mexico—have generally offset solid gains elsewhere, for example, in Canada,

Brazil, and West Africa. In the first quarter of 2008, Russian production declined for the first time in nine years, and this has added to the nervousness about future oil supplies. Non-OPEC production has been hampered by a number of factors: rising costs, limited supply of materials and skilled labor, depletion of aging fields, higher taxes, renegotiation of current contracts or de facto nationalization, and diminishing access to abundant low-cost reserves. The latter is forcing international oil companies to explore and develop in higher-cost and more difficult environments, such as oil sands and deep-water oil deposits. Frontiers still exist to find new reserves in still deeper waters, the Arctic, and other unexplored regions.

With low stocks and limited spare OPEC capacity, temporary oil disruptions (as have occurred in Nigeria and in the North Sea) or potential disruptions (for example, when Venezuela threatened to stop oil shipments to the United States) can easily lead to sharp spikes in prices. Two additional elements made prices even less stable, allowing for even steeper spikes. Investors moving away from loss-generating financial assets in search of yield increased their participation in crude oil futures markets, eager to benefit from rising prices. The number of futures contracts on NYMEX doubled since 2005, although with the sharp run-up in prices since the fourth quarter of 2007, the number of noncommercial participants (often deemed speculators) actually diminished. The weakening dollar and global inflationary pressures have also contributed to oil price increases.

Although the oil market is expected to remain tight over the coming years, there is room for a slight moderation in price as the global economy slows and oil demand turns more subdued, while new, non-OPEC supply (temporarily held back by project delays) should eventually come to market. In addition there are large investments taking place in a number of OPEC countries, which will add significant capacity in the coming years. However, whether these projects will translate into production or whether yet further investments will take place have contributed to supply uncertainty. Still, high prices are inducing all manner of innovation on the demand and supply sides of the market that in addition to environmental pressures, should moderate oil demand going forward. In the medium to longer terms, oil supplies will be supplemented by unconventional oil and other

Figure 1.23 Food prices driven up by biofuels demand

Index, 2000 = 100

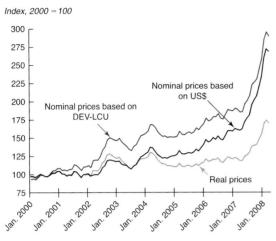

Source: World Bank.

Note: DEV-LCU = developing-country local currency units.

liquids (from coal, gas, and agriculture—mainly cellulosic).

Agricultural commodities. Among various food and agricultural commodities, the dominant drivers for higher prices are the demand for biofuels in the United States and Europe, higher fertilizer and energy prices, and the weak dollar. Price increases were largest for oilseeds, which during the first months of 2008 were nearly twice as expensive as a year earlier; and for grains, for which prices increased 76 percent over the same period (figure 1.23).

High prices are directly linked to the rising production of ethanol from maize in the United States and of biodiesel from vegetable oils in Europe. In each of the past two years, more than half of the growth in global grain demand came from increased U.S. use of maize crops for ethanol production. The share of global maize production used for ethanol was 2.5 percent in 2000, 5 percent in 2004, and 11 percent in 2007. The increase in demand was first met by a reduction in stocks, with limited increase in price. Global maize stocks declined from 32 percent of global demand in 1999 to 13 percent of demand by 2007. Once stocks were reduced to low levels, prices spiked as the possibility of supply shortages became real.

Other sources of demand for food and feed products have not grown at exceptionally rapid

rates. For example, China's feed use this decade has grown at an annual pace of less than 1 percent. And grain imports into developing countries have remained constant in recent years, declining as a share of global production. In a few markets, sudden increases in developing countries' demand did occur in 2007 (for example, a sharp jump in China's imports of soybeans), but these instances were exceptions rather than the rule.

Price increases in international food markets have been amplified by policy responses, especially among grain-exporting countries. These policies—such as a ban on non-Basmati rice exports from India; increases in tariffs or bans on grain exports from Argentina, China, Kazakhstan, Russia and Ukraine, and a decline in import tariffs in food-importing countries—attempt to restrain domestic prices, but they also result in higher international prices, in both the short and longer runs. In the short run, these policies exacerbate shortages in international markets. In the longer run, they discourage supply increases in response to higher prices.

To the extent that increased demand for biofuels is linked to high oil prices, a new and stronger correlation between oil and agricultural markets has been created. But historically oil prices have always influenced agricultural prices through cost structures. Grain production, especially in the United States, is energy and fertilizer intensive. This link was clearly at work in 2007. By the beginning of 2008, fertilizer prices had tripled from their level a year earlier.

Prices of internationally traded food commodities are expected to decline from recent record highs but to remain strong relative to historical levels. Energy prices are likely to remain at elevated levels; new mandates will increase biofuel use in Europe and the United States, whereas trade restrictions prevent the full utilization of the large potential for ethanol production in Brazil. Supply can adjust to sharply increased demand only gradually because it requires substantial time and investment to bring additional cropland into production.

Increasingly, policy makers will be challenged to address both causes and consequences of current high food and energy prices. With respect to causes, mandates for increasing use of biofuels in the United States and Europe—in combination with import restrictions on Brazilian ethanol—could be reconsidered. The high agricultural prices also create an opportunity to reduce distortions in agricultural markets, which is needed to complete the Doha trade negotiations. And oil-producing countries could adjust production quotas upward or eliminate restrictions on the buildup of new capacity.

Just as important, policies should focus on the mitigation of the widespread adverse effects of extraordinarily high commodity prices. The elevated oil prices of the past years have generated large international transfers from oil-importing to oil-exporting countries, increasing current account imbalances across the globe. Oil-importing countries that are already running substantial current account deficits will be strained, especially as international credit supplies tighten. The short-term options for addressing this problem are limited, but the needed long-term adjustment to a higher oil-import bill should be facilitated to the extent possible by prudent fiscal policies, incentives to increase energy efficiency, and measures to promote export competitiveness.

Unlike the case of oil, international income transfers linked to high food prices are relatively small. Two-thirds of global oil production is internationally traded, and increases in oil prices imply large income transfers between countries. The balance-of-payments effects of higher global food prices, however, have been minor. Only 19 percent of global wheat production is internationally traded, and the corresponding shares for maize and rice are 13 percent and 4 percent, respectively. An exception is edible oils, of which 42 percent of global consumption is imported, but the amounts are too small to have large terms-of-trade effects. But for a few small countries, heavily dependent on food imports, the negative terms-of-trade effects have been substantial already and were not offset by increases in other commodity prices. These countries include Cape Verde, Djibouti, Eritrea, The Gambia, Haiti, Lesotho, and São Tomé and Principe. Countries that have enjoyed a more substantial positive terms-of-trade effect due to increased food crop prices include Belize, Fiji, Guyana, Malaysia, Paraguay, and Swaziland.

While balance-of-payments effects are modest, the opposite is true for domestic effects. Terms-of-trade changes are not a particularly good indicator of the potential seriousness of the domestic consequences of higher food prices. For grain-exporting countries, high prices imply terms-of-trade gains, and at the same time, high domestic prices cause

strains for the country's population. More important is the impact on those who live in dire poverty and do not benefit from high agricultural prices because their incomes do not rise in step with these prices. Most of these poor are in urban areas, but many among the rural poor are also net consumers of food. The poor are especially hard hit because they often spend more than half of their incomes on food and energy and they have no accumulated wealth to absorb upturns in costs.

Inflationary consequences. An additional concern is the potential effect of higher commodity prices on domestic inflation. Although food prices have a smaller impact on terms of trade and the current account than do oil prices, effects on domestic inflation tend to be larger, because food accounts for a larger share in consumption than does energy. This is especially true for developing countries. In the same fashion as a large share of the poor's consumption basket consists of food products, food is also a relatively large share of total consumption in poor countries. As a result, spikes in food prices tend to have a bigger impact on consumer price inflation in developing countries than in high-income countries.

Since commodity prices began rising in 2003, the median inflation rate has increased significantly among developing countries, with a particularly sharp jump observed during the course of 2007 as food prices surged (figure 1.24).

Figure 1.24 Rising inflation in developing countries

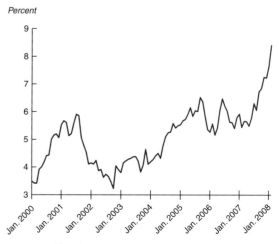

Percent

Source: World Bank.

Figure 1.25 Domestic and imported food prices compared

Percent

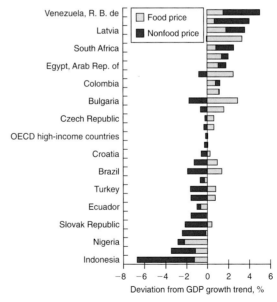

Source: World Bank.

These inflationary pressures present a further challenge for macroeconomic policy in developing countries, as a notable part of their economic success over the past decade originated from policies that stabilized and then reduced inflation. In some cases, price increases tied to international energy and food markets come to augment domestic and other international factors underlying inflation. This is true among some oil-exporting economies and in several Central and Eastern European countries where large capital inflows have created rapid credit growth, as well as in a few countries in Latin America where loose monetary and fiscal policies have created shortages.

In part because of limited data, the correlation between international and domestic food prices for developing economies and the relationship between domestic food prices and overall inflation is difficult to detect. Data for 23 mainly middle-income countries show that upturns in domestic food price indexes are almost universal, albeit by a factor of 5 to 10 times less than the surge in internationally traded food crops (figure 1.25). Almost without exception, food prices have been the dominant force pushing inflation up across developing countries. Indeed, for most countries, the nonfood portion of consumer prices in 2007 decelerated relative to 2006 (figure 1.26). This may be good news, as the recent two-year surge in

Figure 1.26 Contribution of food and nonfood in increase of inflation 2006–07

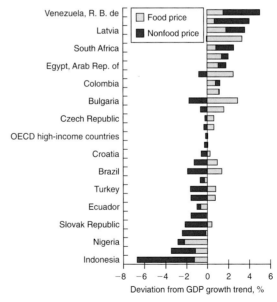

Source: World Bank.

food prices may give way to a degree of easing in the next years, and there are few signs to date that food prices have had substantial second-round effects. Hence, central banks in most developing countries remain cautious, and many are in tightening mode.

27

Key economic risks

The slowdown in high-income countries and tighter credit conditions are expected to curb the rapid pace of growth exhibited by developing countries over the past two years. A slowdown was inevitable, and indeed desirable, in the many countries where overheating had become a major concern. Despite the slowdown, growth in most developing countries is expected to remain above historical averages, and prospects are good that their robust growth can be sustained over the long term. The degree of uncertainty surrounding the economic outlook has been elevated by the turmoil that has disrupted financial markets since mid-2007. The risks have clearly shifted to the downside.

A key risk to the outlook at the current juncture is that the deterioration in global economic and financial conditions will become more severe and prolonged. A sharp relapse in financial markets could trigger a vicious cycle in which economic and financial conditions negatively affect each other, potentially leading to extreme outcomes. The impact of significantly tighter credit conditions in the United States would be pervasive across the U.S. economy. In turn, deteriorating economic conditions have an adverse impact on the financial system, leading to larger loan losses, further balance-sheet consolidation, and tighter credit conditions. Even if the United States continues to bear the brunt of the adjustment, the impact would be transmitted worldwide through waning export opportunities and tighter credit conditions in international markets.

The uncertainty about the outlook for the United States is reflected in increased dispersion of forecasts for economic growth in 2008. Not only did the average GDP forecast, as illustrated by those of Consensus Economics Ltd. surveys, come down rapidly from 3 percent in January 2007 to 1.3 percent in April 2008, the standard deviation of the underlying forecasts increased to an average of 0.45 percent in the first four months of 2008 from 0.27 percent during the same period in 2007 (figure 1.27). In this environment of heightened uncertainty, alternative outcomes for developing countries have to be thought through carefully, and policy makers in developing countries have to be prepared for varying modes of downside risks and scenarios.

A sharper slowdown in the United States, implying a serious recession, would hit U.S.

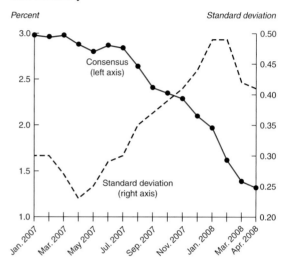

Figure 1.27 Consensus forecasts for the U.S. economy

Source: Consensus Economics Ltd.

Note: Forecasts for 2008 GDP growth were prepared on dates along x-axis.

investment and manufacturing especially hard. These are sectors of the economy that are closely linked to the global economy, with relatively high import content. A simulation using the World Bank's global forecasting model *Isimulate* shows that an autonomous 10 percent additional decline in business fixed investment in 2008, relative to the baseline, yields an additional 7 percentage points contraction in U.S. imports. That shock would carry the United States into a severe recession, with GDP dropping 0.6 percent for the year (a 1.7 percent difference with the baseline) and would—through endogenous feedback—leave investment 17 percent below baseline growth.

The sharp decline in U.S. imports could have quite severe effects for close trading partners. Total exports from Mexico would decline in a such scenario by more than 9 percent (vis-à-vis baseline), as almost all of that country's exports are destined for the U.S. market, and Mexico is specialized in highly cyclical components for inputs to manufacturing. China's export growth would be reduced by 3 percentage points, as that country is more geographically diversified than is Mexico, and the growth of China's exports is driven more by market penetration than by fluctuations in the size of export markets. Several other countries in East Asia and the Pacific that specialize in high-tech exports could see a similar reduction in overall exports, again relative to baseline. Exports from the European Union would decline some 2.5 percent, while the impact of a sharp decline in U.S. imports would be smaller for many other countries.

The simulation effects on developing countries' GDP project a 0.2 percent reduction in GDP growth in 2008, reflecting the fact that effective demand is not the main constraint to growth for many developing countries. Lack of production capacity and infrastructure is a much greater limiting factor. As a result, even in the face of slowing exports, domestic investment continues to increase at rapid rates. These results are consistent with developments during 2006–07, when U.S. imports slowed sharply, contributing to a more than 2 percentage point deceleration in world trade, without measurably affecting the pace of GDP growth among developing countries.

A much larger impact on growth in developing countries is to be expected from further deterioration in international financial markets. Countries with large current account deficits and heavy financing needs are most vulnerable to the risk of an abrupt downturn in the credit cycle. Vulnerable countries include several in the Europe and Central Asia region where a surge in cross-border bank lending over the past few years has supported rapid growth in investment and consumption. Economic conditions in such countries could worsen significantly if external financing were to stop suddenly. Investment would be hardest hit in the affected countries.

A more severe recession in the United States, combined with additional distress in financial institutions, could lead to monetary policy reactions in the United States to diverge further from those in the rest of the world, putting the U.S. dollar under more pressure. Further weakening of dollar would increase uncertainty in the international trading system as it changes relative competitiveness across countries in the short run, depending on their exchange-rate regimes. Similarly, further weakness in the dollar would increase uncertainty about relative yields in the financial markets. And a sharply weakening dollar would boost inflationary expectations in the United States, which could fuel global inflationary expectations, pushing commodity prices up further.

Oil prices have become notoriously difficult to predict. Yet further price increases cannot be ruled out, even in the scenario where there is a moderate slowdown in global growth. Further increases in oil prices would have significantly more severe effects on oil-importing developing countries than the price increases of previous years. In earlier episodes, many countries enjoyed surpluses or small deficits on current account and benefitted from rising export prices for other commodities, while domestic inflation was muted. Now, current accounts of many oil-importing countries have already deteriorated, metals prices are no longer on a strong upward trend, and inflationary pressures are on the rise. And with the current high levels of oil prices, the share of oil in GDP of the importing countries is a multiple of what it was only a few years ago, implying that the same percentage rise in the oil price has a substantially larger impact.

The potential for large exchange-rate movement increases uncertainty in the international trading system as the value of contracts varies with currency denominations. The possibility of a further depreciation of the U.S. dollar runs the risk of accentuating existing inflationary pressures in countries with fixed or managed exchange-rate regimes (linked to the U.S. dollar). A weakening dollar also runs the risk of fueling inflationary expectations in the United States, which could escalate investor interest in commodity markets, pushing commodity prices up still higher.

Soaring food prices over the past years have had a major adverse impact on poverty in some of the poorest countries. Global food markets remain very tight, making them extremely susceptible to supply disruptions. With global grain stocks at near-record lows relative to consumption, a drought affecting the coming harvest would put severe pressure on prices. A moderate drought in a major producing country results on average in a 2 percent decline in global yields from trend. That would reduce grain production by 40 million tons and global stocks by about 12 percent from the projected 320 million tons at the end of the current marketing year. A yield decline of at least that magnitude has occurred approximately 30 percent of the time since 1960, and a decline of 3 percent or greater has occurred about 20 percent of the time. High fertilizer prices may increase the chance of disappointing yields, because farmers can't pay for fertilizer. And average grain prices would, in such a scenario (drought), rise by an estimated 30 percent on top of already very high prices. Further increases in food prices would have a major impact on many of the poorest and most vulnerable, particularly those in urban centers.

Notes

1. The decline in home prices has varied across various measures of price. The National Association of Realtors' (NAR) measure of the median price of a new home declined 7.2 percent (year over year) through February 2008. The U.S. Department of Commerce's measure of the median price of an existing home, similar in concept to the NAR index, declined by the same amount in February 2008. And the Case/Schiller Index of home prices, which encompasses both new and existing homes for 20 major U.S. metropolitan areas fell 10.7 percent in January 2008 (year over year).

2. Based on past experience, about 60 percent will be expended within 90 days.

3. The developing countries of the Middle East and North Africa region can usefully be arrayed into oil-exporting economies and a more economically diversified group. In the former, Algeria, Iran, Oman, the Syrian Arab Republic, and the Republic of Yemen are key players, dominated by the first two countries in terms of oil potential and population density. A group of more diversified exporters would include Egypt (although the country is increasingly viewed as a net oil exporter), Jordan, Lebanon, Morocco, and Tunisia, all largely export-based economies focused on the European and U.S. markets in basic industries such as textiles and clothing.

Reference

World Bank. 2008. *Global Economic Prospects 2008: Technology Diffusion in the Developing World*. Washington, DC: World Bank.

2

Financial Flows to Developing Countries: Recent Trends and Prospects

NET CAPITAL INFLOWS TO DEVELOP-ing countries surged to another record level in 2007, marking the fifth consecutive year of strong gains. Economic expansion in developing countries and ample liquidity in the first half of the year supported a $269 billion increase in net private flows, mainly reflecting continued rapid expansion in equity inflows and net bank lending, which both reached record levels.

But developing countries' easy access to global capital markets deteriorated in late 2007 and into 2008 in the wake of the U.S. subprime mortgage crisis. Uncertainty both about the identity of financial institutions with large exposures and about the potential magnitude of losses gave rise to a volatile financial environment, sparking a sell-off across the entire spectrum of risky assets in mature and emerging markets. At the same time, major financial institutions that have taken sizable write-downs have curbed their lending to restore balance sheets, and further losses are expected over the balance of 2008. Besides reducing capital flows to developing countries, the turmoil has increased borrowing costs, although less so than in previous episodes, when emerging markets themselves were the primary source of difficulty.

This chapter reviews financial flows to developing countries, analyzing recent developments and assessing short-term prospects. The key messages are highlighted below.

- Net private flows to developing countries reached a record level for the year 2007 as a whole, even though economic and financial conditions deteriorated appreciably over the latter part of the year. *Turmoil in international financial markets has curbed private*

debt and equity flows in late 2007 and into early 2008.

- Under our base-case scenario, where global growth moderates and credit conditions remain tight, *private flows are projected to decline modestly in the short term, stabilizing at levels above previous peaks (as a share of GDP) over the medium term.* Under an alternative scenario, where global growth declines abruptly and credit conditions tighten further, private flows are projected to exhibit a sharper decline in the short run, stabilizing at close to historical average levels (as a share of GDP) over the medium term.

- *The financial turmoil that began midyear had a marked impact on emerging debt and equity markets, although to a lesser degree than in previous crises.* Investors' reduced appetite for risk widened spreads on emerging-market sovereign bonds by about 150 basis points between mid-2007 and early 2008, a modest increase relative to previous episodes, such as the Mexican peso crisis in late 1994 and early 1995 and the Russian crisis in August 1998, when sovereign bond spreads widened by 800–1,000 basis points in just a few months. The widening of emerging-market bond spreads during the current episode, however, has coincided with a decline in benchmark U.S. Treasury yields, keeping yields on emerging-market sovereign bonds relatively stable. In contrast, yields on noninvestment-grade corporate bonds in mature and emerging markets rose significantly between mid-2007 and early 2008, suggesting that the turmoil has had a much greater impact on the cost of financing for corporations, particularly the less creditworthy. Emerging-market equity prices peaked in late October 2007, followed by a sharp correction. However, equity returns in emerging markets showed strong gains for the year 2007 as a whole and continued to outperform mature markets by a wide margin, as in the previous four years.

- *The external financial position of many developing countries has deteriorated, leaving many of them more vulnerable to subsequent adverse shocks.* The external financial positions of a small number of countries strengthened. China, for example, accounted for $367 billion of developing countries' $426 billion current account surplus, and five major oil exporters (the Russian Federation, the Islamic Republic of Iran, Algeria, República Bolivariana de Venezuela, and Nigeria) ran a combined surplus of $280 billion. By contrast, almost a quarter of developing countries ran current account deficits in excess of 10 percent of GDP, and current account balances deteriorated in two-thirds of developing countries. The pace of foreign reserve accumulation by developing countries accelerated in 2007. Their reserve holdings expanded by over $1 trillion, more than double the value of their short-term debt and bank loans. However, three-quarters of the increase was concentrated in the BRICs (Brazil, Russian Federation, India, and China).

- *Aside from debt relief, donor countries have made slow progress in fulfilling their commitments to enrich development assistance.* Although private capital flows to developing countries have surged over the past few years, most of the flows have gone to just a few large countries. Many developing countries still depend heavily on concessionary loans and grants from official sources to meet their financing needs. In 2006 net disbursements of official development assistance (ODA) exceeded net private debt flows in almost two-thirds of developing countries. Those countries are less vulnerable to an abrupt downturn in the credit cycle, but many face the daunting challenge posed by the dramatic rise in food and energy prices over the past few years. ODA has increased by less than expected since the United Nations' Conference on Financing for Development in Monterrey, Mexico, in 2002. Participants at the Monterrey conference acknowledged dramatic shortfalls in resources required to achieve the internationally agreed development goals, and donors pledged that debt relief would not displace other components of ODA. Since then, ODA (excluding debt relief) has increased from 0.23 percent of donors' gross national income (GNI) in 2002 to only 0.25 percent in 2007, well below the 0.33 percent level attained in the early 1990s. Existing commitments by donors imply that ODA will increase to 0.35 percent of their GNI by 2010, only half of the UN target (0.7 percent). Meeting the 2010 commitments would require an average annual growth rate of over 14 percent in real terms over the balance of the decade, three times that observed since the Monterrey Consensus in 2002.

Capital market developments in 2007
Private capital flows continue to surge . . .

Net debt and equity inflows to developing countries increased by $269 billion in 2007, reaching a record $1.03 trillion (table 2.1). This marks five consecutive years of strong gains in net private flows, which averaged over 44 percent a year. However, much of the increase in dollar terms reflects the depreciation of the U.S. dollar against most other currencies (box 2.1). The increase in 2007 is much more modest when measured against the income (nominal GDP in U.S. dollars) of developing countries—rising from 6.7 to 7.5 percent.

The rapid expansion in private flows reflects strong gains in both equity and debt components (figure 2.1). Net (foreign direct and portfolio) equity inflows reached an estimated $616 billion in 2007, equal to a record 4.5 percent of GDP, up from 4.1 percent in 2006.[1] Net private debt flows (disbursements less principal payments) reached an estimated $413 billion, rising from 2.5 to 3.0 percent of GDP.[2] Loan repayments by developing countries to official creditors exceeded lending for the fifth consecutive year, although the margin narrowed substantially, from approximately $71 billion in 2005 and 2006 to $4 billion in 2007.

Table 2.1 Net capital flows to developing countries, 2000–07

$ billions

Category	1999	2000	2001	2002	2003	2004	2005	2006	2007e
Current account balance	−17.7	36.3	12.8	62.0	116.9	164.3	309.5	431.0	425.9
as % of GDP	−0.3	0.7	0.2	1.0	1.7	2.0	3.2	3.8	3.1
Financial flows									
Net private and official flows	209.7	181.2	191.3	174.0	262.4	386.4	479.7	689.8	1025.0
Net private flows (debt + equity)	195.7	187.0	164.5	169.1	274.1	412.5	551.4	760.3	1028.9
Net equity flows	188.4	179.0	178.6	166.2	186.0	265.9	357.4	472.3	615.9
Net FDI inflows	177.0	165.5	173.0	160.7	161.9	225.5	288.5	367.5	470.8
Net portfolio equity inflows	11.4	13.5	5.6	5.5	24.1	40.4	68.9	104.8	145.1
Net debt flows	15.1	−0.4	4.5	8.9	72.8	128.8	152.4	217.5	409.1
Official creditors	14.0	−5.8	26.8	4.9	−11.7	−26.1	−71.7	−70.5	−3.9
World Bank	8.8	7.9	7.6	−0.4	−0.8	1.4	2.5	−0.7	3.0
International Monetary Fund	−2.2	−10.6	19.5	14.0	2.4	−14.7	−40.2	−27.1	−4.7
Others official	7.4	−3.1	−0.3	−8.7	−13.3	−12.8	−34.0	−42.7	−2.2
Private creditors	1.5	5.8	−23.0	3.8	84.4	155.2	222.7	288.0	413.0
Net medium- and long-term debt flows	18.9	12.2	1.9	0.7	30.9	87.7	133.1	193.8	283.3
Bonds	25.7	19.5	10.2	8.8	19.6	41.1	52.6	25.3	79.3
Banks	−5.5	−3.9	−2.0	−1.7	15.2	50.4	85.3	172.4	214.7
Others	−1.3	−3.4	−6.3	−6.4	−3.9	−3.8	−4.8	−3.9	−10.7
Net short-term debt flows	−17.4	−6.4	−24.9	3.1	53.5	67.5	89.6	94.2	129.7
Balancing item[a]	−153.1	−172.3	−115.5	−70.6	−83.2	−156.6	−417.5	−481.9	−391.0
Change in reserves (− = increase)	−32.8	−42.6	−80.4	−166.5	−292.4	−402.4	−390.8	−634.2	−1090.7
Memorandum item									
Workers' remittances	77.5	84.5	95.5	115.8	143.4	160.7	191.0	221.0	240.0

Sources: World Bank Debtor Reporting System and staff estimates.
Note: e = estimate; FDI = foreign direct investment.
a. Combination of errors and omissions and transfers to and capital outflows from developing countries.

Figure 2.1 Net private flows to developing countries, 1991–2007

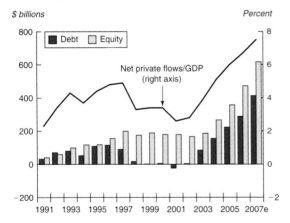

Sources: World Bank Debtor Reporting System and staff estimates.
Note: e = estimate.

. . . despite the turmoil midyear

Global financial markets entered into an episode of heightened volatility beginning about midway through 2007 as the crisis in the U.S. subprime mortgage market spilled over into equity, currency, and bond markets worldwide. The turbulence in financial markets curbed investors' appetite for risk, resulting in a sell-off of risky assets in mature and emerging markets. Although the sell-off has had little impact on the cost of sovereign borrowing from abroad, it has increased the cost of corporate borrowing significantly, particularly for less-creditworthy borrowers. The turmoil has also increased volatility in equity prices, which peaked in October 2007 and have since undergone a sharp correction. Nonetheless, equity returns in emerging markets managed to post impressive gains for 2007 as a whole, and outperformed mature markets by a wide margin.

Current account balances have worsened in most developing countries

Current account balances for developing countries as a group increased slightly in dollar terms in 2007 but declined as a share of GDP, falling from a record surplus of 3.8 percent in 2006 to 3.1 percent in 2007. The $426 billion overall surplus

Box 2.1 The impact of exchange-rate movements on capital flows measured in U.S. dollars

Exchange-rate movements over the past few years have had a major influence on the magnitude of capital flows to developing countries (measured in U.S. dollars). In 2006, almost 40 percent of external debt outstanding in developing countries was denominated in currencies other than the U.S. dollar, mainly in euros (23 percent) and Japanese yen (10 percent). The convention used in this report is to measure all external borrowing in U.S. dollars as the common currency. The choice of common currency has implications for measuring capital flows over time. The surge in net private flows over the past few years is more moderate when euros are used as the common currency instead of U.S. dollars. In 2007, net private flows are estimated to have increased by 35 percent in U.S. dollars, compared with just 24 percent in euros, the difference reflecting the depreciation of the dollar against the euro.

The development potential of capital flows is better measured from the perspective of the recipient country. For this purpose, converting capital flows from U.S. dollars to domestic currency provides a better measure of the purchasing power. The U.S. dollar depreciated significantly against currencies in many developing countries in 2007, in many cases by more than 10 percent. The purchasing power of capital inflows is also eroded by inflation. Countries with currencies appreciating against the dollar and with high inflation rates require a higher level of capital flows (measured in dollars) in order to maintain purchasing power. For example, in the case of Brazil, the real appreciated by 17 percent against the dollar in 2007 and the consumer price index increased by 4.5 percent (in December year over year). Capital inflows to Brazil would have had to increase by over 20 percent in dollar terms just to maintain the same purchasing power.

Measuring the value of capital flows relative to nominal GDP takes into account exchange-rate and domestic price changes, along with real GDP growth. Nominal GDP growth in developing countries as a group averaged 18 percent in 2004–07, 11 percentage points above the average annual rate of real GDP growth. In contrast, nominal GDP growth averaged only 0.5 percent in 1998–2002, 3 percentage points below the average annual rate of real GDP growth. Capital flows to developing countries were quite stable throughout the 1990s, adjusting for exchange-rate changes and inflation (proxied using changes in GDP price deflators), and have increased at an average annual rate of about 31 percent over 2003–07, compared with 44 percent in dollar terms.

Net private capital flows to developing countries, 1991–2007

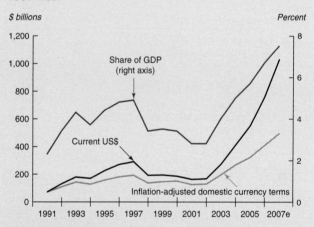

Source: World Bank staff estimates.

Note: e = estimate.

position was dominated by China, where the current account balance increased from $250 billion in 2006 (9.6 percent of GDP) to $360 billion in 2007 (11.7 percent of GDP), along with a number of leading oil exporters, notably Russia ($83 billion), the Islamic Republic of Iran ($49 billion), and Algeria ($27 billion). The overall surplus position for developing countries, however, gives a misleading impression of balances in most countries. One in five developing countries ran current account surpluses below 3 percent of GDP; one in two ran deficits in excess of 5 percent of GDP (figure 2.2).

In 2007 current account balances worsened in two-thirds of developing countries (as a share of GDP). The dramatic rise in imported food and energy prices over the past few years has worsened the trade balance in two-thirds of all developing countries. For example in the case of Lesotho, commodity price increases over the period 2003–07 worsened the trade balance by an estimated $550 million (an amount equal to 28 percent of Lesotho's GDP in 2007), a major factor underlying its current account deficit exceeding 25 percent of GDP in 2007. In the more extreme case of Seychelles,

Figure 2.2 Current account as a share of GDP in developing countries, 2007

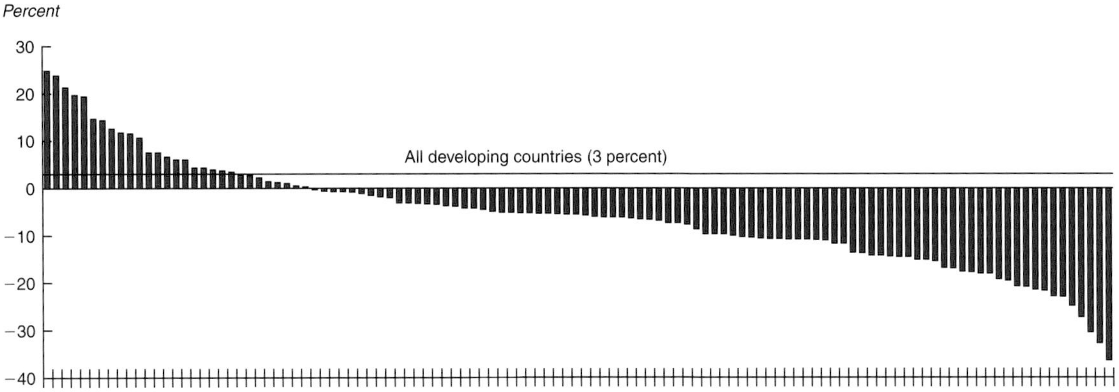

Percent

All developing countries (3 percent)

Source: IMF International Financial Statistics.

commodity price increases worsened the trade balance by an estimated $235 million (equal to 33 percent of GDP in 2007), while the current account deficit in Seychelles increased from around 2 percent of GDP in 2003 to almost 34 percent in 2007. Soaring commodity prices have also had a major impact on larger developing countries such as Morocco, where commodity price increases over the period 2003–07 worsened the trade balance by an estimated $10 billion (equal to 16 percent of GDP in 2007), while Morocco's current account balance deteriorated from a surplus equal to 3.5 percent of GDP to a deficit equal to 3.2 percent.

Foreign reserves continue to cumulate in the BRICs

Foreign exchange reserves rose by $1.03 trillion in 2007, up from $634 billion in 2006 and approximately $400 billion in 2004 and 2005. The BRICs accounted for over two-thirds of the increase: $462 billion in China, $169 billion in Russia, $96 billion in India, and $94 billion in Brazil. Reserve holdings by all developing countries increased from 23 percent of their GDP in 2006 to 27 percent in 2007 (figure 2.3). The share of reserves held by the BRICs rose from 40 percent in 2000 to about 65 percent in 2007. China's share of total reserves held by developing countries has been stable at about 40 percent over the past four years, while the share held by Russia increased from 7.5 percent to 12.5 percent.

Reserve holdings by all four of the BRICs greatly exceed levels required to provide adequate insurance against a sudden shift in private capital

Figure 2.3 Foreign reserve holdings as a share of GDP in developing countries, 2000–07

Percent

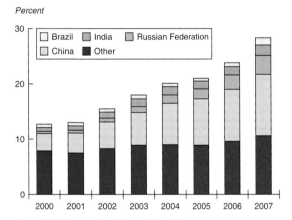

☐ Brazil ▨ India ▨ Russian Federation
☐ China ■ Other

Source: IMF International Financial Statistics.

flows. At the end of 2007, the BRICs held $2.4 trillion in foreign reserves, an amount equal to 5.7 times the value of principal and interest payments due in 2008, compared with 1.8 times for other developing countries. In the case of India, the ratio has risen from 2.5 in 2000 to 8.4 in 2007 (figure 2.4).

Developing countries now account for almost 60 percent of global foreign reserve holdings, up from 40 percent in 2003 (figure 2.5). According to the Currency Composition of Official Foreign Exchange Reserves database maintained by the International Monetary Fund (IMF), the bulk of reserves held by developing countries and newly industrialized economies is denominated in U.S. dollars (60 percent) and euros (28 percent). The

Figure 2.4 Foreign reserves relative to principal and interest payments on debt outstanding, 2000–07

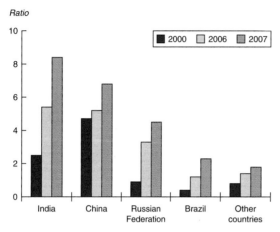

Sources: World Bank Debtor Reporting System; IMF International Financial Statistics.

currency composition has been stable over the past five years.[3]

Several developing countries have shifted a higher proportion of their foreign currency earnings from official foreign currency reserves to sovereign wealth funds. There is wide diversity among sovereign wealth funds, partly because they have been set up for a variety of purposes (see IMF 2008b). These funds have an estimated $600 billion in assets under management in developing countries,[4] dominated by China ($200 billion held by the Chinese Investment Corporation and $68 billion held by the Central Huijin Investment

Figure 2.5 Global foreign reserve holdings, 1997–2007

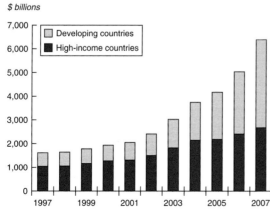

Source: IMF Statistics Department COFER database.

Company) and Russia ($130 billion held in the Reserve Fund and $33 billion held by the Fund of Future Generations). This amount pales in comparison to the total level of reserves held by developing countries ($3.7 trillion at end 2007), but in a few countries the value of assets managed by sovereign wealth funds is sizable relative to reserve holdings. For instance, the Kazakhstan National Oil Fund has assets valued at around $19 billion, exceeding the $15.5 billion in foreign reserves held at end 2007. Sovereign wealth funds also play a prominent role in Azerbaijan, Botswana, Chile, Libya, Oman, and República Bolivariana de Venezuela, where the value of assets under management is estimated to be equal to between one-half and two-thirds of reserve holdings. The value of assets managed by sovereign wealth funds worldwide is dominated by high-income countries. The range of estimates varies considerably (between $2 trillion and $3.5 trillion), implying that sovereign wealth funds in developing countries manage around 20 to 30 percent of the total. The wide range of estimates largely stems from uncertainty about the value of assets managed by the Abu Dhabi Investment Authority and Corporation (estimated at between $250 billion and $875 billion at end 2007), the Government of Singapore Investment Corporation ($100 billion to $330 billion), Temasek Holdings ($66 billion to $160 billion), and the Kuwait Investment Authority ($160 billion to $250 billion).

Private debt market developments
Bank lending showed strong gains over the year 2007 as a whole . . .

The expansion in net private debt flows in 2006–07 has been concentrated in net bank lending (figure 2.6), which accounted for over half of private debt flows in 2007, up from less than 40 percent in 2004. As a share of GDP, net bond flows rebounded in 2007 to levels attained in 2004 and 2005, while short-term debt flows remained relatively constant.

Disbursements of cross-border loans by commercial banks rose by $58 billion in 2007, reaching a record level in dollar terms ($455 billion), with strong gains in East Asia and the Pacific ($23 billion), South Asia ($21 billion), and Sub-Saharan Africa ($14 billion). These gains were partly offset by an $8 billion decline in Europe and Central Asia (table 2.2). Loan disbursements as a share of

Figure 2.6 Net private debt flows as a share of GDP, 1991–2007

Percent

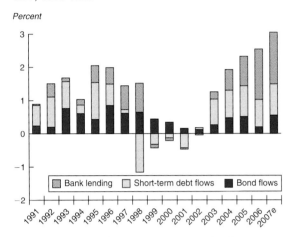

Sources: World Bank Debtor Reporting System and staff estimates.
Note: e = estimate.

GDP declined slightly to 3.3 percent in 2007, from a record 3.5 percent in 2006, while principal repayments continued to decline, reaching 1.75 percent of GDP in 2007, down from 2.5 percent in 2001 and 2002 (figure 2.7).

Figure 2.7 Bank lending as a share of GDP, 1991–2007

Percent

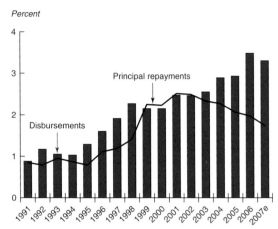

Sources: World Bank Debtor Reporting System and staff estimates.
Note: e = estimate.

Cross-border syndicated loan commitments provide an alternative measure of bank lending to developing countries (box 2.2). According to this measure, loan commitments to developing countries increased by a substantial $118 billion in

Table 2.2 Cross-border bank lending to developing countries, by region, 2000–07

$ billions

Indicator	2000	2001	2002	2003	2004	2005	2006	2007e
Gross bank lending								
Total	116.5	137.6	146.0	175.3	235.2	285.5	397.0	454.7
By region								
East Asia and Pacific	14.9	20.7	27.3	37.2	34.8	43.7	42.4	65.1
Europe and Central Asia	37.9	46.9	61.5	76.3	128.4	170.1	260.3	252.1
Latin America and the Caribbean	56.7	62.9	46.3	47.0	53.3	48.2	76.6	77.9
Middle East and North Africa	2.3	1.9	2.7	2.5	1.9	4.5	3.1	9.4
South Asia	1.5	3.2	5.6	8.7	11.8	11.0	10.7	32.1
Sub-Saharan Africa	3.2	2.1	2.6	3.7	4.9	8.0	3.9	18.1
Principal repayments								
Total	120.4	139.6	147.8	160.1	184.7	200.1	224.6	240.0
By region								
East Asia and Pacific	26.2	32.5	37.5	45.6	34.6	42.1	31.3	36.0
Europe and Central Asia	28.5	39.6	45.6	55.8	81.9	94.1	120.8	136.2
Latin America and the Caribbean	56.1	57.2	52.3	48.4	52.4	49.6	57.0	50.9
Middle East and North Africa	2.1	2.3	3.2	3.7	2.6	3.3	3.9	4.0
South Asia	3.5	4.3	4.6	4.2	10.7	6.8	6.1	7.0
Sub-Saharan Africa	3.8	3.7	4.6	2.4	2.5	4.2	5.5	6.0
Net bank lending (gross lending less principal repayments)								
Total	−3.9	−2.0	−1.7	15.2	50.4	85.3	172.4	214.7
By region								
East Asia and Pacific	−11.3	−11.8	−10.2	−8.4	0.2	1.6	11.1	29.1
Europe and Central Asia	9.3	7.2	15.9	20.4	46.5	76.0	139.5	115.9
Latin America and the Caribbean	0.6	5.6	−6.0	−1.4	0.8	−1.4	19.6	27.0
Middle East and North Africa	0.2	−0.4	−0.5	−1.2	−0.6	1.2	−0.9	5.4
South Asia	−2.0	−1.1	1.0	4.4	1.1	4.1	4.6	25.2
Sub-Saharan Africa	−0.7	−1.6	−1.9	1.2	2.4	3.8	−1.5	12.1

Sources: World Bank Debtor Reporting System and staff estimates.
Note: e = estimate.

Box 2.2 Alternative measures of cross-border bank lending to developing countries

Cross-border bank lending by developing countries reported in table 2.2 is based on annual data collected by the World Bank Debtor Reporting System (DRS). The DRS provides a comprehensive coverage of loan disbursements, commitments, and principal and interest payments but is not available on a timely basis. Currently only preliminary data for 2007 are available for a subset of countries. Estimates are generated for total borrowing by all developing countries and the regional aggregates using various data sources, including monthly data on cross-border syndicated loan commitments collected by Dealogic Loan Analytics (reported in table 2.3). The timeliness of the Dealogic data provides a more up-to-date perspective on emerging trends. The monthly frequency is of particular interest for analyzing the impact of the financial turmoil (which began in mid-2007) on bank lending over the course of the year 2007 and into early 2008.

There are, however, a few important differences between the two data sources that limit their comparability.

First, Dealogic only reports data on loan commitments (loan agreements made), which may not be a good indicator of the net bank lending (loan disbursements less principal repayments) component of net private capital flows. Second, the Dealogic data do not include intrabank lending (loans made from a parent bank to a subsidiary or branch operating in a foreign country), which has played a prominent role in some countries, particularly those in the Europe and Central Asia region. Bank loan disbursements to the Europe and Central Asia region (reported by the DRS) exceeded loan commitments (reported by Dealogic) by $163 billion in 2006, compared with only $15 billion in 2000.

Third, the Dealogic data mostly entail lending by bank syndicates, whereas the DRS also includes loans made by a single bank. Taken together, these factors can explain why the estimate of cross-border bank loan disbursements to developing countries (reported in table 2.2) for 2007 exceeds syndicated loan commitments (reported in table 2.3) by $74 billion.

2007, most of which was concentrated in just three countries: Russia ($50 billion), India ($18 billion), and China ($17 billion) (table 2.3).

Cross-border syndicated loan commitments are dominated by the corporate sector. Governments accounted for only about 3 percent over the past few years, down from about 15 percent in the early 1990s, while private corporations received

just over 70 percent, up from an average level of about two-thirds over the previous 10 years (figure 2.8).

In 2007 there was a dramatic increase in the proportion of bank lending to developing countries denominated in domestic currency. The domestic-currency share increased from under 5 percent in 2005–06 to 11 percent in 2007, led by South Africa

Table 2.3 Top 10 developing countries receiving cross-border syndicated loan commitments, 2000–07
$ billions

Category	2000	2001	2002	2003	2004	2005	2006	2007
All developing countries	114.1	83.9	75.6	98.9	124.0	202.0	262.8	380.3
Top 10 countries								
Russian Federation	4.7	2.9	5.8	7.4	13.9	39.9	38.8	89.1
India	3.0	2.1	1.8	3.0	6.9	11.7	18.0	36.3
China	6.8	3.3	10.2	13.0	9.3	18.6	14.6	31.7
Turkey	11.3	4.6	3.7	4.7	8.4	14.6	26.4	28.8
Mexico	12.8	11.3	7.5	13.9	15.7	18.1	28.4	28.0
Brazil	15.0	11.9	5.4	3.1	9.8	12.7	33.5	27.5
South Africa	8.1	5.5	3.0	3.7	2.5	5.6	15.5	13.4
Malaysia	7.5	4.1	5.6	5.8	7.7	4.4	7.4	12.6
Kazakhstan	0.0	0.6	0.6	1.9	3.9	4.7	8.5	11.9
Ukraine	0.4	0.2	0.0	0.1	0.4	1.5	2.7	7.2
Memorandum item								
BRICs	29.5	20.1	23.2	26.5	40.0	82.9	105.0	184.6

Source: World Bank staff calculations based on Dealogic Loan Analytics data.
Note: BRICs = Brazil, Russia, India, and China.

Figure 2.8 Share of cross-border loan commitments, by debtor, 1991–2007

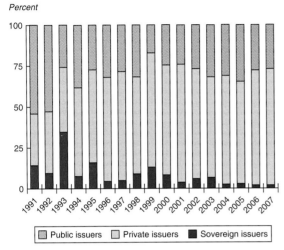

Percent

Public issuers   Private issuers   Sovereign issuers

Source: Dealogic Loan Analytics.

Table 2.4 Currency composition of cross-border syndicated bank loan commitments to developing countries, 2003–07

Share of total (percent)

Currency	2003	2004	2005	2006	2007
U.S. dollar	78.0	85.5	81.7	84.4	77.9
Euro	17.1	8.5	12.8	9.3	9.5
South African rand	0.0	0.0	0.0	0.8	2.5
Brazilian real	0.0	0.0	0.2	0.3	2.2
Russian ruble	0.0	0.0	0.1	0.2	1.8
Chinese renminbi	0.1	0.1	1.0	0.4	1.8
Memorandum items					
Advanced-country currencies	97.4	97.9	95.8	95.7	88.9
Developing-country currencies	2.6	2.1	4.2	4.3	11.1

Source: Dealogic Loan Analytics.

transaction in each case, but this was not the case for bank loans denominated in South African rand and Chinese renminbi, which involved 10 and 20 separate loan agreements, respectively.[5]

. . . as private bond flows rebounded

Net bond flows increased by $54 billion in 2007, after declining by some $27 billion in 2006 (table 2.5). The rebound reflects a combination of more issuance and lower principal repayments

(60 percent), China (36 percent), Brazil (24 percent), and India (20 percent) (table 2.4). The sharp rise in bank loans denominated in Brazilian reals and Mexican pesos in 2007 reflected a single

Table 2.5 Private bond flows to developing countries, by region, 2000–07

$ billions

Indicator	2000	2001	2002	2003	2004	2005	2006	2007e
Bond issuance								
All developing countries	69.4	54.6	49.2	68.2	102.8	115.1	105.9	142.2
By region								
East Asia and Pacific	5.6	6.7	8.0	6.6	16.3	14.4	14.4	12.5
Europe and Central Asia	12.1	7.7	11.6	21.2	35.4	46.1	45.1	68.4
Latin America and the Caribbean	42.5	32.7	20.8	34.7	36.4	42.6	35.1	42.6
Middle East and North Africa	2.1	5.1	6.2	2.8	6.5	4.4	3.6	4.6
South Asia	5.5	0.0	0.1	1.6	7.1	6.3	5.9	8.0
Sub-Saharan Africa	1.5	2.5	2.5	1.4	1.0	1.3	1.9	6.1
Principal repayments								
All developing countries	49.9	44.4	40.4	48.6	61.7	62.5	80.6	62.9
By region								
East Asia and Pacific	6.4	6.3	7.9	4.8	6.6	6.6	8.8	6.0
Europe and Central Asia	6.6	6.6	8.0	12.3	11.8	17.9	11.2	16.4
Latin America and the Caribbean	35.4	29.9	21.6	23.7	36.7	26.6	54.1	34.5
Middle East and North Africa	0.9	0.7	1.2	2.1	3.2	2.1	3.0	1.9
South Asia	0.1	0.4	0.8	4.7	3.0	9.1	1.6	3.8
Sub-Saharan Africa	0.5	0.5	0.9	1.0	0.4	0.0	1.7	0.3
Net bond flows (bond issuance less principal repayments)								
All developing countries	19.5	10.2	8.8	19.6	41.1	52.6	25.3	79.3
By region								
East Asia and Pacific	−0.7	0.4	0.1	1.8	9.7	7.8	5.5	6.5
Europe and Central Asia	5.5	1.1	3.6	8.9	23.6	28.2	33.9	52.0
Latin America and the Caribbean	7.1	2.8	−0.8	11.0	−0.3	16.0	−19.0	8.1
Middle East and North Africa	1.2	4.4	5.0	0.7	3.3	2.3	0.6	2.7
South Asia	5.4	−0.4	−0.7	−3.1	4.1	−2.9	4.3	4.2
Sub-Saharan Africa	1.0	1.9	1.5	0.4	0.6	1.3	0.1	5.8

Sources: World Bank Debtor Reporting System and staff estimates.
Note: e = estimate.

Figure 2.9 Private bond flows as a share of GDP, 1991–2007

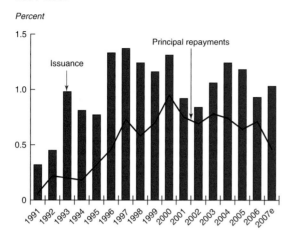

Sources: World Bank Debtor Reporting System and staff estimates.
Note: e = estimate.

Figure 2.10 Share of private bond issuance, by debtor, 1991–2007

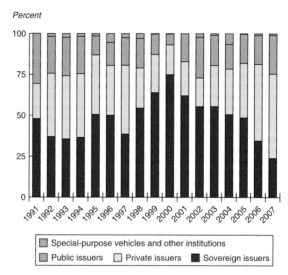

Source: Dealogic DCM Analytics.

(figure 2.9). Bond issuance as a share of GDP also increased in 2007, although it remains below levels attained in 2003–05. Europe and Central Asia accounted for almost half of total issuance in 2007, up from less than 30 percent in 2003, while issuance by countries in Latin America and the Caribbean declined from just above 50 percent to 30 percent over the same time period. Principal repayments by countries in Latin America and the Caribbean declined by $20 billion in 2007, following record-high repayments in 2006 resulting from sovereign debt buybacks by Brazil, Colombia, Mexico, and República Bolivariana de Venezuela totaling almost $30 billion.

Private and public corporations continue to dominate issuance in international bond markets. The sovereign share of bond issuance shrank to below 25 percent in 2007, down from a peak of 75 percent in 2000, while the private corporate share rose to just over 50 percent, up from less than 20 percent in 2000 (figure 2.10).

The volume of emerging-market debt traded worldwide remained constant at $6.5 trillion in 2007 (Emerging Markets Traders Association 2008). Trading volumes in the first three quarters of 2007 outpaced those of 2006. The fourth quarter, however, represented the lowest quarterly volume in more than two years and was 16 percent below the same quarter of 2006. Local instruments accounted for nearly two-thirds of total trading volume, up from less than half in 2005,

reflecting the shift by sovereign borrowers from external to domestic debt markets. Sovereign Eurobond trading declined from $2.1 trillion in 2006 to $1.4 trillion in 2007, while corporate Eurobond trading increased from $458 billion to a record $676 billion in 2007.

As in the case of bank lending, developing countries increased the proportion of external bond issues denominated in domestic currency over the past few years. The domestic-currency share has increased from less than 0.5 percent in 2003 to almost 9 percent in 2007 (table 2.6). In the case of Brazil, external bonds denominated in reals increased from three corporate issues totaling $0.3 billion in 2004 to eight corporate issues totaling $1.4 billion and four sovereign issues totaling $1.9 billion (a total of $3.2 billion) in 2007. Domestic-currency issues accounted for one-quarter of Brazil's total external bond issuance in 2007, the highest proportion among developing countries, followed by Mexico (11 percent), and Russia (5 percent).

Governments in several developing countries have continued to shift more of their financing needs into domestic debt markets where bond issues are mainly denominated in local currency, reducing their exposure to exchange-rate risk. Expanding public debt issuance in the domestic market also helps satisfy the growing needs of institutional

Table 2.6 Currency composition of bond issuance by developing countries, 2003–07

Share of total (percent)

Currency	2003	2004	2005	2006	2007
U.S. dollar	76.9	71.1	69.4	71.8	65.2
Euro	21.0	24.6	21.8	19.7	19.8
British pound sterling	0.8	2.1	1.0	0.9	3.2
Brazilian real	0.0	0.3	1.7	1.2	2.2
Japanese yen	0.8	0.9	1.9	1.5	1.6
Peruvian nuevo sol	0.0	0.0	0.2	0.0	1.1
Russian ruble	0.0	0.0	0.0	1.1	1.1
Memorandum items					
Advanced-country currencies	99.6	98.9	95.6	94.3	91.2
Developing-country currencies	0.4	1.1	4.4	5.7	8.8

Source: Dealogic DCM Analytics.
Note: The calculations refer only to bonds issued in external (not domestic) markets.

investors (notably pension funds and insurance companies) for long-dated, low-risk assets denominated in local currency. The process of developing local-currency bond markets has been supported by a series of initiatives taken by international financial institutions (box 2.3).

A lack of timely, comprehensive data on domestic debt prevents us from gauging countries' progress over time. The analysis to date has mainly focused on the large emerging-market economies that have more-developed domestic debt markets and higher-quality data available. For example, Hanson (2007) reports that the domestic portion of outstanding public debt in

Box 2.3   The Global Emerging Markets Local Currency Bond (Gemloc) Program

Financial sector development in many emerging markets has been hampered by the absence of liquid, long-term domestic investment instruments. In November 2007 the World Bank announced the Global Emerging Markets Local Currency Bond (Gemloc) Program, an initiative designed to support the development of local-currency bond markets and increase their investability so that more institutional investment from local and global investors can flow into local-currency bond markets in developing countries.

The Gemloc program consists of three components: an emerging-market local-currency bond fund; an index; and technical assistance provided by the World Bank. The bond fund, to be branded by the World Bank Group's International Bank for Reconstruction and Development (IBRD) in partnership with PIMCO, a private investment management company, is expected to raise $5 billion from public and private institutional investors by early 2008 for investment in 15 to 20 emerging markets initially, expanding to 40 countries within five years. The index, the Markit iBoxx Global Emerging Markets Bond Index (GEMX), to be created by the World Bank Group's International Finance Corporation (IFC) in partnership with Markit Group Limited, will establish a benchmark for the asset class and allow a wide range of emerging markets to be targeted by global investors. The index aims to set out clear, transparent criteria so that countries can implement reforms to improve their ranking, attract additional investment, and expand their bond markets. Technical assistance will be available to help countries meet the goals of policy reform and improved market infrastructure, funded by fee income from the fund and the IBRD. The technical assistance component includes a sunset provision of 10 years,

during which involvement of the World Bank Group will cease and the private sector is expected to be fully engaged.

Initiatives by international financial institutions to help develop local-currency bond markets date back to 1970, when the World Bank and the Asian Development Bank (ADB) issued yen-denominated bonds in Japan (an emerging-market economy at the time). Regional development banks have been active in helping to develop local-currency bond markets (Wolff-Hamacher 2007). The ADB launched several local-currency bonds in Asia (Hong Kong [China], Republic of Korea, and Taiwan [China]) in the 1990s, followed by China, India, Malaysia, the Philippines, Singapore, and Thailand in 2004. The European Bank for Reconstruction and Development has been active in European transition countries, with local-currency issues in the Czech Republic, Estonia, Hungary, Poland, the Russian Federation, and the Slovak Republic in the mid-1990s. The Inter-American Development Bank launched local-currency issues in Brazil, Chile, Colombia, and Mexico in 2004. In addition, the IFC has borrowed in 31 currencies and was the first nonresident institution to launch local-currency bonds in China, Colombia, Malaysia, Morocco, Peru, and Singapore (with China in partnership with the ADB). In December 2006, the IFC became the first foreign institution to issue a bond denominated in CFA francs, the currency of eight countries in West Africa. The European Investment Bank has issued local-currency bonds in most emerging European economies and has recently extended the program to help develop local-currency debt markets in Africa, with Eurobond issues in Botswana (October 2005), the Arab Republic of Egypt (February 2006), Namibia (March 2006), Mauritius (March 2007), Ghana (October 2007), and Zambia (February 2008).

Table 2.7 Net short-term debt flows to developing countries, by region, 2007
$ billions

Category	2000	2001	2002	2003	2004	2005	2006	2007e
Total	−6.4	−24.9	3.1	53.5	67.5	89.6	94.2	129.7
By region								
East Asia and Pacific	−9.9	1.7	9.9	18.5	32.6	45.2	27.7	31.9
Europe and Central Asia	8.3	−6.0	4.2	30.4	18.3	25.5	55.5	60.0
Latin America and the Caribbean	−0.9	−14.6	−10.3	2.3	7.0	14.5	−3.3	29.4
Middle East and North Africa	−1.9	−3.0	−0.7	2.5	5.4	0.1	0.6	0.9
South Asia	−0.9	−0.9	1.8	0.7	2.6	1.6	3.6	4.0
Sub-Saharan Africa	−1.1	−2.1	−1.8	−1.0	1.6	2.8	10.1	3.6

Sources: World Bank Debtor Reporting System and staff estimates.
Note: e = estimate.

25 large emerging-market economies increased from 38 percent in 1995 to 58 percent in 2004. The World Bank (2007, p. 48) reports that the ratio increased from a little more than half in 1998 to three-quarters in 2006 for a slightly different set of countries. Recent data indicate that the domestic portion of public debt also plays a prominent role in several low-income countries. In 2007, the ratio exceeded 25 percent in almost half of 38 low-income countries where data are available and exceeded 50 percent in five countries—Cameroon, Ethiopia, Guinea-Bissau, Mauritania, and Zambia.

Short-term debt flows—debt instruments with original maturity of less than one year (mostly bank loans and trade credit)—increased by $35.5 billion in 2007; these flows were concentrated in Latin America and the Caribbean, where net flows rebounded from −$3.3 billion to $29.4 billion (table 2.7). Although short-term debt flows to Europe and Central Asia increased by only $4.5 billion, the region still accounted for almost half of total flows.

Large economies receive the vast majority of private debt flows . . .
Bank lending and bond issuance remain highly concentrated in just a few of the largest developing-country economies. In 2007 five countries accounted for over half of syndicated loan commitments and bond issuance; 20 countries accounted for nearly 90 percent (table 2.8). The largest borrower, Russia, accounted for almost one-quarter of the total, well above its share (9 percent) of total developing-country GDP. In contrast, lower-middle-income countries, which accounted for just over half of GDP, received less than 20 percent of syndicated loan commitments and bond issuance.

Table 2.8 Share of total syndicated loan commitments to and bond issues by developing countries, 2007
Percentage of total

Borrower	Bank lending	Bond issuance	Bank lending and bond issuance	Nominal GDP
Russian Federation	23.4	23.1	23.3	9.1
India	9.5	5.7	8.5	8.6
Mexico	7.4	8.0	7.5	6.3
Brazil	7.2	8.3	7.5	8.8
Turkey	7.6	4.9	6.8	3.6
China	8.3	1.5	6.4	22.6
Kazakhstan	3.1	6.5	4.1	0.8
South Africa	3.5	4.9	3.9	1.9
Malaysia	3.3	0.2	2.4	1.2
Venezuela, R. B. de	0.8	5.7	2.2	1.8
Top 5	57.6	51.0	53.7	36.3
Top 10	76.7	72.5	72.7	64.7
Top 20	89.7	90.8	87.6	81.2
Upper-middle-income countries	68.5	76.6	70.8	35.2
Lower-middle-income countries	17.9	16.0	17.4	50.7
Low-income countries	13.6	7.3	11.8	14.1
India	9.5	5.7	8.5	8.6
Sub-Saharan Africa	2.5	1.0	2.1	2.8
Others	1.5	0.7	1.3	2.7

Sources: Dealogic Loan Analytics and World Bank staff estimates.

The concentration of bond issuance among the top five developing-country borrowers has declined over the past several years, particularly among sovereign issuers. The top five countries accounted for half of sovereign bond issuance in 2003–07, compared with three-quarters in 1993–97 (figure 2.11). Corporate issuance, though, remains more concentrated than sovereign issuance. In 2003–07, five countries accounted for two-thirds of issuance by private corporations and three-quarters of issuance by public corporations.

Figure 2.11 Share of bond issuance by top five developing countries

Percent

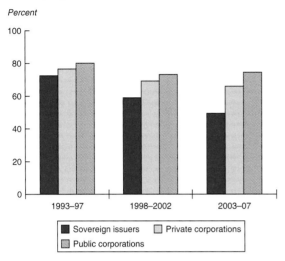

Source: Dealogic DCM Analytics.

In sum, bond issuance has become increasingly dominated by corporations located in just a few large emerging-market economies.

. . . but a few low-income countries have recently gained access to private debt markets

Three in five developing countries have never issued a bond in the international market. Until just a few years ago, India was the only low-income country to access the international bond market on a frequent basis.[6] India has been active since the early 1980s, with bond issues in 14 of the past 18 years. Some low-income countries have accessed the international bond market intermittently. For example, Pakistan issued a series of external bonds in the mid-1990s, before its debt crisis in 1998–99, and reestablished access in 2004. In Sri Lanka, the Bank of Ceylon (a public bank) issued a three-year, $12 million bond (private placement) in 1995, followed by a $50 million sovereign issue in 1997. There were no subsequent bond issues until 2005, when Sri Lanka Telecom launched a $100 million issue (private placement), followed by a $500 million sovereign issue in 2007. A few other low-income countries have gained access recently, notably Vietnam in 2005, followed by Mongolia, Ghana, and Nigeria in 2007.

First-time bond issues by low-income countries over the past few years have been well received by the markets. Vietnam issued a $750 million sovereign Eurobond in 2005, followed by a $187 million issue (denominated in domestic currency) in 2007 by a publicly owned corporation (table 2.9). In 2007, the Trade & Development Bank of Mongolia, a public company, issued a $75 million Eurobond; two Nigerian corporations also issued Eurobonds.

Table 2.9 First-time external bond issues by developing countries, 2005–08

Income/date issued	Country	Issuer	Sector	Value ($millions)	Currency of issue	Yield (percent)	Tenure (years)	Credit rating
Low income								
2005-Oct.	Vietnam	Socialist Republic of Vietnam	Sovereign	750	$US	7.25	10	BB-
2007-Mar.	Vietnam	Vietnam Shipbuilding Industry Corp	Public corporate	187	Viet. dong	9.00	10	—
2007-Jan.	Mongolia	Trade & Development Bank of Mongolia	Public corporate	75	$US	8.94	3	BB
2007-Jan.	Nigeria	GTB Finance BV	Public corporate	350	$US	8.81	5	BB-
2007-Mar.	Nigeria	First Bank of Nigeria PLC	Private corporate	175	$US	10.15	10	B
2007-Sep.	Ghana	Republic of Ghana	Sovereign	750	$US	8.68	10	B+
Lower-middle income								
2005-Jun.	Jamaica	Air Jamaica	Public corporate	200	$US	9.60	10	B+
2005-Jun.	Romania	City of Bucharest	Subsovereign	606	Euros	4.28	10	BB+
2005-Dec.	Macedonia	Republic of Macedonia	Sovereign	177	Euros	4.69	10	BB+
2006-Sep.	Fiji	Republic of Fiji Island	Sovereign	150	$US	7.12	5	BB
2007-Feb.	Georgia	Bank of Georgia	Sovereign	200	$US	9.20	5	BB-
2007-May	Belarus	Polesie Trading House	Private corporate	19	Russ. rubles	13.37	3	—
2008-Apr.	Georgia	Republic of Georgia	Sovereign	500	$US	7.64	5	BB-
Upper-middle income								
2006-Sep.	Seychelles	Republic of Seychelles	Sovereign	200	$US	9.47	5	B
2007-Mar.	Serbia	ProCredit Bank AD	Private corporate	165	Euros	6.00	5	BB-
2007-Dec.	Gabon	Republic of Gabon	Sovereign	1,000	$US	7.85	10	BB-

Source: Dealogic Loan Analytics.
Note: — = not available.

Ghana became the first heavily indebted poor country (HIPC) to issue an external bond, offering a $750 million Eurobond issue in September 2007. The bond issue was oversubscribed several times, despite being launched in the midst of the turmoil in international financial markets.

Gabon, an upper-middle-income country, issued its inaugural sovereign bond in December 2007 when it launched a $1 billion, 10-year Eurobond with a yield of 8.25 percent (a 426 basis-point spread over U.S. Treasury yields at the time of issue) that was used to prepay its Paris Club creditors.

There has been a great deal of diversity in first-time bond issues by developing countries over the past few years. The wide range of issue amounts ($19 million to $1 billion), tenures (3 to 10 years), yields (4.28 to 13.37 percent), and credit ratings (B to BB+) indicate that countries do not need to meet specific threshold levels to access the international bond market. Additionally, borrowers with quite different financing needs and risk circumstances have decided

to tap the international bond market for the first time.

In 6 of the 13 countries that accessed the international bond market for the first time between 2005 and early 2008, corporate issues preceded sovereign issues. In Nigeria, for instance, a private bank and a public bank issued Eurobonds in 2007, while the country's first sovereign issue is expected to be launched in 2008. This pattern goes against the conventional wisdom that countries must first issue sovereign bonds to set a benchmark to price subsequent corporate issues. There are many examples where corporations based in developing countries have issued bonds before the government has. In fact, corporate issues preceded sovereign issues in almost one-third of the developing countries that gained access to the international bond market since 1990.[7] However, in some of these cases, first-time corporate issues entailed relatively small amounts for project financing, backed by collateral or government guarantees or both.

Table 2.10 Net equity inflows to developing countries, 2000–07
$ billions

Indicator	2000	2001	2002	2003	2004	2005	2006	2007e
Net (FDI and portfolio) equity inflows								
Total	179.0	178.7	166.0	185.9	265.9	357.4	472.3	615.9
By region								
East Asia and Pacific	51.8	50.7	63.2	69.3	89.6	130.3	159.8	166.0
Europe and Central Asia	25.5	26.2	26.2	34.2	68.6	80.1	135.7	182.2
Latin America and the Caribbean	78.9	74.6	54.4	45.6	64.0	82.9	81.9	135.3
Middle East and North Africa	5.0	4.2	4.3	8.4	8.0	17.0	29.5	32.6
South Asia	6.8	8.8	7.7	13.4	16.6	22.4	33.3	64.2
Sub-Saharan Africa	11.0	14.2	10.1	15.1	19.2	24.7	32.2	35.5
Net FDI inflows								
Total	165.5	173.0	160.7	161.9	225.5	288.5	367.5	470.8
By region								
East Asia and Pacific	45.2	48.9	59.4	56.8	70.3	104.2	105.0	117.4
Europe and Central Asia	24.8	26.6	26.1	34.9	63.5	72.2	124.6	161.6
Latin America and the Caribbean	79.5	72.1	53.0	42.3	64.6	70.4	70.5	107.2
Middle East and North Africa	4.8	4.2	4.9	8.2	7.1	14.4	27.5	30.5
South Asia	4.4	6.1	6.7	5.4	7.6	10.0	22.9	28.9
Sub-Saharan Africa	6.8	15.1	10.5	14.4	12.5	17.3	17.1	25.3
Net portfolio equity inflows								
Total	13.5	5.7	5.3	24.0	40.4	68.9	104.8	145.1
By region								
East Asia and Pacific	6.6	1.8	3.8	12.5	19.3	26.1	54.8	48.6
Europe and Central Asia	0.7	−0.4	0.1	−0.7	5.1	7.9	11.1	20.7
Latin America and the Caribbean	−0.6	2.5	1.4	3.3	−0.6	12.5	11.4	28.1
Middle East and North Africa	0.2	0.0	−0.6	0.2	0.9	2.6	2.0	2.1
South Asia	2.4	2.7	1.0	8.0	9.0	12.4	10.4	35.4
Sub-Saharan Africa	4.2	−0.9	−0.4	0.7	6.7	7.4	15.1	10.2

Sources: IMF International Financial Statistics; World Bank Debtor Reporting System and staff estimates.
Note: e = estimate.

Private equity market developments
Equity inflows continue to outpace growth

The expansion of equity inflows to developing countries in 2007 follows three years of strong gains. Net (foreign direct and portfolio) equity inflows reached an estimated $616 billion, an amount equal to 4.5 percent of GDP in developing countries, up just slightly from 4.2 percent in 2006 (table 2.10). Foreign direct investment (FDI) continues to account for the bulk of equity inflows, although less so than in previous years (figure 2.12). Portfolio flows have played a more prominent role over the past few years, accounting for just over 20 percent of equity in 2005–07, up from negligible levels in 2001–02.

The increase in equity flows was led by Latin America and the Caribbean, where the share of equity flows increased from 17 to 22 percent between 2006 and 2007, partially reversing a longer-term trend (figure 2.13). Despite the rebound in 2007, the region's share remains only about half of what it was 10 years ago, while shares going to Europe and Central Asia, South Asia, and Sub-Saharan Africa have doubled.

Portfolio equity flows to developing countries increased by $40 billion in 2007, following a $36 billion increase in 2006 (table 2.11). Although the flows increased in dollar terms in 2007, they remained constant as a share of GDP at 0.9 percent. As in past years, most of the flows are concentrated in a few of the largest developing economies—

almost three-quarters are expected to go to the BRICs. Strong gains in portfolio inflows to India ($24.5 billion) and Brazil ($18.5 billion) were partially offset by a decline in China ($8 billion).

The largest emerging-market economies play a prominent role in global equity markets, where issuance is on par with that of high-income countries. China, Brazil, and the Russian Federation ranked above all countries except the United States by value of cross-border initial public offerings (IPOs) in 2007, accounting for almost one-third of the IPO total worldwide (table 2.12).[8] Additionally, companies based in each of the BRICs launched at least one IPO valued at over $2 billion—including an $8 billion issue by the Russian bank, VTB Group—demonstrating the depth of the global market for large equity issues by emerging markets (table 2.13).

Emerging and frontier equity markets continue to outperform mature markets

Equity returns in emerging markets continue to outperform those in mature markets, even though emerging equity markets are more volatile. Though the correction in late 2007 and early 2008 was sharper in emerging markets than in mature markets, so were the gains earlier in the year. Equity prices in all markets peaked in October 2007, with

Figure 2.12 Net equity inflows as a share of GDP, 1991–2007

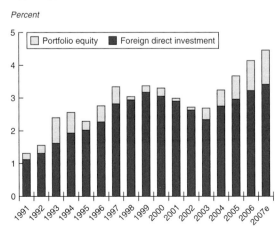

Sources: World Bank Debtor Reporting System and staff estimates.

Note: e = estimate.

Figure 2.13 Share of net equity inflows to developing countries, by region

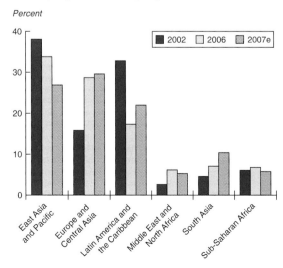

Sources: IMF International Financial Statistics; World Bank Debtor Reporting System and staff estimates.

Note: e = estimate.

Table 2.11 Top 10 portfolio equity destination developing countries, 2000–07
$ billions

Category	2000	2001	2002	2003	2004	2005	2006	2007e
All developing countries	13.5	5.6	5.5	24.1	40.4	68.9	104.8	145.1
Top 10 countries								
China	6.9	0.8	2.2	7.7	10.9	20.3	42.9	35.0
India	2.3	2.9	1.0	8.2	9.0	12.1	9.5	34.0
Brazil	3.1	2.5	2.0	3.0	2.1	6.5	7.7	26.2
Russian Federation	0.2	0.5	2.6	0.4	0.2	−0.2	6.1	14.8
South Africa	4.2	−1.0	−0.4	0.7	6.7	7.2	15.0	10.0
Turkey	0.5	−0.1	0.0	0.9	1.4	5.7	1.9	5.2
Thailand	0.9	0.4	0.5	1.8	1.3	5.7	5.3	4.4
Philippines	−0.2	0.1	0.2	0.5	0.5	1.5	2.4	3.3
Indonesia	−1.0	0.4	0.9	1.1	2.0	−0.2	1.9	3.1
Malaysia	0.0	0.0	−0.1	1.3	4.5	−1.2	2.4	2.8
Memorandum item								
BRICs	12.5	6.7	7.9	19.3	22.3	38.7	66.3	110.0

Sources: IMF International Financial Statistics; World Bank staff estimates.
Note: BRICs = Brazil, Russia, India, and China; e = estimate.

Table 2.12 Worldwide cross-border IPOs, 2007
$ billions

Category	Value	Share of total (percent)	Number of issues	Average issue value ($ millions)
Total	373.6		2397	16
Top 10 countries	276.2	73.9	1504	18
United States	88.3	23.6	300	29
China	65.5	17.5	249	26
Brazil	32.1	8.6	67	48
Russian Federation	18.4	4.9	18	102
United Kingdom	18.2	4.9	129	14
Spain	15.6	4.2	11	141
Canada	10.4	2.8	333	3
Germany	10.0	2.7	46	22
India	9.4	2.5	112	8
Australia	8.3	2.2	239	3
Memorandum item				
BRICs	125.4	33.6	446	28

Source: Dealogic DCM Analytics.
Note: BRICs = Brazil, Russia, India, and China.

gains for the year of 45 percent in emerging markets, compared with 13 percent in mature markets (figure 2.14). As of mid-May 2008, equity prices in emerging markets were up 32 percent from the beginning of 2007, while mature markets posted gains of only 2 percent. Some of the largest, most actively traded emerging equity markets, however, were also the most volatile. Notably, equity prices in China almost doubled between January and October 2007, only to lose 30 percent of their value over the following six months. Similarly, equity prices in Turkey posted gains of over 70 percent and then lost almost 30 percent of their value over the same period.

Investor confidence in emerging equity markets reflects the countries' strong growth potential over the long term, along with their impressive performance in generating high returns over the

Table 2.13 The 10 largest cross-border IPOs, by developing countries, 2007
$ billions

Issuer	Country	Sector	Exchange	Value
VTB Group	Russian Federation	Banking	London and Moscow	8.0
China CITIC Bank Corp Ltd	China	Banking	Hong Kong and Shanghai (China)	4.2
Bovespa Holding SA	Brazil	Finance	São Paulo	3.7
Bolsa de Mercadorias & Futuros	Brazil	Finance (miscellaneous)	São Paulo—Novo Mercado	2.9
Ecopetrol SA	Colombia	Oil and gas	Bogotá	2.8
Redecard SA	Brazil	Finance	São Paulo—Novo Mercado	2.4
DLF Ltd	India	Construction	Bombay	2.3
PIK Group	Russian Federation	Real estate/property	London and Moscow	1.9
SOHO China Ltd	China	Real estate/property	Hong Kong (China)	1.9
Country Garden Holdings Co Ltd	China	Real estate/property	Hong Kong (China)	1.9

Sources: Economist Intelligence Unit Country Reports, *Financial Times,* and other news media.

Figure 2.14 International equity prices, January 2007 – mid-May 2008

Index, Jan 2007 = 100

Sources: MSCI Barra world and emerging market composite indexes.

Figure 2.15 Average annual return in international equity markets, 2003–07

Percent

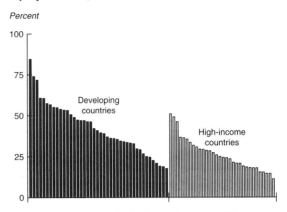

Sources: MSCI Barra; Standard and Poor's/International Finance Corporation.

past few years. Indeed, composite indexes for emerging and frontier equity markets have strongly outperformed those for mature markets in each of the five past years (table 2.14).

Returns on equity in less-developed countries—so-called frontier markets—have been comparable to those in emerging markets, particularly over the past two years. However, foreign investors would have had difficulty realizing such returns because international access to these markets remains limited. Efforts to increase access to frontier markets are being stepped up (box 2.4), but lack of liquidity remains a major concern in many countries, raising the risk of sharp price declines in the event of a sudden swing in investor confidence.

There has been a great deal of diversity in equity returns across equity markets in developing and advanced countries. Almost 80 percent of

developing countries posted average annual returns in excess of 25 percent over the past five years, compared with less than 30 percent of high-income countries (figure 2.15). Moreover, half of developing countries posted average annual returns in excess of 50 percent, compared with only three high-income countries—the Czech Republic, Saudi Arabia, and Slovenia—all of which made the transition to high-income status over the past few years. In general, though, monthly returns in emerging and frontier market have been much more volatile than those in mature markets. The standard deviation of monthly returns over the past five years exceeded 5 percent in three-quarters of emerging and frontier markets, compared to only one-quarter of mature markets.

There has been a great deal of diversity in equity returns across developing countries since equity prices peaked in late October 2007. Between October 2007 and April 2008, equity prices declined in over half of developing countries,

Table 2.14 Returns in international equity markets, 2003–07

Percent

Market type	2003	2004	2005	2006	2007	2003–07	Jan to Oct 2007	Oct 2007 to April 2008	Standard deviation[a]
Mature[b]	30.8	12.1	8.4	17.8	7.1	15.2	11.4	−8.3	2.7
Emerging[c]	51.7	22.4	30.4	29.1	36.5	34.0	45.5	−10.2	5.1
Frontier[d]	35.2	47.8	16.6	33.5	43.3	35.3	38.8	−6.6	3.8

Sources: JPMorgan; Standard and Poor's/International Finance Corporation.
a. Standard deviation of monthly percent changes over the period 2003–07.
b. MSCI world composite index.
c. MSCI emerging markets composite index.
d. Standard & Poor's/International Finance Corporation frontier composite index.

Box 2.4 The development of frontier equity markets

A combination of factors has allowed investor interest in equity markets to spread to a much wider range of developing countries over the past few years. Low interest rates in mature markets have spurred investors' search for yield, while steady improvements in economic fundamentals, along with sustained robust growth, have caused equity returns in many developing countries to exceed those in mature markets by a wide margin. Moreover, institutional investors in mature and emerging-market economies have expanded their holdings of debt and equity securities across a wider range of countries in an effort to exploit potential diversification benefits.

Financial institutions have responded to the growing demand by giving global investors greater access to equity investments in more developing countries. The International Finance Corporations (IFC), in an early effort, began producing standardized equity price indexes for developing countries in 1981. At the time, the IFC covered equity markets in only 10 developing countries. By the late 1990s, coverage had grown to 52 countries, 22 of which are classified as frontier markets because of their low capitalization and lack of liquidity relative to emerging markets (annex 2A). Of the 31 emerging-market countries, 20 are classified as "investable," implying that the market is open to foreign institutional investors based on judgments (by analysts at Standard & Poor's, which acquired the IFC's indexes in 2000) about the extent to which foreign institutions can trade shares on local exchanges and repatriate initial investment capital, capital gains, and dividend income without undue constraint. Countries must have equity markets with a minimum investable market capitalization of $100 million and must meet liquidity requirements (minimum trading volume) to qualify as a frontier market under the S&P/IFC definition. The number of developing countries qualified as frontier markets has expanded from 14 in 1996 to 21 in 2006.

In December 2007 MSCI Barra, a leading provider of international investment analysis, introduced equity price indexes for 19 frontier markets using criteria that appear to be similar to those of S&P/IFC. Yet only 10 of the 19 countries correspond to those covered by S&P/IFC, indicating that there is little agreement on which countries qualify as frontier markets. This is not the case for the emerging-market classification—all 21 countries classified as investable emerging markets by S&P/IFC are also classified as emerging markets by MSCI Barra and are included in the analysis of capital flows to emerging-market economies conducted by the Institute of International Finance. There is, however, little correspondence between the classification of countries' income level (GNI per capita) and equity markets. In particular, equity markets in six high-income countries are classified as frontier markets by MSCI Barra.

In January 2008 Duet Asset Management, a London-based alternative asset manager, started the first Sub-Saharan African index tracking fund, the Duet Victoire Africa Index Fund. The fund is composed of companies listed on the stock exchanges of Botswana, Ghana, Kenya, Malawi, Mauritius, Namibia, Nigeria, Tanzania, Uganda, and Zambia, with capitalization exceeding $250 million.

And in March 2008 the Merrill Lynch Frontier Index was launched. The index is composed of 50 stocks in 17 countries. To be included in the index, stocks must have a minimum market capitalization of $500 million, a minimum three-month average daily turnover of $750,000, and a foreign ownership limit above 15 percent. The index is dominated by companies in the Middle East (50 percent), followed by Asia (23 percent), Europe (14 percent), and Africa (13 percent). Currently the index can be accessed only by institutions such as corporations, mutual funds, and hedge funds.

compared with 90 percent of high-income countries (figure 2.16).

FDI inflows continued to expand despite financial headwinds

Net FDI inflows to developing and high-income countries continued to surge in 2007, marking the fourth consecutive year of solid gains (figure 2.17). Global FDI inflows reached an estimated record $1.7 trillion, just over a quarter of which went to developing countries, on par with the previous five years. Net FDI inflows to developing

countries as a whole increased to an estimated record $471 billion, an amount equal to 3.4 percent of their GDP, up from 3.25 percent in 2006. The estimated $103 billion increase in 2007 was broadly based across most regions (see table 2.8), led by strong gains in Russia ($22 billion) and Brazil ($16 billion) (table 2.15).

China remained the top destination among developing countries for FDI in 2007, although its share continued to decline relative to other countries. FDI inflows to China have shown little change over the past three years in dollar terms,

Figure 2.16 Return in international equity markets, October 2007 – April 2008

Percent

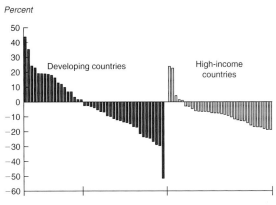

Sources: MSCI Barra; Standard and Poor's/International Finance Corporation.

Figure 2.17 Global FDI inflows, 1991–2007

$ billions

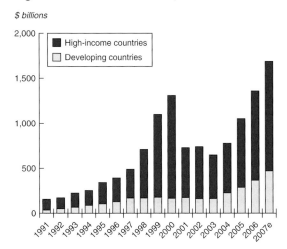

Source: World Bank staff estimates.

Note: e = estimate.

and China's share of inflows to all developing countries has fallen from 30 percent in 2002–03 to 18 percent in 2007, while the shares of Brazil and Turkey have increased substantially. FDI inflows to China in 2006–07 are equal to 8 percent of domestic investment, down from 15 percent in the late 1990s. Although the overall environment for foreign investment in China remains positive, recent developments have made it more difficult for foreign firms to invest. In particular, the Chinese government is becoming more selective in approving investment projects with foreign involvement, instead giving priority to projects in the interior of the country and those that promise a high degree of technology transfer. This trend has been counterbalanced, however, by China's commitments to

the World Trade Organization, which require the gradual opening of sectors including domestic commerce, financial services, insurance, and tourism to foreign investment.

FDI inflows to Russia increased in 2007 despite Russia's lack of progress in improving its investment climate, in particular the unfavorable changes in regulations related to FDI. Foreign investors are drawn by profitable opportunities in extractive industries, along with the potential for continued rapid growth in domestic consumption. The Netherlands and the United Kingdom are main source countries; large flows from Cyprus suggest that "round-tripping" might be playing an important role as well.

Table 2.15 Top 10 FDI destination developing countries, 2000–07

$ billions

Category	2000	2001	2002	2003	2004	2005	2006	2007e
All developing countries	165.5	173.0	160.7	161.9	225.5	288.5	367.5	470.8
Top 10 countries	114.6	123.5	107.9	101.8	147.5	176.2	226.2	288.9
China	38.4	44.2	49.3	47.1	54.9	79.1	78.1	84.0
Russia	2.7	2.7	3.5	8.0	15.4	12.9	30.8	52.5
Brazil	32.8	22.5	16.6	10.1	18.2	15.2	18.8	34.6
Mexico	17.9	29.4	21.1	15.0	22.5	19.9	19.2	23.2
Turkey	1.0	3.4	1.1	1.8	2.9	9.8	20.1	22.0
India	3.6	5.5	5.6	4.3	5.8	6.7	17.5	21.0
Poland	9.3	5.7	4.1	4.6	13.1	10.4	19.2	17.6
Chile	4.9	4.2	2.5	4.3	7.2	6.7	8.0	14.5
Ukraine	0.6	0.8	0.7	1.4	1.7	7.8	5.6	9.9
Thailand	3.4	5.1	3.3	5.2	5.9	8.0	9.0	9.6
Memorandum item								
BRICs	77.5	74.9	75.0	69.5	94.3	113.9	145.2	192.1

Sources: IMF International Financial Statistics; World Bank staff estimates.

Note: BRICs = Brazil, Russia, India, and China; e = estimate; FDI = foreign direct investment.

Table 2.16 The 10 largest privatizations, mergers, and acquisitions in 2007

Seller	Home country	Buyer		Sector	Value ($ billions)
Standard Bank	South Africa	ICBC	China	Banking	5.5
Oyakbank	Turkey	ING	Netherlands	Banking	2.7
El Mutun	Bolivia	Jindal Steel	India	Iron ore	2.3
Ukrsotsbank	Ukraine	Bank Austria Creditanstalt	Austria	Banking	2.1
Petkim	Turkey	Transcentral Asia	Russia/Kazakhstan	Petrochemical	2.1
Transelec	Chile	Management	United States	Electricity	1.7
BTC	Bulgaria	AIG	United States	Telecom	1.5
Sicartsa	Mexico	Arcelor Mittal	Luxembourg	Steel	1.4
Serasa	Brazil	Experian	Ireland	Financial	1.2
Almacenes Exito	Colombia	Cencosud	Chile	Retail	1.1

Source: World Bank staff estimates.

Net FDI inflows to Latin America and the Caribbean increased by $37 billion in 2007, raising the region's share from 19 percent in 2006 to 23 percent, led by strong gains in Brazil ($16 billion), Chile ($7 billion), and Mexico ($4 billion). Despite the rebound, the region's share is still only about half of what it was in the late 1990s, while the share going to Europe and Central Asia has doubled. The surge in FDI inflows to Europe and Central Asia has been dominated by privatization associated with major reforms, as was the case for the large volume of FDI inflows to Latin America in the late 1990s. The more recent pickup in inflows to Latin America stems from investment in the manufacturing sector and higher overall retained earnings, whereas in the late 1990s, the bulk of FDI inflows entailed privatization in the service sector.

FDI inflows to Sub-Saharan Africa surged from $17 billion in 2006 to $25 billion in 2007, largely because of a single transaction, the $5.5 billion purchase of a 20 percent equity stake in the South African commercial bank Standard Bank by the Industrial and Commercial Bank of China (table 2.16).

This is not unusual for South Africa, where large acquisitions over the past few years have resulted in volatile FDI inflows. In 2005, a $5 billion acquisition resulted in net inflow of $6.5 billion, followed by the sale of foreign equity in a mining company in 2006, which resulted in net disinvestment of $0.1 billion. In general, however, FDI inflows to the region have been mainly directed at countries rich in natural resources. In 2006, over 60 percent of FDI inflows to the region went to just three resource-rich countries (Equatorial Guinea, Nigeria, and Sudan).

Equity outflows have also risen dramatically

Rapid growth in equity outflows from developing countries over the past few years has important implications for analyzing capital flows. Net FDI outflows from developing countries increased from $140 billion in 2006 to an estimated $184 billion in 2007, led by Russia ($42 billion), China ($30 billion), and India ($15 billion) (table 2.17). Outflows from Russia increased by $19.5 billion in 2007, fueled mostly by foreign asset acquisitions by Russian firms in the extractive industries of

Table 2.17 Estimated equity outflows from developing countries, 2007
$ billions

Category	FDI and potfolio equity	Category	FDI	Category	Portfolio equity
All developing countries	231.4	All developing countries	183.6	All developing countries	47.8
Top 10 countries	165.1	Top 10 countries	134.0	Top 10 countries	36.3
Russian Federation	44.4	Russian Federation	42.0	Chile	9.9
China	37.0	China	30.0	China	7.0
India	15.0	India	15.0	Poland	5.5
Chile	14.9	Hungary	8.0	Hungary	2.4
Poland	11.5	Kazakhstan	8.0	Russian Federation	2.3
Hungary	10.4	Malaysia	8.0	Kazakhstan	2.1
Kazakhstan	10.1	South Africa	7.0	Peru	2.0
South Africa	8.9	Poland	6.0	South Africa	1.9
Malaysia	8.0	Chile	5.0	Angola	1.7
Venezuela, R. B. de	5.0	Venezuela, R. B. de	5.0	Croatia	1.5

Sources: World Bank staff estimates based on quarterly data from IMF International Financial Statistics.

nearby countries. Outflows from China increased by almost $14 billion and mainly involved major cross-border acquisitions and newly established overseas trade and economic zones. Outflows from Brazil, on the other hand, plummeted to $3 billion in 2007, down from an extraordinarily high level of $28 billion in 2006; the decline was largely the result of a $17 billion acquisition by the Brazilian mining company Compania Vale do Rio Doce of the Canadian mining company Inco.

The bulk of FDI outflows from developing countries entails cross-border mergers and acquisitions, valued at $80 billion in 2007, up from $75 billion in 2006. Driven by ample liquidity and the desire to expand their market share abroad and secure raw materials, developing countries are acquiring companies both in developed countries (South-North investment) and in other developing countries (South-South investment). Developing-country corporations are investing abroad in virtually all sectors; the services sector accounts for almost 60 percent of the total.

Net portfolio equity outflows from developing countries increased from $26 billion in 2006 to an estimated $48 billion in 2007, led by Chile ($10 billion), China ($7 billion), and Poland ($5.5 billion).

Net FDI and portfolio equity inflows to developing countries increased by an estimated $404 billion over the past four years (2003–07), while outflows increased by an estimated $182 billion, revealing that developing countries have been receiving more equity capital than they have been investing abroad. However, the difference—equity inflows less outflows—has not increased significantly over the past 10 years relative to the GDP of developing countries (figure 2.18).

The rapid increase in equity outflows over the past few years also has had a major influence on the relationship between developing countries' overall current account balance and capital inflows. This report uses the convention of comparing the overall current account balance of developing countries to capital (debt and equity) inflows and changes in foreign reserves (see table 2.1). This convention has served to focus the discussion on the main elements of capital inflows to developing countries and is not intended to provide a comprehensive analysis of the balance of payments. Omitted elements of the balance of payments—notably capital outflows from developing countries, official transfers, and errors and omissions—are captured by a

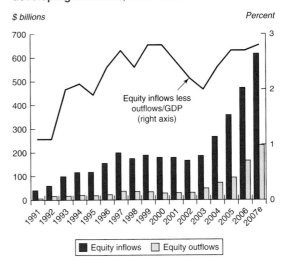

Figure 2.18 Equity inflows to and outflows from developing countries, 1991–2007

Sources: IMF International Financial Statistics; World Bank staff estimates.

Note: e = estimate.

balancing item, which has grown (in absolute value) from under $100 billion in 2002–03 to almost $500 billion in 2006 (table 2.18). In 2007 equity outflows accounted for almost two-thirds of the balancing item—including equity outflows in the analysis reduces the balancing item (in absolute value) from $360 billion to $129 billion.

Net capital inflows are also overstated by intercompany loans, which are included in both private debt flows and FDI inflows. In principle, intercompany loans should be subtracted from net capital inflows to avoid double counting. However, in practice, precise estimates of intercompany loans are hampered by poor data quality. Intercompany loans are estimated to have increased from an average level of around $20 billion in 2002–04 to over $70 billion in 2006 before declining to about $60 billion in 2007. Excluding both equity outflows and estimates of intercompany loans from net capital inflows in 2007 reduces the balancing item from −$360 billion to only −$67 billion.

Net official lending returns to more normal levels

Net official lending continued to decline in 2007, but at a much lower rate than in the past few years. Repayments on loans owed to governments and multilateral institutions exceeded lending by $4 billion in 2007, compared with $70 billion in

Table 2.18 Net capital inflows to and outflows from developing countries, 2000–07

$ billions

Flow type	2000	2001	2002	2003	2004	2005	2006	2007e
Current account balance	36.3	12.8	62.0	116.9	164.3	309.5	431.0	425.9
FDI inflows	165.5	173.0	160.7	161.9	225.5	288.5	367.5	470.8
FDI outflows	21.0	18.0	23.7	39.1	63.5	80.0	140.1	183.6
FDI inflows–outflows	144.5	155.0	137.0	122.8	162.0	208.5	227.4	287.2
Portfolio equity inflows	13.5	5.6	5.5	24.1	40.4	68.9	104.8	145.1
Portfolio equity outflows	7.4	11.4	7.0	9.9	8.7	13.8	25.8	47.8
Portfolio equity inflows–outflows	6.1	−5.8	−1.5	14.2	31.7	55.1	79.0	97.3
Equity inflows	179.0	178.6	166.2	186.0	265.9	357.4	472.3	615.9
Equity outflows	28.4	29.5	30.7	48.9	72.2	93.8	165.8	231.4
Equity inflows–outflows	150.6	149.1	135.5	137.1	193.8	263.6	306.5	384.5
Debt inflows	−0.4	4.5	8.9	72.8	128.8	152.4	217.5	413.0
Debt and equity inflows	178.6	183.1	175.1	258.8	394.7	509.8	689.8	1028.9
Debt inflows and equity inflows–outflows	150.2	153.6	144.4	209.9	322.6	416.0	524.0	797.5
Change in reserves (− = increase)	−42.6	−80.4	−166.5	−292.4	−402.4	−390.8	−634.2	−1090.7
Intercompany loans	20.9	19.6	18.0	21.8	19.6	41.1	73.4	62.2
Balancing item[a]	−172.3	−115.5	−70.6	−83.2	−156.6	−428.5	−486.7	−360.2
excluding equity outflows	−143.9	−86.0	−39.8	−34.3	−84.4	−334.7	−320.8	−128.8
and intercompany loans	−123.0	−66.5	−21.8	−12.5	−64.8	−293.6	−247.5	−66.6

Sources: IFS, World Bank Debtor Reporting System and staff estimates.
Note: e = estimate.
[a]Combination of errors and omissions and transfers to and capital outflows from developing-countries.

Figure 2.19 Net official debt flows to developing countries, 1998–2007

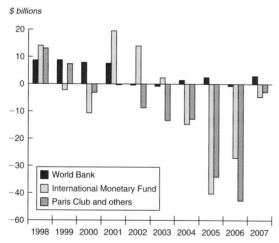

Sources: World Bank Debtor Reporting System and staff estimates.

2005–06 (figure 2.19). Net official lending has declined by a cumulative total of $185 billion over the past five years, as middle-income countries made voluntary prepayments to the Paris Club and multilateral institutions.

High oil prices, in particular, have enabled several major oil-exporting countries to prepay official debt over the past few years. Notably, Russia paid off its Soviet-era debts with a total of $37 billion

prepayments to Paris Club creditors in 2005–06, while Nigeria made $14 billion in prepayments to its Paris Club and London Club creditors.[9] In May 2007 the Paris Club agreed to accept prepayments from Peru for outstanding debt valued at $2.5 billion. The prepayment was partly financed by a $1.5 billion sovereign bond, which enabled Peru to improve the maturity structure of its debt. The Paris Club also agreed to accept buybacks at market value on debt owed by Jordan and Gabon valued at $2.3 billion and $2.5 billion, respectively.[10]

Lending by the IMF (purchases) has continued to decline, reaching $2.5 billion in 2007, down from $4 billion in 2005–06 and dramatically down from levels exceeding $30 billion at the beginning of the decade, when Argentina, Brazil, and Turkey all experienced major financial crises. Favorable global economic and financial conditions have virtually eliminated IMF lending to countries in need of emergency financing, permitting countries such as Argentina, Brazil, and Turkey to repay their outstanding debt. IMF credit outstanding declined to under $15.5 billion at end-December 2007, down from a high of just under $100 billion in 2003.

Net lending by the World Bank averaged only $0.8 billion over the past six years (2002–07). This reflects a number of factors. The favorable economic and financial conditions during this period enabled debtor countries to repay structural adjustment loans to the International Bank for Reconstruction and Development (IBRD) made during the financial crises of the late 1990s. Principal repayments to the IBRD exceeded disbursements by $4.4 billion on average over the period 2002–07, offset by $5.2 billion in net lending by the International Development Association (IDA). The change in the composition of net lending by the World Bank implies a shift away from IBRD lending to middle-income countries toward IDA lending to low-income countries, with a much higher average grant element. Moreover, IDA has provided a growing proportion of financial resources in the form of grants rather than loans, which are not included in the debt flow calculations.

In general, most of the large repayments made to official creditors over the past few years involved nonconcessional loans to middle-income countries. Concessional loans and grants to low-income countries are a better measure of development assistance.

Official development assistance

Some developing countries have recently gained access to the international bond market. However, many countries still need to make significant progress on improving the fundamentals that will enable them to access private debt markets on favorable terms, without endangering debt sustainability over the long term. Many developing countries will continue to depend heavily on concessionary loans and grants from official sources to meet their financing needs for some time. In 2006, official development assistance exceeded 10 percent of GDP in 30 countries (figure 2.20).

Little progress on official aid commitments, aside from debt relief

Net ODA disbursements by the 22 member countries of the Development Assistance Committee (DAC) of the Organisation for Economic Co-operation and Development (OECD) totaled $103.7 billion in 2007, down from $104.4 billion in 2006 and a record $107.1 billion in 2005. The decrease in ODA over the past two years largely reflects the return of debt relief to more normal levels following two extraordinary Paris Club agreements in 2005, under which Iraq and Nigeria received a total of $19.5 billion in debt relief from their Paris Club creditors, followed by another $13 billion in

Figure 2.20 Net ODA disbursements as a share of GDP in developing countries, 2006

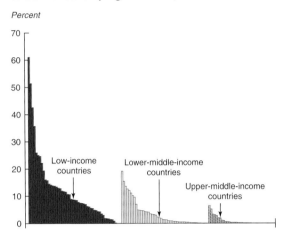

Source: OECD Development Assistance Committee (DAC).

2006. Debt relief continues to play a critical role in the development agenda, especially for many of the poorest countries burdened by heavy debt service payments. At the United Nations' Conference on Financing for Development in Monterrey in 2002, donors pledged that debt relief would not displace other components of ODA. In 2007, however, ODA net of debt relief increased by only 2.4 percent in real terms (adjusted for inflation and exchange rate movements) (table 2.19).

There has been a shift in the share of ODA disbursements (excluding debt relief) provided by DAC member countries since the Monterrey Consensus in 2002. Notably Japan's share has declined from 14.5 percent in 2002 to only 8 percent in 2007, while the U.S. share has risen from 20 percent to 23.5 percent. Existing commitments imply a substantial shift from the United States to the 15 DAC EU countries. The share provided by these countries is projected to increase from 55.6 percent in 2007 to 64 percent in 2010, while that provided by the United States is projected to decline from 23.5 to below 19 percent (OECD 2007, table 3).

Relative to GNI in DAC donor countries, ODA net of debt relief was unchanged at 0.25 percent in 2007, just slightly above the 0.23 percent level recorded in 2002, the year of the Monterrey Consensus, and well below the 0.33 percent level attained in the early 1990s (figure 2.21). ODA by DAC member countries is projected to increase to 0.35 percent of GNI based on commitments made in 2005 (OECD 2008a). This would require an average annual growth rate of over 14 percent in

Table 2.19 Net disbursements of official development assistance excluding debt relief, 1990–2007

Constant 2005 $ billions

Donor	1990	1995	2000	2002	2003	2004	2005	2006	2007e
All donors	69.9	61.7	68.1	73.9	73.7	80.8	89.0	90.4	
DAC donors	69.8	60.6	66.6	69.8	69.8	77.0	85.1	85.4	87.4
United States	14.1	8.9	11.2	13.9	15.9	20.2	23.9	21.3	20.6
United Kingdom	4.1	4.8	6.2	5.7	7.3	7.2	7.3	9.6	9.4
Germany	7.9	7.3	6.9	6.5	6.3	7.1	6.7	7.6	8.4
France	9.1	8.1	6.1	7.6	6.0	7.0	7.0	7.0	7.4
Japan	11.2	11.2	12.3	10.1	9.1	8.6	10.0	9.2	7.0
Netherlands	3.7	3.7	4.8	4.2	4.2	4.1	4.8	5.1	5.2
Sweden	2.2	1.9	2.4	2.7	2.7	2.7	3.4	3.9	4.0
Canada	3.2	2.7	2.4	2.9	2.5	2.9	3.8	3.4	3.5
Spain	1.3	1.8	2.0	2.5	2.3	2.3	2.5	3.2	4.7
Norway	1.9	1.9	2.0	2.5	2.6	2.5	2.8	2.7	3.1
Australia	1.3	1.6	1.5	1.5	1.5	1.6	1.7	2.1	3.0
Italy	4.4	2.2	2.1	3.3	2.8	2.5	3.4	2.2	2.5
Switzerland	1.0	1.1	1.3	1.2	1.4	1.5	1.8	1.6	2.4
Belgium	1.2	1.0	1.2	1.3	1.3	1.3	1.5	1.5	1.5
Ireland	0.1	0.2	0.4	0.6	0.6	0.6	0.7	1.0	1.3
Finland	0.9	0.4	0.5	0.6	0.6	0.7	0.9	0.8	0.9
Austria	0.2	0.6	0.6	0.5	0.5	0.6	0.7	0.7	0.7
Korea	0.1	0.1	0.3	0.4	0.4	0.5	0.8	0.4	0.4
Greece	..	0.2	0.4	0.4	0.4	0.3	0.4	0.4	0.4
Portugal	0.3	0.3	0.4	0.5	0.4	1.1	0.4	0.4	0.4
Luxembourg	0.0	0.1	0.2	0.2	0.2	0.2	0.3	0.3	0.3
New Zealand	0.1	0.2	0.2	0.2	0.2	0.2	0.3	0.3	0.3
Non-DAC donors	0.1	1.1	1.5	4.1	3.9	3.8	3.9	5.0	
Arab Countries	..	0.7	0.8	3.4	3.0	2.1	1.4	2.4	
Turkey	..	0.2	0.1	0.1	0.1	0.3	0.6	0.7	
Korea	0.1	0.1	0.3	0.4	0.4	0.5	0.8	0.4	
Memorandum items									
G-7 countries	53.9	44.2	46.3	48.8	49.2	55.2	61.5	60.1	59.4
DAC EU countries	37.0	33.6	36.0	37.9	36.7	39.6	41.6	45.4	49.4

Source: OECD Development Assistance Committee (DAC).

Note: e = estimate; EU = European Union; G-7 = group of seven countries (Canada, France, Germany, Italy, Japan, the United Kingdom, and the United States).

Figure 2.21 Net ODA disbursements by DAC donors, 1991–2007

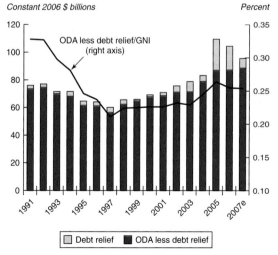

Source: OECD Development Assistance Committee (DAC).

Note: e = estimate; ODA = official development assistance.

real terms over the balance of the decade, three times the observed rate of 4.6 percent since the Monterrey Consensus in 2002.

The amount of ODA allocated to Sub-Saharan Africa has increased significantly since the early part of the decade, rising from $11.5 billion in 2000 to $39 billion in 2006 in real terms (figure 2.22). However, much of the increase has come in the form of debt relief. Excluding debt relief, the region received 37.5 percent of total ODA in 2006, up from 34 percent in 2006 but slightly below its 38 percent share in 2004. To meet their pledged increase to Sub-Saharan Africa of $50 billion (in real terms) by 2010, ODA donors would have to increase the flow of aid to the region by an average annual rate of 18 percent over the balance of the decade (in real terms), well above the 9 percent rate observed in 2002–06. This would also require that donors allocate 46 percent of their projected ODA commitments to countries in Sub-Saharan Africa.

Figure 2.22 Net ODA disbursements to Sub-Saharan Africa, 1990–2010

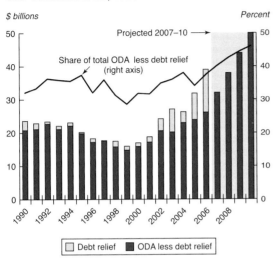

Source: OECD Development Assistance Committee.

Figure 2.23 Share of ODA disbursements excluding debt relief to low-income countries, 1990–2006

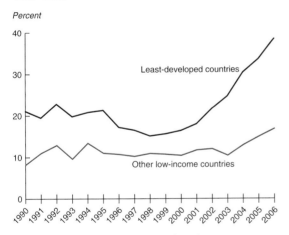

Source: OECD Development Assistance Committee.

The amount of aid going to the 49 low-income countries designated by the United Nations to be least developed (LDCs) has increased significantly since the late 1990s. The share of ODA disbursements excluding debt relief allocated to the LDCs rose from a low of 15 percent in 1998 to 38.5 percent in 2006. ODA allocated to other low-income countries over the same period increased more modestly, from 11 to 17 percent (figure 2.23).

Several empirical studies have examined whether donors have become more selective in allocating aid across countries on the basis of equity

and performance criteria.[11] A central issue in this line of research is whether donors have allocated a higher portion of aid to countries in most need (typically measured using income levels) and with better economic policies and institutions. The existing empirical evidence on this issue is mixed. Dollar and Levin (2004) and Claessens, Cassimon, and Van Campenhout (2007) find that donors have become more selective in allocating ODA to countries on the basis of GDP per capita and measures of policy performance and institutional quality, but Easterly (2007) and Easterly and Pfutze (2008) report conflicting results. Following this line of research, regression analysis was used to examine how equity and performance criteria have influenced donors' allocation of ODA over the past few years. The results (reported in annex 2B) indicate that the allocation of ODA in 2006 was influenced by cross-country differences in GDP per capita, and by the World Bank Worldwide Governance Indicators. Moreover, we find that donors have allocated a higher portion of aid to countries in Sub-Saharan Africa, controlling for their income and performance levels. The estimates imply that countries in Sub-Saharan Africa with a GDP per capita of $480 (the median level for low-income countries in 2006) received ODA disbursements equal to about 19.5 percent of their GDP, on average, while countries outside of Sub-Saharan Africa with a GDP per capita of $760 (one standard deviation higher) received only about 12.5 percent. Estimates obtained in each year over the period 2002–06 suggest that the influence of all three explanatory variables has declined since 2004, implying that donors have become less selective.

Developing countries have become important sources of aid for other developing countries. Unfortunately, there is little comprehensive, up-to-date data on the activities of "emerging donors," making it difficult to gauge their impact. Non-DAC donors' share of ODA disbursements (excluding debt relief) has been relatively stable, averaging around 5 percent in 2002–06.[12] China is estimated to have provided between $2 billion and $3 billion in concessional loans in 2005; India, an additional $1 billion (Kharas 2007, p. 12). Concessional loan commitments made by China, Brazil, and India to other developing countries increased from $2.5 billion in 2005 to $3.5 billion in 2006.[13] The average grant element of all loan commitments made by China, Brazil, and India was about

Figure 2.24 Net ODA disbursements excluding debt relief, 1960–2006

Constant 2005 $ billions

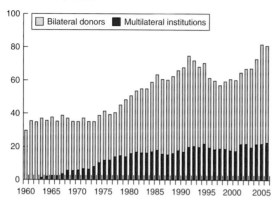

Source: OECD Development Assistance Committee.

Figure 2.25 Net ODA disbursements by bilateral donors, 1960–2006

Constant 2005 $ billions

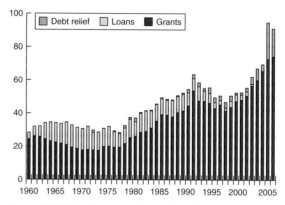

Source: OECD Development Assistance Committee.

one-third in 2005–06, equal to the average for other countries.

The volume of ODA disbursed by multilateral institutions has been stable at around $20 billion in real terms (constant 2005 dollars) since the early 1990s, while that disbursed by bilateral donors has fluctuated widely (figure 2.24). However, there has been a significant shift in the composition of disbursements across multilateral institutions. In 1990 UN agencies accounted for almost 30 percent of multilateral disbursements, while the European Commission (EC) accounted for just over 20 percent. By 2006, the share disbursed by UN agencies had fallen to less than 15 percent, while the EC share had doubled to just over 40 percent.

The International Development Association (IDA) has accounted for around 30 percent of net ODA disbursements by multilateral institutions on average since 1990. IDA's share is expected to increase somewhat over the balance of the decade as a consequence of the 15th replenishment of IDA (IDA15) completed in December 2007. The IDA15 replenishment of $41.6 billion represents an increase of $9.5 billion over the previous replenishment (IDA14), the largest expansion in donor funding in IDA's history. Forty-five countries, the highest number of donors in IDA's history, made pledges to the IDA15 replenishment, with six countries—China, Cyprus, the Arab Republic of Egypt, Estonia, Latvia, and Lithuania—joining the list of donors for the first time. IDA15 will support low-income countries by increasing its activities in combating climate change, facilitating regional integration and cooperation, boosting

infrastructure investment, and providing greater support to postconflict countries, notably in Sub-Saharan Africa.

Net ODA disbursements by bilateral donors have become dominated by grants. In 2002–06, repayments on ODA loans to bilateral creditors exceeded disbursements by almost $2 billion, on average. This is in sharp contrast to the late 1960s, when net lending accounted for about one-third of net ODA disbursements (figure 2.25).

Debt burdens continue to decline

Along with the major debt relief initiatives, the shift from bilateral ODA loans to grants, ongoing over the past 40 years, has significantly reduced the debt burdens of many low-income countries, particularly for those that have reached the HIPC completion point and received additional debt relief from the Multilateral Debt Relief Initiative. In 2007, 14 of the 21 HIPCs that had reached completion point by the end of 2006 had external debt-to-GDP ratios below 37.5 percent, the median for other developing countries (figure 2.26).[14] In 2000 the median external debt-to-GDP ratio for those same 22 countries was 109 percent, twice the median level for other developing countries (53 percent).

The external debt burden of all developing countries continues to decline, especially the portion owed to public creditors (or that is publicly guaranteed). The nominal value of public and publicly guaranteed external debt declined from 25 percent of GDP in 1999 to 10 percent in 2007, while private nonguaranteed debt remained stable at 9 percent of GDP (figure 2.27).

Figure 2.26 External debt as a share of GDP in
21 HIPCs

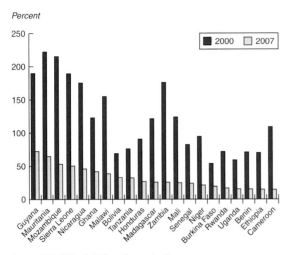

Source: World Bank Debtor Reporting System.
Note: HIPCs = heavily indebted poor countries.

Figure 2.27 External debt as a share of GDP in
developing countries, 1991–2007

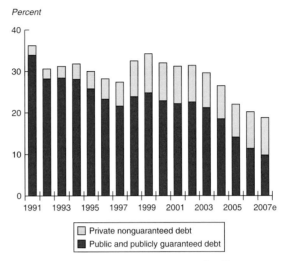

Source: World Bank Debtor Reporting System and staff estimates.
Note: e = estimate.

Recent trends in remittances

Officially recorded remittance transfers to developing countries are estimated to have increased to $240 billion in 2007, an amount equal to 1.8 percent of GDP, down from an average level of 2.0 percent of GDP over the previous five years (table 2.20).[15] The actual size of migrant remittance flows, including unrecorded flows through formal and informal channels, is arguably much larger (World Bank 2006b). In particular, remittance flows to Sub-Saharan Africa are grossly underestimated, with wide deficiencies in data reporting for several countries and a predominance of informal channels for the transmission of remittances.

Latin America and the Caribbean continued to receive the largest amount of remittance flows

among developing regions. However, the rate of growth of remittances to the region (particularly to Mexico) slowed markedly, a result of slower growth in output (which has reduced demand for labor in the construction sector in particular) and increased anti-immigration sentiment in the United States.[16] Apprehensions along the U.S.-Mexico border have declined by nearly 50 percent from the level in 2000, indicating a reduction in the number of undocumented migrants trying to enter the United States. Recent enforcement efforts appear to have reduced the number of seasonal migrants and their ability to send remittances, especially through formal channels (Ratha and others 2007).

By contrast, remittance receipts in developing countries in Europe and Central Asia increased significantly. Strong demand for labor in oil-exporting

Table 2.20 Remittance flows to developing countries, 2000–07
$ billions

Category	2000	2001	2002	2003	2004	2005	2006	2007e
Total	84.5	95.6	115.9	143.6	161.3	191.2	221.3	239.7
By region								
East Asia and Pacific	16.7	20.1	29.5	35.4	39.1	46.6	52.8	58.0
Europe and Central Asia	13.1	12.7	14.0	16.7	21.1	29.5	35.1	38.6
Latin America and the Caribbean	20.0	24.2	27.9	34.8	41.3	48.6	56.5	59.9
Middle East and North Africa	12.9	14.7	15.3	20.4	23.1	24.2	26.7	28.5
South Asia	17.2	19.2	24.1	30.4	28.7	33.1	39.8	43.8
Sub-Saharan Africa	4.6	4.7	5.0	6.0	8.0	9.3	10.3	10.8

Source: World Bank Debtor Reporting System and staff estimates.
Note: e = estimate.

Figure 2.28 Top remittance-receiving countries, by dollars and percentage of GDP

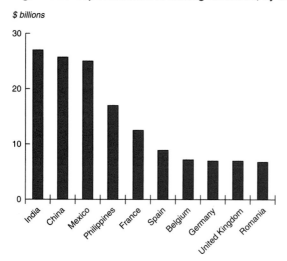

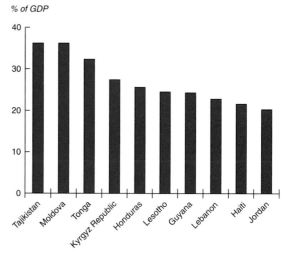

Source: World Bank staff estimates.

Note: e = estimate.

Middle Eastern countries boosted remittances to Bangladesh by 19 percent and to Pakistan by 17 percent in 2007 and contributed to South Asia and the Middle East and North Africa having the highest share of remittance receipts relative to their GDP. In the Philippines, remittances rose by 14 percent year over year during the first 11 months of 2007. Remittances to India rose by 30 percent in the first half of the year.

India, China, and Mexico were the top three recipients of remittances in 2007 and accounted for nearly one-third of remittances received by developing countries (figure 2.28). The countries receiving the most remittances as a share of GDP were small, poor economies such as Tajikistan, Moldova, Tonga, Kyrgyz Republic, and Honduras, where these flows exceeded 25 percent of GDP (see figure 2.28). In general, remittance receipts represent a significantly larger share of output in low-income countries (3.6 percent) than in middle-income countries (1.7 percent).

High-income countries are the dominant source of global remittance flows, led by the United States ($42 billion) and followed by Saudi Arabia ($15.6 billion) (figure 2.29). Developing countries receive somewhere between 10 and 29 percent of their remittance flows from other developing countries (South-South flows) equivalent to $18 billion to $55 billion (Ratha and Shaw 2007). Russia and Malaysia, both middle-income countries, are important sources of remittance flows to other developing countries.

Figure 2.29 Top remittance-sending countries

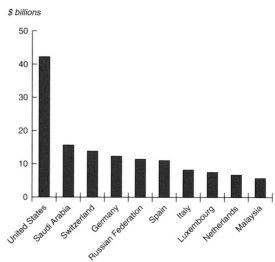

Source: World Bank staff estimates.

Prospects for capital flows
The impact of the financial turmoil on development finance

The turmoil that gripped financial markets worldwide began with a credit shock in the U.S. subprime mortgage market in mid-2007, amplified by highly leveraged financial institutions holding related securities. This led to a surge in demand for short-term financing, resulting in a liquidity crisis.

The origin of the crisis in the U.S. subprime mortgage market can be traced back to 2002–06, a period characterized by very favorable financial and economic conditions. An extended period of abundant liquidity and low interest rates world-wide sparked a search for yield that induced some investors to take on additional risk with little in the way of extra compensation. These factors were supported by robust global growth, fueling a four-year expansion in the global credit cycle.

At the same time, rapid growth in the market for asset-backed securities and structured financial products (such as collateralized debt obligations) in major financial centers facilitated both lending (by reducing the costs entailed in assessing and managing the risks) and borrowing (by effectively increasing liquidity and the availability of credit). These financial innovations boosted the level of exuberance that tends to set in during a prolonged expansion in the credit cycle. Spreads on corporate and emerging-market bonds declined to record lows; equity prices rallied in many countries. The degree of risk was especially underestimated in the low-quality segment of the U.S. mortgage market (subprime loans), where lending standards had loosened significantly.

By midyear 2007 it became apparent that the default rate on U.S. subprime mortgages would be substantially higher than initially projected by credit rating agencies, implying that the credit quality of assets backed by those mortgages would be downgraded substantially. However, little was known about the size of exposures held by the various financial institutions involved in the mortgage intermediation process. Moreover, the complex nature of structured financial instruments made it very difficult to price the underlying assets. The lack of transparency and the difficulty of pricing complex securities undermined the secondary market for asset-backed securities. The cost of issuing such securities increased sharply in August, as financial markets recognized that the magnitude of loan losses was more severe than originally envisaged.

The resulting sell-off in risky assets caused emerging-market sovereign bond spreads (measured using the JP Morgan Emerging Markets Bond Index [EMBI] Global composite index) to widen to over 300 basis points in March 2008, up from a record low of 150 basis points in early June 2007 (figure 2.30). Volatility in global financial markets soared amid high uncertainty surrounding the rapid turnaround in financial conditions. Investors' appetite for risk waned, leading to a sell-off in risky assets in mature and emerging markets alike, which was

Figure 2.30 Bond spreads, January 2007 – mid-May 2008

Basis points

Source: JPMorgan.

Note: EMBIG = JPMorgan Emerging Markets Bond Index Global.

intensified by forced selling resulting from margin calls and redemption orders by hedge fund investors.

Uncertainty about counterparty risk spread throughout the financial system, causing a surge in demand for short-term financing (IMF 2008a). This had a marked impact on the interbank market, where spreads between interbank borrowing rates and yields on government securites rose dramatically (see chapter 3). Notably, the spread between the three-month London Interbank Offered Rate in U.S. dollars ($US/LIBOR) and the yield on three-month U.S. Treasury bills exceeded 200 basis points in late 2007 and again in March 2008, compared with an average level of less than 50 basis points in the 12 months before the subprime crisis (figure 2.31).

Central banks in mature markets introduced unprecedented measures in an effort to provide the liquidity needed to keep markets functioning in an orderly manner. In the United States, the Federal Reserve began easing monetary policy in August 2007 out of concern that the disruption in the financial system could lead to an abrupt economic slowdown. A series of interest-rate cuts reduced the federal funds rate from 5.25 percent in mid-August 2007 to 2.00 percent in mid-April 2008. The dramatic decline in U.S. short-term interest rates reduced the $US/LIBOR by over 200 basis points between August 2007 and early 2008. In contrast, LIBOR lending denominated in euros increased during this period, reaching 485 basis points in mid-May 2008, up by over 100 basis points since early 2007.

Figure 2.31 Three-month LIBOR and yield on three-month U.S. Treasury bills, January 2007 – mid-May 2008

Source: U.S. Board of Governors of the Federal Reserve System.
Note: LIBOR = London Interbank Offered Rate.

Figure 2.32 Yields on 10-year government bonds and emerging-market sovereign bond spreads, January 2003 – mid-May 2008

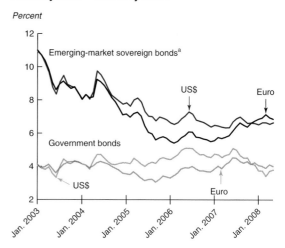

Source: JPMorgan.
a. Government bond yields plus emerging-market sovereign bond spread (EMBI Global) composite index.

Yields on U.S. government securities declined in response to the reductions in the U.S. federal funds rate and the sharp increase in the demand for liquid, safe assets by financial institutions. The yield on one-month U.S. Treasury bills fell from 5 percent in early August 2007 to under 1 percent in March 2008, the lowest rate since mid-2004. During the same time period, the yield on 10-year U.S. Treasury bonds fell from 4.75 percent to below 3.5 percent, the lowest level since mid-2003 (figure 2.32). The decline in the benchmark yields on dollar-denominated emerging-market sovereign bonds offset the rise in bond spreads, keeping the yield relatively stable. Yields on euro-denominated emerging-market sovereign bonds, however, increased by over 125 basis points between January 2007 and mid-May 2008.

The turmoil had a much larger impact on the cost of credit provided to the corporate sector, particularly for less-creditworthy borrowers. In the United States, spreads on non-investment-grade corporate bonds increased by over 500 basis points between early 2007 and March 2008, while spreads on U.S. investment-grade corporate bonds increased by only 160 basis points over the same period, indicating that the adverse economic and financial developments were expected to have a greater impact on less-creditworthy corporations. A similar pattern was observed in emerging markets, indicating that financial markets were discriminating mainly on the basis of risk characteristics of

corporations, irrespective of location. In other words, credit conditions tightened significantly for less-creditworthy corporate borrowers domiciled in mature- or emerging-market economies alike.

The implicit yield on five-year investment-grade corporate bonds in the United States declined by over 1 percentage point between early 2007 and early 2008, while yields on non-investment-grade corporate bonds have increased by over 1.5 percentage points (figure 2.33). Yields on non-investment-grade bonds issued by corporations in the Euro

Figure 2.33 Yields on 5-year U.S. corporate bonds, April 2003 – mid-May 2008

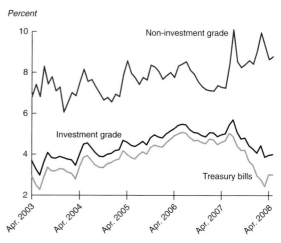

Source: Market CDX indexes for 5-year U.S. corporate bonds.

Figure 2.34 Yields on 5-year Euro Area corporate bonds, April 2003 – mid-May 2008

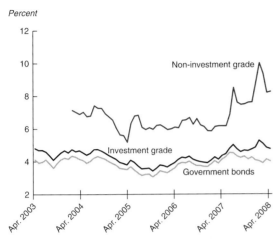

Percent

Source: Market iTraxx index for 5-year Euro Area corporate bonds.

Area increased by around 2 percentage points during the same period, exceeding levels observed over the past five years (figure 2.34).

Although corporations issuing non-investment-grade bonds face higher financing costs, a growing proportion of bonds issued by emerging-market economies carries investment-grade ratings. In the mid-1990s only about one-quarter of emerging-market bonds were rated investment grade, compared with one-half in 2007. On the whole, improved credit ratings have reduced the cost of bond issuance by governments and corporations in developing countries.

The discussion above examines the cost of external financing faced by developing countries in foreign currency (U.S. dollars and euros), reflecting the need to measure financing costs across several countries on a common basis. Measuring financing costs in domestic currency is more relevant for governments and corporations whose revenues and expenditures are largely denominated in domestic currency. Exchange-rate movements over the past few years have had a major influence on the cost of debt service and the value of outstanding debt in many developing countries. For instance, in 2007 the Turkish lira appreciated by 17.5 percent against the U.S. dollar and 7 percent against the euro, which significantly reduced debt service payments on its debt denominated in U.S. dollars and euros (as measured in lira). Moreover, developing countries have significantly increased their external borrowing denominated in domestic currency (see tables 2.5 and 2.6).

In sum, the turbulence in financial markets has had little impact on the cost of sovereign borrowing from abroad, but it has significantly raised the cost of non-investment-grade corporate issues.

Early indications suggest that capital flows have declined

The turmoil in global financial markets appears to have had a marked impact on bond issuance worldwide. Global bond issuance surged to a record $4 trillion in the first half of 2007 but then fell sharply to $2 trillion in the second half of the year, the lowest second-half volume since 2002. Bond issuance by developing countries declined from $108 billion to only $40 billion from the first to the second half of 2007. The decline was concentrated in the corporate sector; corporate issues fell sharply from a record $85 billion in the first half of 2007 to only $25 billion in the second half, while sovereign issuance has declined gradually since early 2006 and was evenly shared between investment-grade and non-investment-grade securities.

Global bond issuance continued to decline into the first quarter of 2008, with a total volume of $1 trillion, down almost 50 percent from the first quarter of 2007. Much of the decline has been concentrated in structured financial instruments, particularly asset-backed securities and collateralized debt obligations. The pace of bond issuance by developing countries dropped off sharply in mid-2007, with monthly volumes averaging only $6 billion from July 2007 to March 2008, down from an average of $15 billion during the same period in 2006 (figure 2.35).

The sharp decline in bond issuance since mid-2007 reflects both supply and demand factors. On the demand side, the reassessment of credit risks and increase in risk aversion on the part of international investors has led to wider bond spreads, particularly for less-creditworthy corporations. And for their part, borrowers are reluctant to launch major bond issues in an environment characterized by high volatility and uncertainty surrounding the demand for new issues. Many governments and corporations that have been active in the past do not have pressing financing needs and hence prefer to postpone their issuance programs until the market settles. In some countries, governments and corporations have been able to meet more of their financing needs by borrowing in the domestic bond market. The decline in corporate bond issuance has

Figure 2.35 Bond issuance by developing countries, January 2004 – March 2008

$ billions

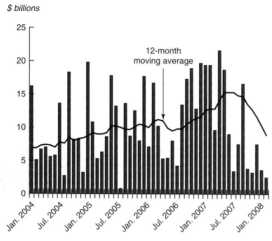

Source: Dealogic DCM Analytics.

been more prominent among non-investment-grade issues, which comprised only 18 percent of corporate issues between October 2007 and March 2008, compared with 55 percent over the same period the previous year.

The turmoil has also curtailed cross-border bank lending and equity issuance by developing countries, but less so than for bond issuance. The volume of syndicated loan commitments to developing countries posted strong gains until October 2007 (figure 2.36). However, some of the increase reported in the third quarter of the year represented transactions agreed to in the preceding few

months. Monthly loan commitments averaged $23 billion from October 2007 to March 2008, down from an average of $28 billion over the same period in the previous year. Equity issuance by all countries totaled $118.5 in the first quarter of 2008, the lowest level in five years. Equity issuance by developing countries increased throughout most of 2007, reaching a record $26 billion in October, which coincided with the peak in equity prices, and then fell sharply in early 2008 as equity prices declined. Equity issuance by developing countries averaging only $5 billion in January and March 2008, the lowest level in five years (figure 2.37). A total of 91 IPOs were withdrawn or postponed during this period, the highest on record since 2001 following the sharp correction in equity prices.

The turmoil also seems to have significantly dampened merger and acquisition (M&A) activity. The value of M&A deals worldwide announced in the first quarter of 2008 totaled $652 billion, down 40 percent year over year and the lowest level in four years. Difficulty in arranging financing for leveraged buyouts is believed to be a major factor. That has been most evident for private equity firms; their participation in M&A deals fell to $52 billion in the first quarter of 2008, down 70 percent year over year. The decline in M&A activity by private equity firms has been partially offset, however, by the growing role of sovereign wealth funds, which invested $25 billion in M&A deals in the first quarter of 2008, compared with $60 billion

Figure 2.36 Cross-border syndicated loan commitments to developing countries, January 2004 – March 2008

$ billions

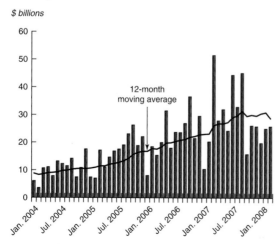

Source: Dealogic Loan Analytics.

Figure 2.37 Equity issuance by developing countries, January 2004 – March 2008

$ billions

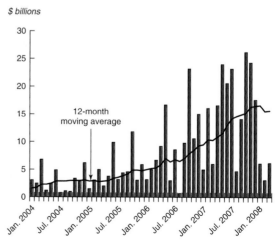

Source: Dealogic Loan Analytics.

over the entire year 2007, accounting for 35 percent of world M & A activity (Global Insight 2008, p. 3).

In sum, early indications are that the turmoil has curtailed private debt and equity flows to developing countries. However, it is unclear whether this constitutes a turning point in the credit cycle or a temporary interruption in borrowing activity.

Private capital flows to developing countries are expected to decline moderately

Tighter credit conditions, together with more moderate global growth, are expected to curb the expansion of private capital flows over the balance of 2008 and into 2009. Corporations in developing countries will find it more difficult to obtain credit; those that do will face higher financing costs, particularly the less creditworthy. It is important to recognize, however, that financing conditions have been very favorable over the past few years. Ample liquidity and investors' search for yield reduced bond spreads to record lows, while private capital flows to developing countries surged to record levels. An orderly adjustment in the credit cycle at the current juncture is desirable to the extent that capital flows fall to levels that can be sustained over the longer term.

As in past episodes, investor sentiment will have a major influence on whether the adjustment will be gradual or abrupt. Despite high volatility, investor confidence in emerging market assets has remained high. However, that could change quickly given the high degree of uncertainty surrounding current market conditions. This uncertainty makes projecting capital flows much more difficult, even over the short term. With this in mind, we prefer to characterize the realm of possibilities with reference to two alternative scenarios.

Under our base-case ("soft-landing") scenario, private capital flows are projected to decline moderately over the balance of 2008 and into 2009, falling from 7.3 percent of GDP ($1.03 trillion) in 2007 to 5.0 percent ($850 billion) in 2009, which is still above the previous peak reached in 1996 (4.4 percent) just before the East Asian financial crisis (figure 2.38). Under our "hard-landing" scenario, private capital flows are projected to decline more abruptly, falling to 3.5 percent of GDP ($550 billion) in 2009, just slightly below the average level over the period 1993–2002 (3.7 percent).

In addition to the moderation in global growth projected for 2008–09 (see chapter 1),

Figure 2.38 Net private capital flows to developing countries, 1990–2009

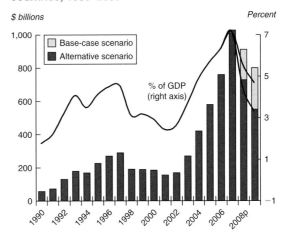

Sources: World Bank Debtor Reporting System and staff estimates.
Note: Estimate was made for 2007; p = projections for 2008–09.

tighter financing conditions are also expected to curb private capital flows. The intermediation process underlying the provision of credit has been impaired by the fallout from the U.S. subprime crisis, and some time is likely to be needed before normal financial operations are restored. In the few years leading up to the turmoil, ample liquidity supported a surge in M&A activity by providing easy financing for leveraged buyouts. Investment banks had little difficulty arranging financing for syndicated bank loans, which also expanded rapidly. These forces swiftly reversed in late 2007 when major financial institutions in mature markets (mainly the United States and Europe) began announcing large write-downs resulting from sharp declines in the market value of their holdings of asset-backed securities, along with major trading losses in some cases. Losses on unsecured U.S. loans are estimated at $225 billion as of March 2008, along with an additional $720 billion in mark-to-market losses on related securities (IMF 2008a, table 1.1).[17] Major international banks are expected to bear roughly half of these loses, with the balance spread among a wide range of institutional investors (such as insurance companies, pension funds, money market funds, and hedge funds) (IMF 2008a, p. 12). Estimates of additional write-downs suggest that the process will continue over the course of 2008. In mid-March one major financial institution—Bear Stearns—required financial support from the U.S. Federal Reserve when it failed to meet margin calls by creditors concerned about the declining market value of collateral (notably asset-backed securities) put up by Bear Stearns to secure its short-term financing needs. Other major financial institutions have been able to restore their capital-to-asset ratios by curtailing dividend payments, terminating share buybacks, and raising equity capital (from sovereign wealth funds in many cases).

Although capital adequacy has not been a major problem so far (other than in the case of Bear Stearns), hoarding of liquidity and concerns about counterparty risk have continued to strain interbank and other short-term lending markets (see chapter 3). This has impaired the intermediation process, causing assets to accumulate on bank balance sheets. Investment banks are reported to have a substantial inventory of loans that they have been unable to syndicate. Leveraged loans held by investment banks have lost around 15 percent of their market value in the United States and Europe between mid-2007 and early 2008, before recovering partially in the spring.[18] Banks have also come under pressure to expand credit to off-balance-sheet entities (conduits and structured investment vehicles) and borrowers that normally fund their operations in the segments of the financial market that have ceased to function. In particular, companies that have been unable to access short-term financing from the asset-backed commercial paper market have drawn on lines of bank credit. Moreover, hedge funds under pressure to finance margin calls and redemptions have also accessed bank credit lines. Faced with the financial pressures outlined above, many of the major banks, securities firms, and financial guarantors have curtailed their lending activity in an effort to restore their balance sheets.[19] There is also the possibility that global banks may significantly curtail lending activities by their subsidiaries operating abroad in an effort to restore balance sheets in the parent bank (see chapter 3). Moreover, heightened uncertainty surrounding the availability of interbank liquidity may also curtail cross-border lending to developing countries (see chapter 3).

The deleveraging process is being complicated by the lack of transparency and valuation difficulties for some credit instruments and is likely to continue over the balance of 2008 and into 2009. The adjustment will curtail the ability of investment banks to arrange leveraged financing for large M&A transactions and syndicated bank loans. This will provide investment opportunities for those private equity firms that have capital to be deployed, particularly those with expertise in emerging markets, along with sovereign wealth funds and state-owned enterprises looking to expand their operations abroad. Moreover, institutional investors' holdings of emerging-market assets are well below levels implied by their capitalization value and hence are expected to rise significantly over the medium term. Assets under management worldwide by pension, insurance, and mutual funds are estimated to be in the $55 trillion to $60 trillion range at end 2006, which greatly exceeds the value of assets managed by sovereign wealth funds ($2.5 trillion to $3.5 trillion), hedge funds ($1.5 trillion), and private equity funds ($0.7 trillion to $1.0 trillion) (Farrell and others 2007, Exhibit 2; Global Insight 2008, p 16). Expectations of continued rapid growth in emerging-market economies and the potential diversification benefits make investments in emerging markets very attractive to institutional investors in advanced and developing countries alike. However, given concerns about overvaluation in some emerging equity markets along with the risk of an abrupt slowdown in global growth, fund managers may prefer to postpone taking on more exposure to emerging-market assets until global economic and financial conditions have improved.

Given the nature of the adjustment process outlined above, we expect private debt flows to decline by more than equity flows. This assessment partly reflects the observation that private debt flows tend to have a larger cyclical element than FDI inflows, the East Asian crisis being a prime example. Although this has also been the case for portfolio equity flows as well, we believe that equity flows more generally will be supported by the growing demand for equity investments by institutional investors, sovereign wealth funds, and state-owned enterprises over the medium term.

Donors need to enhance aid significantly to meet their commitments

For the many developing countries that depend heavily on capital flows from official sources to meet their financing needs, their short-term prospects will be largely determined by the extent to which donors meet their commitments to augment ODA. Under existing commitments, DAC member countries have pledged to raise ODA to

Figure 2.39 Net ODA disbursements by DAC donors, 1960–2010

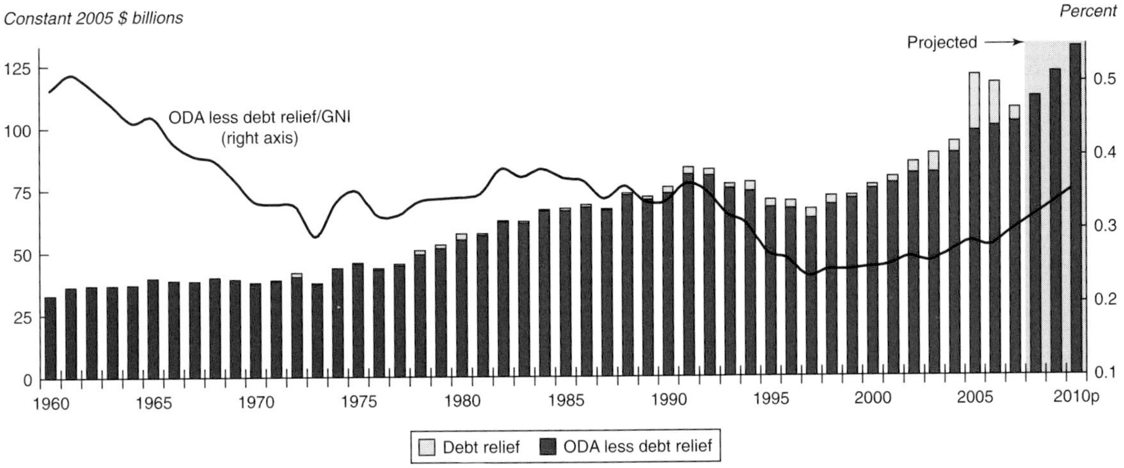

Constant 2005 $ billions

Percent

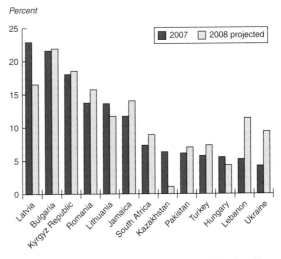

Projected →

ODA less debt relief/GNI (right axis)

☐ Debt relief   ■ ODA less debt relief

Source: OECD Development Assistance Committee (DAC).

Note: ODA = official development assistance; p = projected 2008–10.

0.35 percent of their GNI by 2010, which would be well short of the UN target of 0.7 percent but would represent more rapid progress than that achieved over the past four years since the Monterrey conference in 2002 (figure 2.39).

The moderation in growth in high-income countries projected for 2008–09 will make it more difficult for donors to honor their ODA commitments, particularly in donor countries with sizable fiscal deficits. However, the ODA commitments are small relative to countries' other fiscal expenditures and hence will not prevent them from attaining their overall fiscal objectives. Moreover, honoring ODA commitments over the balance of the decade would raise ODA as a share of GNI to levels observed throughout much of the 1970s and 1980s.

Key financial risks

If financial conditions in mature markets were to deteriorate significantly over the balance of 2008, developing countries would likely experience a pronounced decline in private capital flows. A state of heightened uncertainty would make it more difficult for the major investment banks to attract equity capital, which would accentuate their need to curtail lending activities in an effort to restore their balance sheets. The deleveraging process coupled with a further decline in investors' appetite for risk could reduce the supply of global capital significantly, raising its cost, particularly for less-creditworthy corporations.

Most developing countries are well placed to withstand a sharp downturn in the credit cycle, but some may be vulnerable, particularly those with large external imbalances and heavy financing needs. In 2007, current account deficits exceeded 15 percent of GDP in Bulgaria, the Kyrgyz Republic, Latvia, and Lebanon and are projected to improve only marginally in 2008 (figure 2.40). Moreover, current account deficits in Lebanon, Pakistan, Romania, South Africa, and Ukraine are expected to widen in 2008. Many of these countries are already saddled with high debt burdens, especially

Figure 2.40 Current account deficits as a share of GDP in 13 countries, 2007–08

Percent

■ 2007   ☐ 2008 projected

Sources: IMF International Financial Statistics; World Bank staff.

Figure 2.41 Foreign reserves as a share of short-term debt in 11 countries, 2006–07

Percent

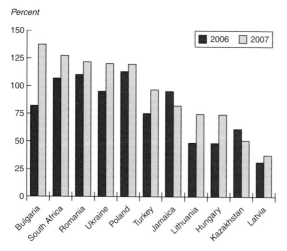

Sources: World Bank Debtor Reporting System; IMF International Financial Statistics.

Figure 2.42 FDI inflows and current account deficits as a share of GDP in 13 countries, 2007

Percent

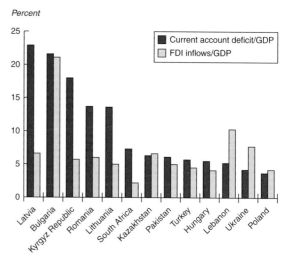

Sources: IMF International Financial Statistics; World Bank staff.

Note: FDI inflows are estimates based on quarterly data.

Hungary, Latvia, and Lebanon, where external debt obligations exceed 90 percent of GDP, compared with 25 percent for developing countries as a group.

Many developing countries have ample foreign reserves to provide a buffer should they encounter external financing problems. At the end of 2007, foreign reserve holdings in three-quarters of developing countries exceeded the amount of principal and interest payments due in 2008. However, this is not the case in countries such as Hungary, Jamaica, Kazakhstan, Latvia, and Lithuania, all of which have current account deficits in excess of 5 percent of GDP (figure 2.41). In Latvia, reserve holdings at end 2007 cover only 38 percent of principal and interest payments due in 2008.

Countries where the current account deficit is financed largely by FDI inflows (rather than debt-creating capital flows) are less vulnerable to external financing difficulties. By and large, FDI inflows have tended to provide a more stable source of external financing than private debt and portfolio equity flows, especially in times of turbulence (World Bank 2003, box 2.4; World Bank 2004, pp. 86–87). This is of particular importance in Bulgaria, Kazakhstan, Lebanon, Pakistan, Poland, Turkey, and Ukraine, where the value of FDI inflows is estimated to have covered their entire current account deficit in 2007 (figure 2.42). However, FDI outflows have risen significantly in some of these countries (namely, Hungary, Poland, and South Africa), reducing the

amount of external financing provided by FDI when inflows are netted against outflows. In the case of South Africa, FDI outflows are estimated to be roughly equivalent to FDI inflows in 2007, providing no net external financing.

A surge in private debt inflows to the banking sector in some countries has fueled rapid credit growth and intensified inflationary pressures over the past few years (World Bank 2007, p. 115). The pace of borrowing has declined in most countries since the turmoil began in mid-2007, but remains high relative to previous years. In particular, Kazakh banks borrowed $2 billion (1.7 percent of GDP) between October 2007 and April 2008, down from $13 billion (12.2 percent of GDP) during the same period the previous year and below the $5.5 billion (6.7 percent of GDP) borrowed the year before that (figure 2.42). Russian banks borrowed $10.6 billion between July 2007 and February 2008, down from $19 billion during the same period the previous year but just slightly below the $11 billion borrowed the year before that (figure 2.43). Banks in Russia, Kazakhstan, and Ukraine did very little borrowing in January and February 2008, giving the impression of a credit squeeze. However, banks in other countries have continued to access syndicated bank loans and issue bonds in the international market. Banks in Latvia, for example, received syndicated bank loan commitments totaling $0.5 billion in January and February 2008,

Figure 2.43 Cross-border bank loan commitments to and bond issuance by the banking sector as a share of GDP in 8 countries, July 2005 – February 2008

$ billions

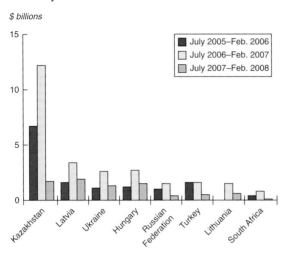

Sources: Dealogic DCM Analytics and Loan Analytics.

Figure 2.44 Domestic credit growth in 9 countries, 2006–07

Percent

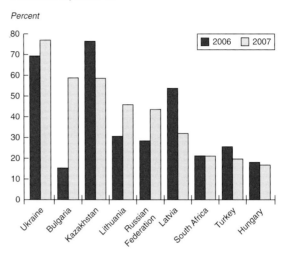

Source: IMF International Financial Statistics.

following $2 billion in borrowing over the entire year 2007 (an amount equal to over 60 percent of the country's GDP). Banks in Hungary borrowed a total of $1.7 billion in January and February 2008, following $2.7 billion in total borrowing in 2007.

It is important to recognize that monthly data on syndicated bank loan commitments do not include lending by parent banks to subsidiaries operating abroad; such lending has played a prominent role in the surge in bank lending to the countries discussed above.[20] Moreover, monthly fluctuations in syndicated loan commitments and bond issuance are quite volatile, making it difficult to ascertain whether recent events mark the beginning of a protracted downturn in the credit cycle or whether borrowers and lenders are waiting for financial conditions to settle.

The pace of domestic credit growth has declined somewhat in some countries (Kazakhstan, Latvia, and Turkey) but has picked up in others (Bulgaria, Lithuania, Russia, and Ukraine) (figure 2.44). Inflation has increased significantly in most developing countries, mainly because of a sharp rise in commodity and food prices (see chapter 1). Inflation has risen above 10 percent in most of the countries experiencing rapid credit growth, namely, Bulgaria, Kazakhstan, Latvia, Lithuania, Russia, and Ukraine (figure 2.45).

The rally in emerging-market equity prices since 2002 raised concerns that asset prices were

Figure 2.45 Inflation in 12 countries

Percent

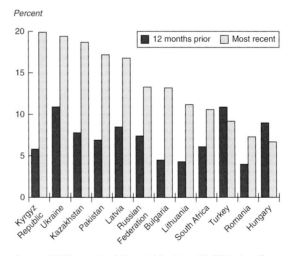

Sources: IMF International Financial Statistics; World Bank staff.
Note: 12-month change in the consumer price index

overvalued in some countries, raising the risk of a sharp correction. Equity prices have declined significantly from their peak in October 2007, notably in China and Turkey (a drop of almost 30 percent as of early May 2008). However, in most cases the recent correction brings equity prices back to levels attained in mid-2007 before the turmoil. Despite the correction, equity prices in 40 of 43 developing countries recorded overall gains between January 2007 and April 2008, compared with just 15 of

Figure 2.46 Equity market returns in 8 countries, January 2007 – early May 2008

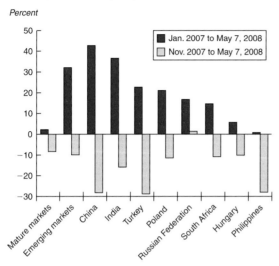

Percent

Legend:
■ Jan. 2007 to May 7, 2008
□ Nov. 2007 to May 7, 2008

Categories: Mature markets, Emerging markets, China, India, Turkey, Poland, Russian Federation, South Africa, Hungary, Philippines

Sources: Morgan Stanley; Standard & Poor's.

23 high-income countries (figure 2.46). Equity prices have increased more than threefold in 17 developing countries over the past five years. This increase reflects several factors, including improved fundamentals in many cases, but concerns remain that some countries need a further correction.

So far the impact of the turmoil in financial markets on the more vulnerable countries has been mixed. Sovereign bond spreads widened by more than 200 basis points in Lebanon, South Africa, and Ukraine between early June 2007 and the end of March 2008, compared with 165 basis points for the EMBI Global composite index, but spreads have been less affected for other vulnerable countries, notably Poland (60 basis points) and Hungary (55 basis points). Few currencies have come under pressure, with the exception of the South African rand, which depreciated by 14 percent against the U.S. dollar (and almost 30 percent against the euro) between January and March 2008. Equity prices have declined sharply in countries with large current account deficits (notably South Africa and Turkey), but also in countries with sizable surpluses (China and the Philippines).

Vulnerable countries can help alleviate the risk of a hard landing by implementing close surveillance of potential exposures in their banking systems and by managing demand pressures using monetary and fiscal policy measures with a strong focus on medium-term objectives.

Annex 2A

Table 2A.1 List of countries in emerging- and frontier-market indexes
$ dollars

Income/country	GNI per capita in 2006	Emerging markets				Frontier markets	
		IIF	MSCI	S&P/IFC Investable	S&P/IFC Noninvestable	MSCI	S&P/IFC
High income (> $11,116)							
Kuwait	..	0	0	0	1	1	0
United Arab Emirates	..	0	0	0	1	1	0
Israel	..	0	1	1	0	0	0
Qatar	..	0	0	0	1	1	0
Slovenia	18,890	0	0	0	0	1	1
Bahrain	..	0	0	0	1	1	0
Korea, Rep. of	17,690	1	1	1	0	0	0
Taiwan, China	17,230	0	1	1	0	0	0
Saudi Arabia	..	0	0	0	1	0	0
Trinidad and Tobago	13,340	0	0	0	0	0	1
Czech Republic	12,680	1	1	1	0	0	0
Estonia	11,410	0	0	0	0	1	1
Number of countries in index		2	3	3	3	4	3
Upper-middle income ($3,956 < $11,115)							
Oman	..	0	0	0	1	1	0
Hungary	10,950	1	1	1	0	0	0
Slovak Republic	9,870	1	0	0	0	0	1
Croatia	9,330	0	0	0	0	1	1
Poland	8,190	1	1	1	0	0	0
Latvia	8,100	0	0	0	0	0	1
Mexico	7,870	1	1	1	0	0	0
Lithuania	7,870	0	0	0	0	0	1
Chile	6,980	1	1	1	0	0	0
Venezuela, R. B. de	6,070	1	0	0	1	0	0
Botswana	5,900	0	0	0	0	0	1
Russian Federation	5,780	1	1	1	0	0	0
Malaysia	5,490	1	1	1	0	0	0
Lebanon	5,490	0	0	0	0	1	1
Mauritius	5,450	0	0	0	0	1	1
Turkey	5,400	1	1	1	0	0	0
South Africa	5,390	1	1	1	0	0	0
Uruguay	5,310	1	0	0	0	0	0
Argentina	5,150	1	1	1	0	0	0
Romania	4,850	1	0	0	0	1	1
Brazil	4,730	1	1	1	0	0	0
Bulgaria	3,990	1	0	0	0	1	1
Number of countries in index		15	10	10	1	5	9

(continued)

Table 2A.1 List of countries in emerging- and frontier-market indexes *(Continued)*
$ dollars

Income/country	GNI per capita in 2006	Emerging markets				Frontier markets	
		IIF	MSCI	S&P/IFC Investable	S&P/IFC Noninvestable	MSCI	S&P/IFC
Lower-middle income ($906 < $3,955)							
Kazakhstan	3,790	0	0	0	0	1	0
Jamaica	3,480	0	0	0	0	0	1
Namibia	3,230	0	0	0	0	0	1
Algeria	3,030	1	0	0	0	0	0
Thailand	2,990	1	1	1	0	0	0
Tunisia	2,970	1	0	0	0	1	1
Peru	2,920	1	1	1	0	0	0
Ecuador	2,840	1	0	0	0	0	1
Colombia	2,740	1	1	0	1	0	0
Jordan	2,660	0	1	0	1	0	0
China	2,010	1	1	1	0	0	0
Ukraine	1,950	1	0	0	0	1	1
Morocco	1,900	1	1	0	1	0	0
Indonesia	1,420	1	1	1	0	0	0
Philippines	1,420	1	1	1	0	0	0
Egypt, Arab Rep. of	1,350	1	1	1	0	0	0
Sri Lanka	1,300	0	0	0	1	1	0
Number of countries in index		**12**	**9**	**6**	**4**	**4**	**5**
Low income (< $906)							
Côte d'Ivoire	870	0	0	0	0	0	1
India	820	1	1	1	0	0	0
Pakistan	770	0	1	0	1	0	0
Vietnam	690	0	0	0	0	1	1
Nigeria	640	0	0	0	1	1	0
Kenya	580	0	0	0	0	1	1
Ghana	520	0	0	0	0	0	1
Bangladesh	480	0	0	0	0	0	1
Number of countries in index		**1**	**2**	**1**	**3**	**3**	**4**

Source: World Development Indicators.
Note: IIF = International Institute of Finance; MSCI = Morgan Stanley Capital Internation—Barra; S&P/IFC = Standard & Poor's/International Finance Corporation.

Annex 2B: Econometric analysis of aid selectivity

Regression analysis was used to gauge the extent to which donors allocated aid to countries on the basis of equity and performance criteria. This entailed estimating equations of the form:

$$aid_i = \beta_0 + \beta_1 equity_i + \beta_2 SSA + \beta_3 performance_i + \varepsilon_i ,$$

where aid = net ODA disbursements as a percent of GDP; equity = GDP per capita (in log form); SSA = dummy variable (1 for countries in Sub-Saharan Africa, 0 otherwise); performance = average value of six World Bank Worldwide Governance Indicators (WGI); and ε_i = random error term.

The estimates reported below indicate that equity (GDP per capita) played a significant role in donors' allocation of aid in 2006 (β_1 is statistically significant in regressions 1 to 4). Regression 1 indicates that donors allocated aid to countries in Sub-Saharan Africa much the same as they did to other countries (β_2 is statistically insignificant). However, the SSA dummy variable becomes significant when two outliers are excluded from the analysis (regression 2).

Three alternative measures were used as indictors of performance: the average value of the six Worldwide Governance Indicators, the IDA Resource Allocation Index (IRAI) and International Country Risk Guide (ICRG) composite index. Only the WGI average was found to be statistically significant (regressions 3 and 4). The main component indexes of the WGI, IRAI, and ICRG were not significant either. These inferences partly reflect the fact that the IRAI and ICRG have more limited country coverage than the WGI (the IRAI and ICRG are available only for 72 and 92 countries respectively, compared with 124 for the WGI). None of the explanatory variables were found to have a significant influence on donors' allocation of ODA on a per capita basis (not reported). The year-over-year change in the WGI was found to be positively correlated with ODA allocations but was insignificant as well.

Regression 3 was estimated for each of the years 2002–06 separately and pooled (with fixed effects). The results (reported below) indicate that the influence of GDP per capita on donors' aid allocations (β_1) has steadily declined since 2003, as has donors' preference for allocating a higher portion of aid to countries in Sub-Saharan Africa (β_2) and to countries with higher performance ratings (β_3).

Table 2B.1 Estimates obtained for 2006

Regression	Dependent variable	β_1	β_2	β_3	R^2	Nobs
1	ODA / GDP	−4.78 (0.76) [0.00]	1.49 (2.00) [0.46]		0.423	127
2	ODA / GDP	−3.45 (0.48) [0.00]	3.43 (1.26) [0.007]		0.575	125
3	ODA / GDP	−4.56 (0.54) [0.00]	2.95 (1.20) [0.016]	2.98 (0.72) [0.00]	0.633	124
4	ODA ex. debt relief / GDP	−4.44 (0.51) [0.00]	2.00 (1.12) [0.077]	3.00 (0.68) [0.00]	0.613	124

Source: World Bank staff.
Note: Nobs = number of observations; ODA = official development assistance. Standard error of estimate is reported in parentheses; p-value, in square brackets. Regressions 2 to 4 exclude two outliers—Burundi and Solomon Islands, where ODA exceeds 50 percent of their GDP.

Table 2B.2 Estimates of regression 3, 2002–06

Regression 3	2002	2003	2004	2005	2006	2002–06
β_1	−5.56	−6.96	−6.21	−4.77	−4.56	−5.56
(SE)	(0.83)	(1.35)	(0.74)	(0.714)	(0.54)	(0.39)
[P-value]	[0.00]	[0.00]	[0.00]	[0.00]	[0.00]	[0.00]
β_2	4.71	4.51	3.74	3.53	2.95	3.93
(SE)	(1.73)	(2.81)	(1.57)	(1.53)	(1.20)	(0.83)
[P-value]	[0.008]	[0.11]	[0.02]	[0.02]	[0.016]	[0.00]
β_3	4.25	3.43	5.04	2.69	2.98	3.60
(SE)	(1.18)	(1.91)	(1.05)	(0.95)	(0.72)	(0.54)
[P-value]	[0.00]	[0.075]	[0.00]	[0.005]	[0.00]	[0.00]
R^2	0.52	0.40	0.61	0.54	0.63	0.49

Source: World Bank staff.

Annex 2C: Commercial Debt Restructuring

Developments between April 2007 and April 2008

Developing countries continued their proactive liability management exercises during the past year. Between April 2007 and April 2008, seven countries carried out buyback operations to retire about $4 billion of its outstanding external debt. Of these, Peru and the Philippines bought back about $964 million of Brady bonds by exercising the embedded call option to eliminate nearly all of their outstanding Brady debt, joining Brazil, Colombia, Mexico, and República Bolivariana de Venezuela as countries that have retired all of their Brady bonds. Other bond markets also saw major buyback activities as part of the developing countries' general liability management strategy to clean up external debt and rebalance debt profile. It is also notable that Mexico and the Philippines issued debt-exchange warrants, which have been used successfully to replace external debt with domestic debt. Finally, although it is not discussed in this review, Brazil has reportedly redeemed about $480 million of global bonds during the year. (Detailed information on Brazil's transactions is currently not available.)

Debt buyback operations in developing countries

Colombia. In June 2007, the Colombian government agreed to buy back around $850 million, at face value, of its dollar-denominated global bonds due 2008, 2009, 2010, and 2011. The transaction reflects the country's long-term liability management strategy to reduce its dollar-denominated debt and its currency. The buyback operation was financed by the issue of a new $1 billion peso-denominated global bond due in 2027. The new issue priced at par to yield 9.85 percent, which was rated Ba2 by Moody's Investor Service and BB+ by Standard & Poor's. The government also agreed to retire 50 percent of the global peso-denominated TES bonds due 2010 and 25 percent of the floating-rate notes due 2013.

Mexico. In March 2008, Mexico carried out a debt-management operation to retire about $714 million of its dollar-denominated global bonds (with 10 different maturities) between 2009 and 2034 through an open-market purchase. According to the finance ministry, the buyback was to be financed by local bond issues and loans from international institutions. This transaction reflects the Mexican government's strategy to improve the terms and conditions of its external debt and to strengthen its benchmark global bonds. In April 2008, the government announced the issuance of a debt-exchange warrant, Mexico's fourth offering since launching the first one in November 2005. This warrant entitles holders to exchange about $1.25 billion of various foreign currency bonds for a combination of peso-denominated and inflation-linked bonds.

Nicaragua. In December 2007, the government of Nicaragua reached an agreement with creditors to a cash buyback of more than $1.3 billion of the country's commercial external debt, out of total eligible claims of $1.4 billion. The agreement was reached with the support of a grant of up to $62 million from the World Bank's Debt Reduction Facility (DRF) and with contributions from various northern European countries, Russia, and the United Kingdom. The first closing of the operation was scheduled to take place in mid-December, and the second closing was expected in the first quarter of 2008. The Ministry of Finance and Public Credit said in a statement that the $1.3 billion accepted for buyback was tendered by Nicaragua at a price of 4.5 percent of the debt's current face value, with the participation of more than 99 percent of creditors (including investors who had won judgments in foreign courts). As a result, the government said in the statement that the country's external debt is expected to fall to 57 percent of GDP in 2007 from 130 percent in 2003.

Peru. The Peruvian government bought back about $838 million of Brady bonds (FLIRB, PDI, and discounts) at the redemption price of 70 percent of the par amount in March 2008, retiring nearly all of Peru's remaining Brady debt. According to the government, the buyback will be financed with cash from the Treasury and a future sale of local currency bonds. In December 2007, the government had already approved a local issue of bonds for the equivalent of $485.8 million in one or more tranches. This debt management operation is in line with the government strategy to restructure its foreign debt by extending maturities and replacing it with sol-denominated debt. In February 2007, the government carried out a liability management operation that swapped and bought back about $2.5 billion of outstanding Brady bonds (FLIRB, PDI, Pars, and discounts) and Global 12s for new securities and cash.

The Philippines. In May 2007, the Philippine government exercised a call option to buy back $126 million of Principal Collateralized Interest Reduction Bonds due in 2018, fully redeeming its Brady bonds issued in 1992 as part of a debt restructuring program. The buyback operation will enable the government to realize about $12.6 million in debt-service savings and to free up $82.3 million in collateral. This transaction marked the third time that the government used an early redemption provision provided under the Brady bonds. In 2006, the sovereign undertook two buyback operations to redeem about $701 million of Brady bonds ($410 million in June and $165 million in December). In February 2008, the Philippines announced it would issue as many as $2 billion of debt-exchange warrants to holders of

its foreign currency bonds. The warrants will allow investors to exchange the dollar- and euro-denominated bonds due 2017 with 10-year treasury bonds (with a yield of 5.875 percent) due 2018, in the event of a default.

Poland. In March 2008, the Polish government undertook a buyback operation to retire $125.5 million of its Brady bonds through the secondary market at below par value. This operation redeemed $104.1 million of RSTA bonds and $21.4 million of par bonds. After the buyback, the country's remaining Brady debt stands at $420 million, down from the original $8 billion in 1994. The transaction reflects the commitment of the Polish government to repay old obligations created by the conversion of debt to the London Club.

Uruguay. In December 2007, the government of Uruguay successfully completed its latest debt management exercise, retiring a total of $240 million in global and local bonds maturing in or before 2012. Through the transaction, Uruguay bought back $116 million in global bonds, including $91 million from seven sets of dollar bonds due between 2008 and 2012, and $25 million from two sets of euro-denominated bonds maturing in 2011 and 2012. The government also repurchased $124 million from 17 sets of local bonds denominated in dollars and others in pesos, which are linked to the Uruguayan inflation rate. The transaction was part of Uruguay's strategy to reduce its foreign currency debt and to improve its debt profile by rebalancing from dollars to local currency.

Annex 2D: Debt Restructuring with Official Creditors

This annex lists official debt restructuring agreements concluded in 2007. Restructuring of intergovernmental loans and officially guaranteed private export credits takes place under the aegis of the Paris Club. These agreements are concluded between the debtor government and representatives of creditor countries. Paris Club treatments are defined individually with the consensus of all creditor countries. Most treatments fall under predefined categories, listed below by increased degree of concessionality: "Classic terms," the standard treatment; "Houston terms" for highly indebted lower-middle-income countries; "Naples terms" for highly indebted poor countries; and "Cologne terms" for countries eligible for the HIPC Initiative. To make the terms effective, debtor countries must sign a bilateral implementing agreement with each creditor.

Agreements with countries

Sierra Leone. In January 2007, the Paris Club creditors agreed on a 91 percent debt reduction for Sierra Leone, who had reached the completion point under the enhanced HIPC Initiative on December 15, 2006. Of the $240 million due to the Paris Club creditors as of December 2006, roughly $218 million was cancelled because of the Paris Club's share in the enhanced HIPC Initiative effort, and additional debt relief of $22 million was granted on a bilateral basis. As a result of the agreement and the additional bilateral assistance, Sierra Leone's debt to the Paris Club will be completely cancelled.

FYR Macedonia. On January 24, 2007, the Paris Club creditors agreed to FYR Macedonia's offer to prepay up to $104 million of it debt at par. The buyout operations are to be carried out, on a voluntary basis, between January 31, 2007, and April 30, 2007, we don't after conclusions of bilateral agreement by participating Paris Club members. This prepayment offer translates into interest savings for FYR Macedonia, and it improves the credit quality of the country.

Central African Republic. In April 2007, the government of the Central African Republic reached an agreement with the Paris Club creditors to restructure $36 million of its external public debt. This decision followed the IMF's approval (on December 22, 2006) of the country's contract under the Poverty Reduction and Growth Facility (PRGF) and the examination by the IMF and the World Bank (IDA) of the preliminary document under the enhanced HIPC Initiative in March 2007. The agreement with the Paris Club reschedules roughly $28.4 million in arrears and maturities falling due during the consolidation period (between December 1, 2006 and November 30, 2009) under the "Naples terms." Loans made as official development assistance (ODA) before the cutoff date are to be repaid progressively over 40 years, with 16 years of grace, at an interest rate equal to or greater than the rate of the original loans. For non-ODA commercial credits, the pre-cutoff debts are cancelled by 67 percent, and the remaining payments will be rescheduled over 23 years, with a 6-year grace period.

Peru. In May 2007, the Paris Club creditors agreed on Peru's offer to prepay up to $2.5 billion of its non-ODA debt falling due between 2007 and 2015. Under the agreement, the principal of a prepayment would be made at par and offered to all creditors. For the participating Paris Club members, the prepayment will be made on October 1, 2007, after the bilateral implementation agreements are concluded. The Peruvian government is expected to finance the Paris Club payment with the issuance of debt in the domestic market.

São Tomé and Principe. On May 24, 2007, the Paris Club creditors agreed to a significant debt reduction for *São Tomé and Principe*, who reached the completion point under the enhanced HIPC Initiative in March 2007. To restore the country's debt sustainability, the Paris Club decided to cancel the debt valued at $23.9 million in nominal terms. As a result, the debt owed to Paris Club creditors would be reduced to $0.6 million in nominal terms. Creditors also committed on a bilateral basis to grant additional debt relief so that the country's debt will be fully cancelled.

Gabon. In July 2007, The Paris Club creditors agreed in principle to accept Gabon's buyback of its non-ODA debt at market value. According to the Paris Club, the face value of eligible debt for early repayment amounts to roughly $2.33 billion (as of July 1, 2007), which was previously rescheduled in 1994, 1995, 2000, and 2004, and falls due up to 2019. Several of Gabon's Paris Club creditors will likely participate in the early repayment operation, although it will be up to each country to decide. This debt buyback operation is in line with the Gabon government's reform policy to reduce its exposure to potential external shocks. This policy also led to a 3-year IMF Stand-By Arrangement that was approved in May 2007.

Jordan. In October 2007, the Paris Club creditors agreed to Jordan's offer to prepay up to $2.5 billion of its non-ODA debt, which had been previously rescheduled by the Paris Club in 1994, 1997, 1999, and 2002. For the participating Paris Club members, this early repayment operation is scheduled to take place between January 1 and March 31, 2008, after conclusion of bilateral implementation agreements. It is expected that around $2.1 billion in debt will be retired at a discount averaging 11 percent, for a total of $1.9 billion. The prepayment is to be largely financed by privatization proceeds, which stood at $1.1 billion as of August 2007.

Notes

1. This report uses the convention of analyzing net equity inflows from the perspective of equity claims by foreigners on the country receiving the investment (the net change in domestic liabilities in the balance of payments). This definition does not include net equity *outflows* associated with the net change in equity claims by domestic residents on other countries (the net change in domestic assets in the balance of payments), which is the convention used by other organizations such as the Institute of International Finance (2008) and the IMF (2008c).

2. Private debt refers to bonds and loans intermediated through private financial markets. Creditors include both private and public institutions (notably public pension funds, government sponsored agencies, and sovereign wealth funds). In contrast, official debt refers to loans from multilateral organizations (such as the World Bank, regional development banks, and other multilateral and intergovernmental agencies), and bilateral loans from governments.

3. The data, however, cover only about half of reserves held by developing countries and newly industrializing economies, down from 60 percent in the mid-1990s.

4. Based on estimates reported by Farrell and others (2007), Hildebrand (2007), Truman (2007), Griffith-Jones and Ocampo (2008), Global Insight (2008), and IMF (2008b).

5. In the case of Brazil, a syndicated bank loan to the telecom company Tele Norte Leste Participacoes accounted for $6.5 billion of the $6.9 billion total. In the case of Mexico, a syndicated bank loan for an infrastructure project (highway development) accounted for $3.4 billion of the $3.9 billion total.

6. Exceptions include the following. Papua New Guinea issued a seven-year, $20 million sovereign bond (private placement) in 1984. The Republic of Congo issued a five-year, $600 million sovereign Eurobond in 1994.

7. This calculation is based on the Dealogic Loan Analytics database. "First-time" bond issuance is defined as a situation in which a government or corporation issues a bond in the international market after 1989 in a country that had no external bond issues during the 1980s.

8. "Cross-border" IPOs refer to issues that can be purchased by nonresidents. The values reported in table 2.10, however, refer to the total value of the IPOs, not just the portion purchased by nonresidents. Moreover, nonresident purchases that exceed 10 percent of the issuing company's capitalization are classified as an FDI inflow.

9. The London Club of creditors, an informal group of commercial banks that join together to negotiate their claims against sovereign debtors, received $1.5 billion of this amount.

10. The buyback transactions between Gabon and its Paris Club creditors took place in December 2007 and January 2008, while Jordan's buyback transactions took place between January and March 2008.

11. See the literature survey in Claessens, Cassimon, and Van Campenhout (2007) and the references therein.

12. Non-DAC donors are 15 countries that are not members of the DAC but that nevertheless report their aid activities to the DAC. They have not yet reported their ODA disbursements for 2007.

13. Based on public and publicly guaranteed loan commitments using the same concessionality criteria as that used by the OECD DAC to define ODA (loans a grant element of at least 25 percent calculated with a 10 percent discount factor).

14. São Tomé and Principe reached its completion point under the enhanced HIPC Initiative in May 2007, followed by The Gambia in December 2007, bringing the number of HIPCs that have reached their completion points to 23.

15. Remittances are defined as the sum of workers' remittances, compensation of employees, and migrant transfers; for definitions and to access the entire data set, see www.worldbank.org/prospects/migrationandremittances.

16. Remittances to Mexico grew only by 1 percent from January to December 2007, compared with an annual growth of over 20 percent from 2002 through 2006.

17. Recent mark-to-market losses of around $700 billion greatly exceed estimates of default loses ($422 billion) calculated by the OECD (2008), suggesting that the size of

the actual write-downs could turn out to be much lower than implied by current asset prices.

18. Based on the Leveraged Loan Index reported by Standard & Poor's and the Loan Syndications and Trading Association (S&P/LSTA).

19. Greenlaw and others (2008) estimate that mortgage losses could prompt banks and other lenders to reduce their total assets by $2 trillion.

20. In 2006, bank loan disbursements to the Europe and Central Asia region totaled $260 billion (according to the World Bank Debtor Reporting System), while syndicated loan commitments totaled only $97 billion (according to Dealogic Loan Analytics). The $163 billion difference results largely from lending by parent banks and from subsidiaries operating abroad, categories that are included in the data collected by the DRS but not in that collected by Dealogic Loan Analytics.

References

Claessens, Stijn, Danny Cassimon, and Bjorn Van Campenhout. 2007. "Empirical Evidence on the New International Aid Architecture." IMF Working Paper WP/07/277, International Monetary Fund, Washington, DC.

Dollar, David, and Victoria Levin. 2004. "The Increasing Selectivity of Foreign Aid, 1984–2002." Policy Working Paper 3299, World Bank, Washington, DC.

Easterly, William. 2007. "Are Aid Agencies Improving?" *Economic Policy* 52 (October): 635–78.

Easterly, William, and Tobias Pfutze. 2008. "Where Does the Money Go? Best and Worst Practices in Foreign Aid." *Journal of Economic Perspectives* 22 (2).

Emerging Markets Private Equity Association. 2008. *EMTA Survey*. New York, NY (February 19).

Farrell, Diana, Susan Lund, Eva Gerlemann, and Peter Seeburger. 2007. *The New Power Brokers: How Oil, Asia, Hedge Funds, and Private Equity Are Shaping Global Capital Markets*. McKinsey Global Institute. Available at http://www.mckinsey.com/mgi/publications/The_New_Power_Brokers/.

Foster, Vivien, William Butterfield, and Chuan Chen. Forthcoming. "Building Bridges: China's Growing Role as Infrastructure Financier for Africa."

Global Insight. 2008. *Sovereign Wealth Fund Tracker*. (April). Available at http://www.imf.org/external/np/pp/eng/2008/022908.pdf.

Greenlaw, David, Jan Hatzuis, Anil Kashyap, and Hyun Song Shin. 2008. "Leveraged Losses: Lessons from the Mortgage Market Meltdown." Paper presented at U.S. Monetary Policy Forum Conference, New York, February 29.

Griffith-Jones, Stephany, and José Antonio Ocampo. 2008. "Sovereign Wealth Funds: A Developing Country Perspective." Paper prepared for workshop on sovereign wealth funds organized by the Andean Development Corporation, London, February 18.

Hanson, James. 2007. "The Growth in Government Domestic Debt: Changing Burdens and Risks." Policy Research Working Paper 4345, World Bank, Washington, DC.

Hildebrand, Philipp. 2007. "The Challenge of Sovereign Wealth Funds." Speech given at the International Center for Monetary and Banking Studies, Geneva, December 18.

International Institute of Finance. 2008. "Capital Flows to Emerging Market Economies." Washington, DC (March 6).

IMF (International Monetary Fund). 2008a. *Global Financial Stability Report* (April, 2008). Washington, DC.

———. 2008b. "Sovereign Wealth Funds—A Work Agenda." (February). Washington, DC. Available at http://www.imf.org/external/np/pp/eng/2008/022908.pdf.

———. 2008c. *World Economic Outlook* (April, 2008). Washington, DC.

Kharas, Homi. 2007. "Trends and Issues in Development Aid." Wolfensohn Center for Development Working Paper 1, Brookings Institution, Washington, DC (November).

Mohapatra, Sanket, and Ratha, Dilip. 2008. "U.S Dollar Depreciation and Remittance Flows to Developing Countries." Migration and Development Brief, Development Prospects Group, Migration and Remittances Team, World Bank, Washington, DC.

OECD (Organisation for Economic Co-operation and Development). 2007. "Final ODA Flows in 2006." DAC Senior Level Meeting, Paris, December 11–12.

———. 2008a. "Debt Relief Is Down: Other ODA Rises Slightly." (April 4). Available at http://www.oecd.org/document/8/0,3343,en_2649_33721_40381960_1_1_1_1,00.html.

———. 2008b. "The Subprime Crisis: Size, Deleveraging and Some Policy Options." (April). Available at http://www.oecd.org/dataoecd/36/27/40451721.pdf.

Ratha, Dilip, Sanket Mohapatra, K. M. Vijayalakshmi, and Zhimei Xu. 2007. "Remittance Trends 2007." Migration and Development Brief 3. Development Prospects Group, World Bank, Washington, DC.

Truman, Edwin. 2007. "A Scoreboard for Sovereign Wealth Funds." Paper presented at the Conference on China's Exchange Rate Policy, October 19, at the Peterson Institute, Washington, DC.

Wolff-Hamacher, Stefanie. 2007. "Local Currency Bond Issues by International Financial Institutions." Bank for International Settlements, Basle, Switzerland (July 6). Available at http://www.bis.org/publ/wgpapers/cgfs28wolff.pdf.

World Bank. 2003. *Global Development Finance 2003*. Washington, DC.

———. 2004. *Global Development Finance 2004*. Washington, DC.

———. 2006a. *Global Development Finance 2006*. Washington, DC.

———. 2006b. *Global Economic Prospects 2006*. Washington, DC.

———. 2007. *Global Development Finance 2007*. Washington, DC.

3

The Changing Role of International Banking in Development Finance

THE RELATION BETWEEN THE INTER-national banking industry and the developing world is changing, with implications for the growth and financial health of both sides. Significant transformation in the structure of the industry, coupled with rapid economic growth and financial liberalization in the developing world, has created a new locus of mutual interest and new dynamics of engagement extending well beyond the traditional realm of provision of trade credit and financing sovereigns in distress. With over 2,027 local offices established in 127 developing countries, the international banking industry now has the operating infrastructure and technology platforms to book overseas transactions from a large network of local agencies, subsidiaries, and branches located in developing countries. Aided by growing cross-border lending activity, international banks play an increasingly important—in some countries, even dominant—role in the financing structure and growth prospects of developing countries. In many developing countries, international banks now provide the primary gateway through which corporations, sovereigns, and banks transfer funds abroad, borrow in short and medium terms, and conduct foreign exchange and derivatives operations. Foreign claims on developing-country residents held by major international banks reporting to the Bank for International Settlements (BIS) currently stand at $3.1 trillion and account for 9.5 percent of global foreign claims, up from $1.1 trillion in 2002. As of end-June 2007, developing-country residents' deposits with international banks amounted to $917 billion, a threefold increase since the end of 2002.

The resilience of the relationship between international banks and developing countries, however, is being tested by the current episode of financial turmoil. The realization of how powerfully shocks to a relatively small segment of the U.S. credit markets spilled over to capital markets in other developed countries in the summer of 2007 and onward to emerging markets highlights the type of new challenges policy makers and market participants are likely to face in an environment of securitized credit and an increasingly interlinked international banking system. Nine months into the turmoil, it is evident that conventional policy prescriptions borne out of the experience of the string of emerging-market financial crises of the 1990s and early 2000s offer some, but not definitive, guidance. The fact that the primary source of instability this time around resides in mature capital markets with significant global impact calls for stronger international cooperation in monetary policy, banking regulation, and liquidity management, all of which need to account for the growing financial links between emerging and mature markets. Although policy coordination to date has mainly taken the form of collaboration in liquidity provision, policy makers, regulators, scholars, and market participants have begun to focus on a longer-term reassessment of the stringency of financial regulation and the role of asset markets in financial stability.

This chapter highlights the growing importance of international banking activity for development finance, focusing on financial intermediation, economic benefits, and financial stability consequences of increased presence of foreign banks in developing countries. It identifies the universe of international banks active in developing countries; examines the characteristics of these banks in terms of country exposure, home country jurisdiction, and links with global money markets; and considers how international banks may serve as a vehicle of transmission of global financial shocks to developing countries. The chapter also maps out the broad policy challenges facing developing countries in dealing with the current turmoil, while underlining the longer-term benefits of their integration into global financial system.

The key messages of this chapter are highlighted below:

- *The participation of foreign banks in developing countries' financial systems has increased rapidly in recent years.* As of 2006, 897 foreign banks had established a majority-ownership stake in developing countries. Foreign-owned lenders account for a particularly high proportion of local banking assets in two regions—70 percent in several Eastern European countries, and approximately 40 percent in some Latin American countries—compared with less than 10 percent in developed economies such as France and Italy. The presence of foreign banks has increased in developing regions for different reasons: in Sub-Saharan Africa because of the limited reach of local banking infrastructure; in Europe and Central Asia along with regional integration into the European Union; and in Latin America as a way for governments to increase openness to foreign competition. In many countries, however, foreign bank presence was permitted after a financial crisis with local banks suffering from massive nonperforming loans and was motivated by the need to recapitalize and reestablish a functioning banking system. On the supply side, home country legislation has allowed banks to expand in foreign markets, advances in information technology have enabled banks to automate and manage large information flows across national borders, and a fundamental shift in business strategy has brought global banks close to customers through local activities.

- *The increased presence of foreign banks has generated substantial economic benefits to some developing countries through efficiency gains in banking systems, increased access to capital, more sophisticated financial services, and expertise in dealing with ailing banks.* Foreign banks operating in regions such as Europe and Central Asia tend to have lower overhead costs and net interest margins than their privately owned and government-owned domestic counterparts, although the impact varies depending on the mode of entry and the policy and institutional environment of the host country. Foreign bank entry can also lead to consolidation of fragmented local banking systems and the realization of economies of scale and scope. These improvements in financial sector development have provided an important avenue for increasing growth in developing countries.

- *Like globalization in general, the increased role of foreign banks can also expose developing countries to certain macroeconomic risks.* During the current episode, such risks have played out in developing countries' greater vulnerability to foreign shocks. Preliminary econometric investigation establishes a statistically significant relationship between international bank lending to developing countries and changes in global liquidity conditions, as measured by spreads of interbank interest rates over overnight index swap (OIS) rates and U.S. Treasury bill rates. A 10 basis-point increase in the spread between the London Interbank Offered Rate (LIBOR) and the OIS sustained for a quarter, for example, is predicted to lead to a decline of up to 3 percent in international bank lending to developing countries. Evidence from the international syndicated loan market already reflects this prediction: both the number of syndicated loans signed and the total volume of lending declined considerably in the fourth quarter of 2007 and first quarter of 2008 compared with the same periods in previous years. Countries particularly active in interbank markets—Brazil, China, Hungary, India, Kazakhstan, the Russian Federation, South Africa, Turkey, and Ukraine—need to be concerned about the possibility that their domestic banks will face funding difficulties in international markets should liquidity pressures in interbank markets remain at elevated levels. Also, several countries in Eastern Europe and Central Asia have experienced rapid private credit expansion in recent years on account of their banks borrowing extensively overseas and significant foreign bank presence in their credit markets.

- *A balanced mix of macroeconomic and regulatory policy measures are called for to maximize the benefits of increased foreign bank presence in developing countries.* Ultimately, policies must take into account differences across countries in the monetary framework (such as inflation targeting), exchange-rate regime, regulatory and supervisory capability, regional integration, level of financial sector development, and nature of exposure to the international banking system. Because the efficiency gains associated with foreign banks depend on the mode of entry as well as on host country factors, public policy interventions can enhance both competition and banking sector efficiency. Countries that are especially vulnerable to foreign monetary shocks should consider establishing backstop foreign currency lines of credit or foreign currency swaps to be made available to domestic banks in the case of severe financial distress. In countries where regulatory and financial institutions are still developing and possibly weak, particular attention would need to be placed on the quality of entry requirements, by relying, for example, on home countries' regulation and prudential supervision of banking institutions. A high premium should also be placed on the parent bank's compliance with international norms and standards regarding capital adequacy, corporate governance, and transparency.

- *The high level of uncertainty and anxiety in global financial markets calls for greater international policy coordination in the areas of financial regulation, liquidity provision, and macroeconomic management.* Although unusual in its scale, the coordinated liquidity provision by the Federal Reserve, the European Central Bank (ECB), and other central banks in December 2007 and subsequent months is consistent with central banks' common goal of maintaining financial stability. Tension in global interbank markets has been moderated by the moves. The fact that the magnitude of the credit turmoil was not on financial regulators' radar screens, however, reveals a significant shortcoming in the current framework of financial market supervision and regulation. This realization has, in turn, prompted a growing consensus on the need to foster greater transparency about the nature of complex financial instruments and each institution's exposure to them, as well as the need to somehow institutionalize market discipline as a complement to regulation, as envisaged under the third pillar of the Basel II Accord. Toward this end, the United States has launched a far-reaching rethinking of its financial regulation system. In Europe, growing cross-border banking consolidation is driving increased recognition of the need for revised regulation and supervisory arrangements. At the international level, lack of both a coherent cross-border banking regulatory framework between home countries and host countries and guidelines surrounding the lender of last resort and crisis management mechanism is a cause for concern. Given that foreign bank penetration has been more extensive in developing countries than in high-income countries, developing countries should have a strong stake in the development of a coherent approach to the governance of cross-border banking. And though recent efforts in macroeconomic stabilization and external debt management have contributed to the relative resilience of developing countries during the recent financial turmoil, these countries still need to intensify efforts to monitor foreign borrowing by their banks and risk management strategies pursued by their corporations with access to external debt markets.

Growth and transformation of international banking activity in developing countries

Although foreign banks have operated in developing countries for decades, their presence has expanded rapidly since the early 1990s. Today international banks are a growing force in shaping the economic transformation and global competitive position of many developing countries. Their importance results from the interaction of three sets of structural factors: closer integration of developing countries into the world economy through greater trade and foreign direct investment (FDI) flows that raise demand for international banking services; technological advances allowing banks to book assets, control operations, and automate processes across the global supply chain in an integrated manner; and regulatory reforms in both developed and developing countries authorizing banks based in one country to invest and operate in the banking sectors of other countries. These factors have resulted in a number of important changes in international banking activity in developing countries—the secular growth in lending exposure, a shift from cross-border to local-market delivery of financial services, and substantial foreign investment through cross-border acquisitions and establishment of local affiliates.

Demand for international banking services in developing countries (defined as services rendered by foreign banks to developing-country residents) has evolved over time in response to the changing position of developing countries on the global economic and financial stage. Attracted by the prospects of asset growth and risk diversification, foreign banks have responded eagerly in expanding their overseas businesses in developing countries through both cross-border and local market activity.

Quantitatively, the most comprehensive measure of international banking activity in developing countries, total foreign claims on developing countries held by banks reporting to the BIS, stood at $3.1 trillion in the third quarter of 2007 (figure 3.1), almost six times larger than in 1992, when banks were recovering from the Latin American debt crisis of the early 1980s.[1] Sixty percent of this exposure is in international claims (claims denominated in

Figure 3.1 International bank claims on developing countries

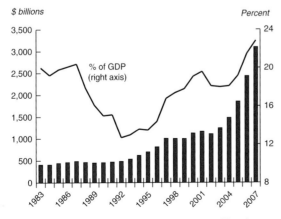

Sources: Bank for International Settlements (BIS); World Bank.
Note: These are the foreign assets of banks reporting to the BIS. GDP is aggregate GDP for developing countries.

Figure 3.2 International claims outstanding, by region, third quarter, 2007

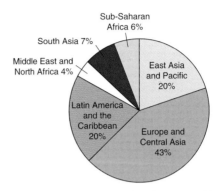

Sources: Bank for International Settlements; World Bank staff calculations.

foreign currency), including cross-border loans and loans extended by banks' foreign offices, mostly to residents of countries in Latin America, East Asia, and Europe and Central Asia (figure 3.2). Despite a steady shift in international banks' strategy from cross-border lending to lending through local affiliates, their exposures to developing countries remains mostly denominated in foreign currency, of which about 44 percent are in short-term maturity.

Because foreign-denominated exposures are typically funded in international markets, they tend to be highly sensitive to movements in global interbank rates and conditions. Furthermore, exposure to foreign-currency loans is widespread across developing-country borrowers, with a majority of borrowers (77 percent) holding more than half their foreign bank debt in loans denominated in foreign currency.

The strong overall growth in international banking has been interrupted, however, by several episodes of credit contractions and economic downturns. Scaled by aggregate GDP of developing countries, a measure that serves as a proxy for demand-side factors, international bank claims declined sharply in the late 1980s and early 1990s (to 13 percent of GDP in 1992), increased steadily through the remainder of the 1990s, paused during the global slowdown of 2001–02, and mostly accelerated since 2003 (reaching 23 percent of GDP in 2007). The latest expansion—from 2003 until the onset of global financial turmoil in mid-2007—coincided with an epoch of excessive global liquidity, large-scale securitization, and cross-border banking sector consolidation (box 3.1).

Box 3.1 Rapid expansion of the international banking industry

The international banking industry has witnessed phenomenal growth and financial innovation over the past two decades, punctuated by episodes of consolidation. The spread of modern international banking is conventionally traced to the establishment of the Eurocurrency market in the late 1950s and early 1960s, initially in London and then in other European financial centers. As measured by foreign assets of banks reporting to the BIS, international banking activity expanded at a very fast pace over the past decade, reflecting expanding world trade, the rise of multinational firms, growth in financing of global payments imbalances, and the assimilation of transition economies into global banking system (figure below). Looking back, international banking has gone through three distinct phases in the post–World War II era:

- The establishment of the Eurocurrency market in the late 1950s and early 1960s, stimulated initially by prevailing capital controls and restrictions on international transactions in the United States and Western Europe, which prompted national banks to establish offices abroad to service the overseas business of their clients.
- The growing role of banks in Japan in the 1980s as the Japanese government attempted to open its markets and promote the international role of yen. This phase also coincided with the growth of syndicated bank lending and the expansion of currency and interest-rate derivatives markets that enhanced banks' scope to expand their geographical reach in both funding and lending.
- The increased securitization of credit in recent years, facilitated by the originate-and-distribute model of bank lending on the one hand and by rapid growth in the market for asset-backed structured financial products (such as collateralized debt obligations) and development of the credit derivatives market on the other. From a public policy perspective, securitization has contributed to a shift in regulatory or oversight responsibility from official agencies to the private marketplace, including credit rating agencies and security underwriters.

A wave of cross-border mergers and acquisitions over the past decade or so has resulted in a significant consolidation of the international banking industry and a concentration of assets in the hands of a few major banks. As of 2007, the top 10 banks held 19 percent of the industry's assets, and the top 100 banks accounted for 75 percent, higher than the corresponding values of 13 and 59 percent in 1996 (figure below).

Financial innovation and technological change pioneered by the banking industry itself has transformed the nature and reach of the international banking business, allowing banks greater market reach and new business areas, including underwriting, asset management, investment banking, and proprietary trading. Rapid growth of the markets for risk transfer—credit derivatives and various types of asset-backed securities—has facilitated highly leveraged exposures by banks themselves and by new players such as hedge funds and private equity firms.

Banking consolidation has increased over time

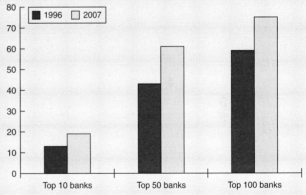

% of assets

Source: World Bank staff calculations based on The Banker database.

International banking expansion, 1970–2007

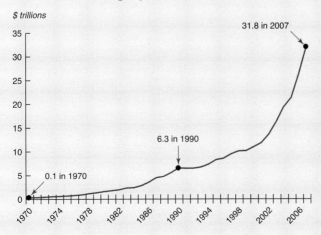

$ trillions

Source: Bank for International Settlements (BIS).

Significant expansion in the credit derivatives market

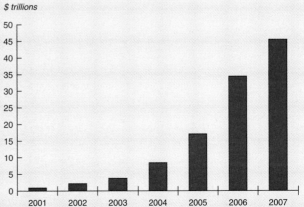

$ trillions

Source: International Swaps and Derivatives Association 2007.

Figure 3.3 Composition of foreign claims on developing countries, by nationality of reporting banks

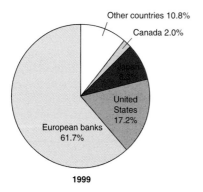

1999

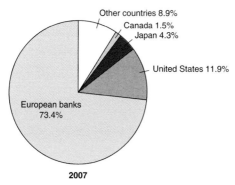

2007

Sources: Bank for International Settlements; World Bank staff calculations.

Note: European banks include those from Austria, Belgium, Denmark, Finland, France, Germany, Greece, Ireland, Italy, the Netherlands, Norway, Portugal, Spain, Sweden, Switzerland, and the United Kingdom.

The regional composition of creditor banks to developing countries has also changed since the early 1990s. Largely reflecting the growing weight of claims by residents of Eastern Europe and Central Asian countries, the role of Western European banks has increased, accounting for 73 percent of total foreign claims on developing countries in 2007, compared with 62 percent in 1999 (figure 3.3). By contrast, banks from Japan and the United States lost market share during this period as they adopted a more cautious approach to overseas expansion.

International banks service their overseas businesses through local market participation
Foreign banks' direct investment in developing countries' banking sectors accounted for a cumulative $250 billion over 1995–2006, fueled by both greenfield (new) investments and mergers and acquisitions (M&A).[2] As of end-2006, the 897 foreign

Figure 3.4 Foreign banks' increasing involvement in developing countries, 1995–2006

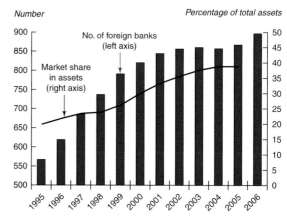

Source: World Bank staff estimates based on data from Bankscope.

Note: Foreign banks are those in which foreign shareholders hold 50 percent or more of total capital. Because asset data for 2006 are missing for a significant number of banks, asset information is presented only to 2005.

banks with a presence in developing countries controlled combined assets of over $1.2 trillion and accounted for more than 39 percent of total banking assets in these countries (figure 3.4), compared with $157 billion 10 years earlier, when they accounted for approximately 20 percent of total banking assets. Since 2000 the majority of the increase in assets has resulted from increased banking sector consolidation and better economic integration between existing and new EU members. Indeed, the number of foreign banks in the countries that joined the European Union in 2004 jumped from 121 in 1995 to 330 in 2006, and the value of their assets surged from $41 billion to $528 billion.

The share of banking assets held by foreign banks with majority foreign ownership stake, however, varies dramatically among developing regions and is to some extent dependent on regulatory restrictions. Overall, foreign ownership of the banking sector is substantially higher in Europe and Central Asia, Sub-Saharan Africa, and Latin America than in East Asia, South Asia, and the Middle East and North Africa (figure 3.5). Foreign ownership also varies considerably intraregionally. While many small Sub-Saharan African countries have shares exceeding 50 percent, Ethiopia, Nigeria, and South Africa have minimal or no foreign bank participation with majority foreign ownership stake (table 3.1). In Latin America, large economies such as Peru and Mexico have foreign presence accounting for 95 and 82 percent of the

Figure 3.5 Share of banking assets held by foreign banks, by region

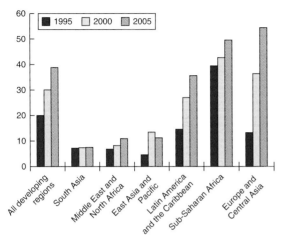

Percent

Source: World Bank staff estimates based on data from Bankscope.

Note: Foreign banks are those in which foreign shareholders hold 50 percent or more of total capital.

banking sector, respectively, while in small economies such as Guatemala and Ecuador, the share is 8 and 5 percent, respectively. Within Europe and Central Asia, foreign banking presence is low in the two largest regional economies, Russia and Turkey, but extensive in most other

countries. In recent years banks from developing countries have begun to invest in other (particularly low-income) developing countries. And as of 2006, 256 of the 897 foreign banks operating in developing countries were based in other developing countries. Typically, these foreign banks are from middle-income countries such as Hungary, Malaysia, and South Africa, and like their high-income competitors they invest mainly within their own regions.

International banks tend to seek out markets where institutional familiarity provides them with a competitive advantage over other foreign banks (Claessens and Van Horen 2008). As such, foreign bank penetration tends to be particularly high in developing countries with similar legal systems, banking regulations, and institutional setups as certain home countries, presumably because such similarities tend to reduce risk and operational costs (Galindo, Micco, and Serra 2003). Foreign bank presence also tends to follow lines of economic integration, common language, and geographical proximity. In Latin America and the Caribbean, for example, 60 percent of foreign banks are headquartered in the United States and Spain, whereas in Europe and Central Asia more than 90 percent of foreign banks are headquartered in the European Union (figure 3.6). Even

Table 3.1 Share of banking assets held by foreign banks with majority ownership, 2006

Country	0%–10%	Country	10%–30%	Country	30%–50%	Country	50%–70%	Country	70%–100%
Algeria	9	Moldova	30	Senegal	48	Rwanda	70	Madagascar	100
Nepal	9	Honduras	29	Congo, Dem. Rep. of	47	Côte d'Ivoire	66	Mozambique	100
Guatemala	8	Ukraine	28	Uruguay	44	Tanzania	66	Swaziland	100
Thailand	5	Indonesia	28	Panama	42	Ghana	65	Peru	95
India	5	Cambodia	27	Kenya	41	Burkina Faso	65	Hungary	94
Ecuador	5	Argentina	25	Benin	40	Serbia and Montenegro	65	Albania	93
Azerbaijan	5	Brazil	25	Bolivia	38	Cameroon	63	Lithuania	92
Mauritania	5	Kazakhstan	24	Mauritius	37	Romania	60	Croatia	91
Nigeria	5	Pakistan	23	Burundi	36	Niger	59	Bosnia-Herzegovina	90
Turkey	4	Costa Rica	22	Seychelles	36	Mali	57	Mexico	82
Uzbekistan	1	Malawi	22	Lebanon	34	Angola	53	Macedonia	80
Philippines	1	Tunisia	22	Nicaragua	34	Latvia	52	Uganda	80
South Africa	0	Mongolia	22	Chile	32	Jamaica	51	El Salvador	78
China	0	Sudan	20	Venezuela, R. B. de	32	Zimbabwe	51	Zambia	77
Vietnam	0	Morocco	18	Georgia	32	Namibia	50	Botswana	77
Iran, Islamic Rep. of	0	Colombia	18	Armenia	31			Kyrgyzstan	75
Yemen, Rep. of	0	Malaysia	16					Poland	73
Bangladesh	0	Jordan	14					Bulgaria	72
Sri Lanka	0	Russian Federation	13					Paraguay	71
Ethiopia	0	Egypt, Arab Rep. of	12						
Togo	0								

Source: World Bank staff estimates based on data from Bankscope.

Note: A bank is defined as foreign owned only if 50 percent or more of its shares in a given year are held directly by foreign nationals. Once foreign ownership is determined, the source country is identified as the country of nationality of the largest foreign shareholder(s). The table does not capture the assets of the foreign banks with minority foreign ownership.

Figure 3.6 Home countries of foreign banks in developing regions, 2000–06

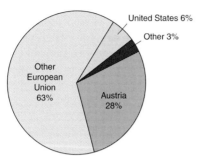

Europe and Central Asia

Latin America and the Caribbean

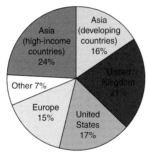

East Asia and the Pacific and South Asia

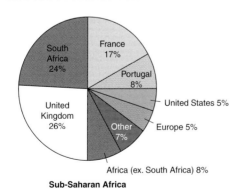

Sub-Saharan Africa

Source: World Bank staff estimates based on data from Bankscope.

excluding HSBC, which moved its headquarters from Hong Kong (China) to the United Kingdom in 1993, Asian banks account for 40 percent of foreign banks in East Asia. In Sub-Saharan Africa, more than 30 percent of foreign banks are from the region, and the rest are mainly from countries with which Sub-Saharan Africa has had economic links since colonial times.

The regional focus of banks investing in developing countries is also evident in data on the 20 foreign banks with the largest asset holdings in developing countries. For example, all majority-owned foreign banking assets of two Spanish banks, Santander and BBVA, and Canadian Scotia Bank, are in Latin America. Other European banks, including Italy's Unicredito and Intesa Sanpaolo and Austria's Erste Bank, Raiffeisen, and HVB, have a significant presence in the Europe and Central Asia region. On the other hand, top 20 banks such as BNP Paribas (France), ING (Netherlands), Deutsche Bank (Germany), and Citibank (United States) are more diversified. All in all, developing countries still account for a relatively small share of these banks' total assets, ranging from 1 to 15 percent.

The mode of foreign bank entry has shifted from greenfield investments to M&A and from branches to subsidiaries

Cross-border consolidation has been an important driver of recent expansion in the amount of FDI in developing countries' banking sectors. Available data show about 750 cross-border M&A transactions in developing countries over 1995–2006, totaling $108 billion.[3] Meanwhile, the share of global cross-border M&A transactions involving banks based in developing countries rose from 12 percent in 1995–2002 to 21 percent in 2003–06. The size of these transactions varied considerably, however. The largest was Citigroup's acquisition of Mexico-based Banamex (table 3.2). M&A transactions resulting in majority ownership accounted for 407 of 587 recorded entries of foreign banks in developing countries during 1995–2006 (figure 3.7). The share of M&A in total foreign bank entry has jumped dramatically—to approximately 90 percent—since 2004.

When a foreign bank enters a country through M&A, it generally operates as a subsidiary—a legally independent entity with powers defined by

Table 3.2 Major cross-border M&A sales by developing countries, 2001–07

Year	Acquired bank	Host country	Acquiring bank	Home country	% of the asset bought	Value ($ billions)
2001	Banamex	Mexico	CitiGroup	United States	100	12.5
2007	ICBC	China	Standard Bank	South Africa	20	5.5
2006	BCR	Romania	Erste Bank	Austria	62	4.8
2006	Akbank	Turkey	CitiGroup	United States	20	3.1
2005	Bank of China	China	Merrill Lynch	United States	10	3.1
2004	Bank of Communications	China	HSBC	United Kingdom	20	2.1
2005	Disbank	Turkey	Fortis	Belgium	90	1.3
2001	Banespa	Brazil	Banco Santander	Spain	30	1.2
2005	Avalbank	Ukraine	Raiffesen	Austria	94	1.1

Source: World Bank, *Global Development Finance,* various years.

Figure 3.7 Mode of entry of foreign banks with majority ownership

No. of bank entities

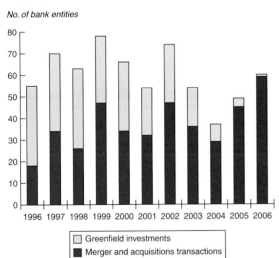

Source: World Bank staff estimates based on data from Bankscope.
Note: Foreign banks are those in which foreign shareholders hold 50 percent or more of total capital.

its own charter in the host country. In the case of a greenfield investment, however, the foreign operation may be either a branch or a subsidiary. A branch is licensed by the host country but its powers are defined by its parent bank's charter (subject to limitations imposed by the host country). Subsidiaries seem to be strongly preferred by the 100 largest foreign banks in Latin America and Eastern Europe, where they accounted for 65 and 82 percent, respectively, of local operations in 2002 (Cerrutti, Dell'Ariccia, and Martinez Peria 2005; Baudino and others 2004).

The decision to enter a developing county through a branch or a subsidiary is found to be affected by several host country factors and the nature of the foreign bank's business (Cerrutti, Dell'Ariccia, and Martinez Peria 2005). Regulations and institutional factors are of paramount importance in the decision, as foreign banks are less likely to operate as branches in countries that limit their activities. In some cases, the organizational structure is shaped by government policies favoring one form over the other, for example, in Malaysia, Mexico, and Russia, where investment through branches is not allowed. When branches are allowed, they are most common in countries with high corporate taxes and in poor countries, perhaps in the latter because of lack of market opportunities. The bank's desired business in the host country market is also an important factor: branches are more prevalent than subsidiaries when foreign operations are small in size and do not provide retail services. Branches are less common in countries with risky macroeconomic environments. However, when the risks are mostly related to government intervention or other political events, foreign banks may prefer to operate as branches.

The distinction between branches and subsidiaries also implies different levels of parent-bank responsibility and financial support. While subsidiaries are legally separate entities from their parent banks, parent banks are responsible for the liabilities of their branches under most circumstances. Parent-bank support can play an important role during times of financial turmoil. For example, following the financial crisis in Argentina in the early 2000s, Citibank increased the capital of its branch operations in the country but sold its subsidiary there. This said, special contractual agreements (such as ring-fencing provisions) and reputational considerations may at times blur distinctions between branches and subsidiaries. For example, in recent years, a number of banking groups have adopted ring-fencing provisions that generally establish that parent banks are not required to repay the obligations of a foreign branch if the branch faces repayment problems because of extreme circumstances (such as war or civil conflict) or because of certain actions by the host government (such as exchange controls, expropriations, and the like).[4] However, concerns about loss of reputation have in certain instances led parent banks to rescue and recapitalize subsidiaries, even if they were not legally forced to do so. For example, HSCB injected a significant amount of capital into its subsidiary in Argentina following the crisis. Portugal's Banco Espiritu Santo did the same for its Brazilian subsidiary following the losses due to the real's devaluation in 1999 (Cerutti, Dell'Ariccia, and Martinez Peria 2005).

Foreign bank expansion has been fostered by financial liberalization and deregulation

Since the mid-1990s, restrictions facing foreign banks, including limitations on form of investment and level of foreign ownership, have been gradually eased through unilateral liberalization policies, bilateral and regional trade and investment agreements such as the North American Free Trade Agreement (NAFTA), and World Trade Organization (WTO) membership requirements. In particular, the General Agreement on Trade in Services (GATS) encourages greater openness among WTO members in provision of financial services from foreign entities. The agreement addresses 17 specific issues related to foreign bank presence in member countries, including foreign bank entry and licensing requirements (such as minimum capital entry requirements), method of entry, expansion after entry, limitations on share of foreign presence in the banking sector, and permissible activities and operations. A close examination of reported practices, however, indicates that some developing-country members of the WTO are more restrictive in practice than they should be according to their WTO commitments (Barth and others 2008).

In many countries, financial sector liberalization came after a financial crisis and was motivated by the need to reestablish a functioning banking system (Cull and Martinez Peria 2007). In general, though, the driving forces behind and timing of financial sector liberalization—and the level of allowed foreign ownership (table 3.3)—continue to vary considerably among developing countries.[5]

In the early 1990s many countries in the Europe and Central Asia region allowed foreign banks to start operations within their borders only through greenfield investment (through licensing) and through purchase of minority stakes in local banks. Majority ownership was allowed only after banking crises hit many of these economies (Baudino and others 2004). Although foreign bank entry was pervasive in the early 1990s for 2004 EU accession countries (in particular Hungary and Poland), it occurred later in the 2007 accession economies, Bulgaria and Romania (Hagmayr, Haiss, and Sümegi 2007). In Turkey foreign banks invested significantly only after the start of the country's official EU accession negotiations in 2005.

Most Latin American countries began opening their banking systems to foreign entry following a series of financial crises in the region in the mid-1990s (ECLAC 2002). In Mexico, for example, all banks (except one foreign bank) were nationalized in 1982 and remained under state control until a progressive easing of restrictions

Table 3.3 Foreign ownership restrictions in banking sector, 2004 or latest available year

Percentage allowed	Country
Not allowed	Ethiopia
1%–49%	Algeria, China, India, Indonesia,[a] Kenya, Pakistan, Sri Lanka, Thailand, Uruguay[a]
50%–99%	Brazil, Arab Republic of Egypt, Malaysia, Mexico, the Philippines, Poland, Romania, Russian Federation
No restrictions	Argentina, Bolivia, Chile, Colombia, Costa Rica, Dominican Republic, Ecuador, El Salvador, Guatemala, Hungary, Jamaica, Mauritius, Mongolia, Morocco, Mozambique, Nigeria, Paraguay, Peru, Republic of Korea, Senegal, South Africa, Trinidad and Tobago, Tunisia, Turkey, Uganda, Tanzania, República Bolivariana de Venezuela

Source: UNCTAD 2006.
a. Denotes 100 percent minus the government ownership percentage, that is, the share of business held by the private sector.

Figure 3.8 Restrictions on FDI in the banking sector, 2005

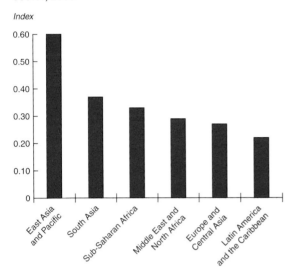

Source: World Bank staff estimates based on data from UNCTAD (2006).

Note: Regional averages are the simple average of the index for each country within the region. The country index is measured on a 0–1 scale, with 0 representing full openness and 1 a de facto probation. The index is based on government policies related to foreign bank ownership restrictions, screening and approval, and operational restrictions (in the order of highest weighted restriction to the lowest).

in the 1990s.[6] Similarly, in Argentina foreign bank entry was permitted starting in the early 1990s but the privatization of state banks accelerated in the fallout of Mexico's Tequila crisis. By contrast, in Brazil, where restrictions were eased in the late 1990s, foreign bank entry is still evaluated on a case-by-case basis (Peek and Rosengren 2000).

Other regions remain relatively less open to foreign bank entry (figure 3.8), although many East Asian countries, including Indonesia, Thailand, and the Philippines, lowered barriers to banking sector FDI following their 1997–98 financial crises (Coppel and Davies 2003). In China, where banking sector FDI traditionally has been limited, the country has recently taken steps toward liberalization in order to meet its WTO commitments.[7] Countries in South Asia and the Middle East and North Africa also tend to have relatively high restrictions on foreign bank entry. India, for example, provides a limited number of licenses for opening branches and permits foreign banks to hold only a 5 or 10 percent equity stake in domestic private banks (and this only since

2005), with a few exceptions for stakes in selected domestic banks. Further liberalization for foreign bank acquisitions is expected in 2009. The Arab Republic of Egypt and Algeria have notable restrictions on foreign investment, although Morocco and Tunisia have no restrictions.

Technological progress has facilitated FDI in the banking industry

Innovations in data transmission, storage, and processing have facilitated the unprecedented growth of FDI in emerging economies' banking sectors. Reliable global payment systems and real-time settlement systems across time zones have allowed intermediaries to increase the efficiency of back-office operations, thereby freeing up resources for front-office activities that permit them to enter new markets. Predictably, however, banks from developed countries have a marked advantage over local banks in developing countries in adopting new technologies because of easier access to required expertise and the economies of scale involved in already having absorbed the very high fixed costs of deploying the same technologies in their home operations.

Commentators have identified four areas in which technological progress has been especially important for the geographic expansion of banks. First, the dawn of market-segment and bank-specific credit-scoring methodologies, combined with the collection of borrower-specific information through credit bureaus, has allowed banks to more efficiently assess the creditworthiness of customers in new markets. As a result, banks have been able to lend over greater distances in both their home and foreign markets. Second, important innovations in risk management systems, often driven by the Basel II Accords, have allowed banks to increase the size of their balance sheets for a given capital base. Improvements in the quantification of expected losses for both individual positions (through credit scoring, for example) and aggregate exposures (through value-at-risk analysis, for example) and the analysis of balance-sheet behavior under alternative market scenarios have enabled banks to better account for the risks of moving into new markets. Third, improved instruments for securitization and hedging have helped banks better manage their international risk exposure (Barth, Caprio, and Levine 2001). Finally, new ways of collecting deposits and interacting with customers—the Internet, automated teller machines (ATMs), and mobile phones—have improved access to finance for unserved or underserved residents of countries such as India, Kenya, the Philippines, South Africa, and Zambia.

Economic benefits of international banking

Developing countries stand to reap substantial gains from their increased engagement with the international banking industry. Access to international banking increases potential sources of credit to firms and households, enhances provision of sophisticated financial services, and encourages efficiency improvements in domestic banks, although the impact of all of these factors varies depending on the characteristics of banks and the policy and institutional environment of host countries. As a result of these influences, increased international banking in developing countries has helped ease credit constraints on firms, thereby contributing to growth and development.

Foreign banks have improved access to financial services

The ability of international banks to frequently offer more sophisticated, higher-quality, and lower-priced services than domestic banks to developing-country borrowers derives from several factors, including access to the technology, the presence of skilled personnel, and the ability to seize opportunities of scale in operational systems already in place in providing services to their domestic clients. For example, Arnold, Javorcik, and Mattoo (2007) document that foreign banks in the Czech Republic were the first or leading banks to offer ATM transactions and remote banking and that they have greatly sped up the process of loan applications. Garber (2000) notes the ability of foreign banks to offer new financial products such as over-the-counter derivatives, structured notes, and equity swaps. Levine (2001) cites a dramatic reduction in fees on letters of credit and letters of guarantee in Turkey following liberalization of bank entry rules. And Wooldridge and others (2003) highlight that foreign banks have also supported the development of local financial markets in many developing countries, particularly in local securities and derivatives markets by investing considerable

capital and expertise. Foreign banks participate as primary dealers in some local government bond markets, and as pension fund managers and swap dealers in other markets.

Increased foreign bank presence can also improve the soundness of the financial system by encouraging stronger regulation and supervision. Numerous studies have found that investments by foreign banks in developing countries spur improvements in bank supervision, with spillover effects that improve the structure of regulation (Goldberg 2004). Levine (2001) argues that foreign banks may encourage the emergence of institutions such as rating agencies, accounting and auditing firms, and credit bureaus, citing the example of improvements in supervision and accounting standards in Mexico as a consequence of opening the banking sector to U.S. institutions under NAFTA.[8] Foreign bank entrants also can bring more advanced safeguards against fraud, money laundering, and terrorism financing, and domestic banks may emulate such safeguards to gain a competitive advantage in access to international financial markets.

Foreign banks have improved the efficiency of domestic financial systems

The entry of foreign banks may improve the efficiency of financial systems in developing countries, either because foreign banks are more efficient than their domestic counterparts or because competition from foreign banks in formerly protected and oligopolistic markets forces domestic banks to improve their own efficiency.[9] Adequate levels of competition are generally viewed as important to reducing costs and increasing innovation in financial markets, while empirical work confirms that foreign bank entry has helped maintain competition during a process of banking consolidation in many developing countries (Gelos and Roldos 2004). An evaluation of data comparing the simple efficiency measures for foreign and domestic banks shows decidedly mixed results (table 3.4). In developing countries as a group, foreign banks average significantly higher overheads and costs, but lower loan loss reserves, than domestic banks. These results vary substantially by region, however, with Europe and Central Asia recording particularly efficient indicators for foreign banks. In Latin America and the Caribbean, foreign banks have had smaller net interest margins than

Table 3.4 Average foreign and domestic bank performance indicators in developing regions, 1998–2005

Category	Net interest margin (%)	Overhead to assets ratio (%)	Taxes to assets ratio	Loan loss reserves to assets ratio	Loan loss reserves to gross loans	Pretax profits to assets ratio	Cost to income ratio
Developing countries							
Domestic	7.27	5.72	0.53	4.51	8.32	1.69	69.60
Foreign	6.86	6.30	0.63	3.63	7.27	1.29	76.52
East Asia and Pacific							
Domestic	3.84	2.68	0.35	3.26	6.01	0.66	63.98
Foreign	3.83	3.03	0.57	10.35	11.85	2.04	62.10
Europe and Central Asia							
Domestic	7.71	6.55	0.67	5.24	8.13	2.08	67.86
Foreign	6.02	5.59	0.41	2.92	5.70	1.43	73.73
Latin America and the Caribbean							
Domestic	9.79	7.55	0.44	3.06	7.23	1.84	76.74
Foreign	7.83	8.05	0.83	2.74	7.52	0.63	81.30
Middle East and North Africa							
Domestic	3.57	2.16	0.25	5.84	12.66	1.08	59.78
Foreign	3.71	2.69	0.27	8.25	16.07	0.90	76.09
South Asia							
Domestic	2.85	2.52	0.44	2.47	6.35	0.92	64.75
Foreign	3.75	2.38	1.02	1.62	7.06	2.46	51.07
Sub-Saharan Africa							
Domestic	10.08	7.76	0.79	8.52	12.56	2.55	74.08
Foreign	9.07	7.24	0.81	3.31	5.54	1.89	81.40
Developed countries							
Domestic	2.63	2.20	0.27	1.92	3.19	1.01	59.78
Foreign	1.80	1.74	0.23	1.40	2.69	1.26	55.86

Source: World Bank staff estimates based on data from Bankscope.
Note: Pairs in bold indicate difference in means of corresponding indicators for foreign and domestic banks and are statistically significant at the 10 percent level. Net interest margin is net interest income as a percentage of earning assets.

domestic banks but no difference in costs, whereas in Sub-Saharan Africa, foreign banks performed better compared with domestic banks but only significantly so in loan loss ratios.

These diverse results reflect the wide range of both foreign banks and domestic banking conditions in developing countries. Characteristics of foreign banks that might affect their efficiency include the efficiency and origin of the parent bank, the type of operation (such as wholesale versus retail), the motive (following the client versus market-seeking), the market share of the foreign banks, and the mode of entry (Berger and others 2008; Sturm and Williams 2005). Factors related to the host economy, such as initial financial, economic, and regulatory conditions, may also affect the efficiency of foreign banks. One factor affecting the relationship between efficiency and mode of entry is the advantage that a greenfield entry offers in allowing investors greater scope and choice in setting up a new facility, compared with an

M&A transaction, which is typically burdened by overhang costs and organizational structure in the existing business. Entry through M&A may involve higher organizational and operational costs, which may delay the improvement in efficiency of the foreign banks, although an immediate increase in the market share after acquisition may increase efficiency through economies of scale. The efficiency advantage of the new investment mode of entry is borne out by the experience of foreign banks entering Europe and Central Asia (as it is in developed countries as a whole), though not by the experience of Sub-Saharan Africa, where foreign banks entering through M&A have superior efficiency to those entering through greenfield investment (figure 3.9). In other regions the difference in efficiency associated with new investment and M&A mode of foreign entry is not sufficiently pronounced to project a clear point of view, in part because of a lower number of M&A transactions in South Asia.

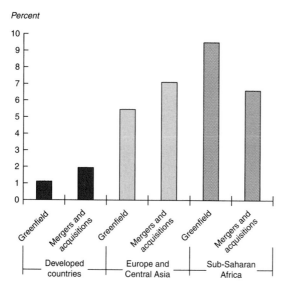

Figure 3.9 Ratio of overhead cost to total assets in select regions, by mode of foreign bank entry, 1998–2005

Source: World Bank staff estimates based on data from Bankscope.

Foreign bank presence has helped ease domestic credit constraints on manufacturing firms

Access to international banking, whether cross-border or through foreign banks' local investments, increases the potential sources of credit available to developing-country firms. If markets are perfectly competitive and if all lenders have access to full information, foreign banks' increased access to technology, improved opportunities for risk diversification, and perhaps better corporate governance should enable them to offer lower interest rates and a higher volume of credit. However, barriers to information and limits on competition to protect safety and soundness are pervasive in financial markets, greatly complicating an analysis of the impact of foreign banks.

Most empirical studies conclude that the presence of foreign banks increases access to credit. For example, Giannetti and Ongena (2005), in a cross-country study using firm-level data, find that foreign lending increased growth in firm sales, assets, and leverage in Eastern European countries. (The effect was dampened, although still positive, for small firms.) A survey of firms operating in 35 developing countries suggests that all firms, including small and medium-size firms, report lower obstacles to obtaining finance in countries with higher levels of bank presence (Clarke, Cull, and Martinez

Peria 2006). Beck, Demirgüç-Kunt, and Maksimovic (2004) conclude that greater foreign bank presence tends to alleviate the impact of bank concentration on setting obstacles to credit access. Even if foreign banking tends to improve access to credit on average, the impact may vary significantly among countries or firms. Some studies have found that foreign banks tend to "cherry pick" the best borrowers, thus limiting credit expansion (Mian 2004; Detragiache, Gupta and Tressel 2006). Therefore, given the existing mixed empirical evidence, focusing on the informational requirements of banking and on the efficiency and real benefits of foreign bank presence can thus provide insight into the potentially differentiated impact and also help determine whether foreign banks might help to mitigate connected-lending problems and improve capital allocation.

Econometric analysis (detailed in annex 3A of this chapter) shows that foreign banks are particularly important for industries in developing countries that rely heavily on external financing. For instance, in a country in which the banking sector is 20 percent foreign owned, such as Brazil, the difference in growth between companies with low financial dependence (at the 25th percentile of all companies) and those with high financial dependence (at the 75th percentile) is less than 1 percentage point on average (figure 3.10). The difference increases exponentially when foreign bank presence is stronger. In countries where foreign ownership of the banking sector is 40–60 percent, such as Bolivia and Romania, companies

Figure 3.10 Real effects of foreign bank presence

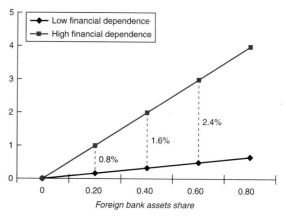

Sources: World Bank staff estimates based on Bankscope and World Bank data.

with high financial dependence grow 1.6 and 2.4 percentage points more, respectively, than those with low financial dependence. As a whole, these results show not only the importance of foreign bank presence for industry growth in developing countries but also the crucial role of such banks in particular industries, namely, those most in need of external financing.

Transmission of financial shocks through the international banking system

The international banking industry's adjustment to the current global financial turmoil bears importantly on the prospects of foreign credit supply to developing countries. A large body of literature and empirical evidence indicates that banks tend to react to adverse financial conditions through balance-sheet adjustments in order to meet a variety of risk management standards (such as value at risk), performance indicators (return on equity), and regulatory requirements (Basel I or II). The response of Japanese banks to the stock and real estate market collapse of early 1990s, when they pulled back from foreign markets—including the United States—in order to reduce liabilities on their balance sheets and thereby meet capital adequacy ratio requirements, is indicative of how banks can transmit domestic financial shocks to foreign markets.

Three trends are important in the transmission of financial shocks to developing countries: first, mounting pressure on major banks' capital positions as they recognize balance-sheet losses; second, deteriorating liquidity conditions in interbank markets; and third, tightening credit standards in the face of global economic slowdown. The fact that all three transmission channels are currently operating simultaneously raises the possibility of a sharp global credit downturn, with particularly negative implications for developing countries whose corporate sectors depend on banks as their primary source of external financing. As of March 2008, credit write-downs and losses disclosed by major banking institutions exposed to U.S. subprime-related securities amounted to $206 billion, with roughly one-half attributable to European banks ($98.5 billion) and the rest attributable to U.S. banks ($92.3 billion) and others

($15.2 billion). Because it seems too early to evaluate the implications of bank-specific balance-sheet problems on the overall banking sector's willingness to lend to developing countries, the following analysis focuses on developments in global interbank markets and the downturn in the lending cycle. A useful start would be to highlight some of the key characteristics of the top 200 international lenders to developing countries (box 3.2).

In the current grouping of the top 200 lenders to developing countries, 18 have experienced considerable credit deterioration and asset price losses from exposure to subprime-related securities and structured investment vehicles. Those not directly affected by the subprime turmoil have suffered from tightening liquidity conditions in global interbank markets and an associated rise in funding costs.

Tightening of global liquidity has heightened short-term funding pressures

Although bank borrowing in the interbank and commercial-paper markets has increased steadily since the early 1990s, short-term funding of lending activities skyrocketed after 2002, as liquidity in global financial markets increased because of easy monetary policy responses to the global slowdown in 2001. As a result, global banks have increasingly relied on short-term financing sources not only for managing liquidity but also for funding their balance-sheet expansion. In essence, banks have engaged in maturity transformation on an unprecedented scale, taking advantage of relatively steep yield curves by borrowing short and lending long.

In recent months, however, this strategy has exposed banks to interest-rate risk from maturity mismatch (flattening of the yield curve) and liquidity risk (the inability to roll over interbank debt). Though the former risk is related to monetary and macroeconomic conditions, the latter arises from counterparty risk (informational asymmetries among market participants). When perceived counterparty risk increases, as it has during the current financial market turmoil, banks become more reluctant to lend to each other. And since most interbank lending occurs among a clearly defined group of global institutions and leads to interrelated claims by the same group of institutions, denial of credit to some market participants is likely to be followed by a chain of denied credit

Box 3.2   Profile of the top 200 lenders to developing countries

The universe of international banks with exposure to developing-country-based borrowers (a population of approximately 2,500) spans a large number of institutions of diverse size, country of origin, funding structure, balance-sheet health, and access to global interbank markets. The top 200 lenders include global banking giants such as ABN AMRO, Citigroup, Goldman Sachs, HSBC, Morgan Stanley, and Standard Chartered, which typically have exposure in multiple countries and provide a wide range of underwriting and investment banking services in addition to bank lending, as well as a multitude of smaller banks with more limited and focused exposure. By asset size, the top 200 lenders range from $970 million (CIMB Investment Bank based in Malaysia) to $2 trillion (UBS), as of end-2006.

The market share of the top 200 lenders is substantial: together, they account for about 80 percent of cross-border lending to developing countries. The top 50 lenders account for 50 percent (figure below).

Top lenders to developing countries entered the recent financial turmoil with strong profitability and sound capital positions (figures below), reflecting the strong performance of the banking industry during

the boom years of 2002–06. Banks' ability to retain these percentages in coming months will reflect the severity of the credit squeeze.

Cumulative international bank lending to developing countries

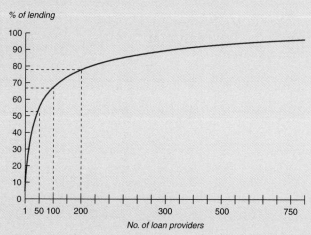

Source: World Bank estimates based on data from Dealogic Loan Analytics.

Top 200 lenders to developing countries

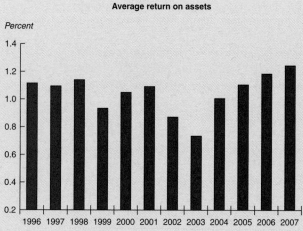

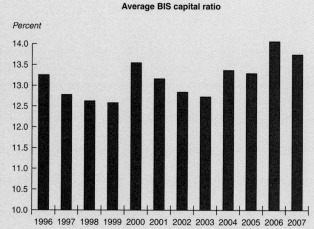

Source: World Bank staff calculations based on data from *The Banker*.
Note: BIS = Bank for International Settlements.

requests, thereby restricting the availability of liquidity. Several episodes since 1990 illustrate the mechanics of such liquidity strain in global interbank markets (box 3.3).

In the context of the current credit market turmoil, growing uncertainty about counterparty quality resulted in a significant tightening of liquidity conditions and a widening of spreads

estimation, with country fixed effects and clustered standard errors or regional dummy variables.

The lagged OIS spread as an indicator of the availability (low) or tightness (high) of interbank liquidity persistently comes out negative and statistically significant (p-values in parentheses) across all specifications, whereas the contemporaneous policy spread is statistically less significant and positive but the (steady state) net effect is generally negative. This result reflects banks' operational policies that will offer credit only after having secured the necessary funding on their part in advance so that past access to liquidity matters more than current access.

To examine the impact of tightening credit standards in developed countries on lending to developing countries, we looked at another set of multivariate regressions with country fixed effects and clustered standard errors or regional dummy variables, in which we related the (logarithm of) foreign bank claims on emerging economies to the fraction of U.S. banks reporting tighter credit standards in a given quarter, its lags, and macroeconomic and institutional control variables. As shown in table 3B.2, the results confirm that there is a statistically significant negative impact of tightened lending standards in the United States on lending to developing countries.

Table 3B.2 Multivariate analysis of credit to emerging economies

Dependent variable	Log(foreign claims)			1st diff log(foreign claims)		
	(1) Fixed effects	(2) Fixed effects	(3) Fixed effects	(4) Region	(5) Region	(6) Region
Lagged log(fc)	0.811	0.81	0.88			
	(0.000)***	(0.000)***	(0.000)***			
Log(GDP)	0.233	0.225	0.212	0.001	0.001	0.001
	(0.000)***	(0.000)***	(0.000)***	−0.761	−0.776	−0.604
Inflation	0.024	0.017	0.01	−0.044	−0.044	−0.005
	−0.786	−0.85	−0.863	−0.468	−0.473	−0.902
Growth	0.182	0.169	−0.045	0.184	0.175	0.164
	−0.266	−0.303	−0.702	−0.174	−0.197	(0.083)*
Tighter U.S. credit standards	−0.054		0.079	−0.067		0.056
	(0.068)*		(0.065)*	(0.005)***		−0.194
Lag1 tightening		−0.066	−0.117		−0.07	−0.115
		(0.035)**	(0.057)*		(0.003)***	(0.007)***
Lag2 tightening			0.036			
			−0.395			
ICRG composite			−0.002			0.001
			−0.283			(0.050)*
Europe and Central Asia				0.034	0.034	0.054
				(0.087)*	(0.085)*	(0.000)***
Latin America and the Caribbean				−0.023	−0.024	−0.006
				−0.219	−0.215	−0.661
Middle East and North Africa				−0.027	−0.027	−0.013
				−0.267	−0.269	−0.426
South Asia				−0.01	−0.01	0.019
				−0.705	−0.705	−0.354
Sub-Saharan Africa				−0.024	−0.024	0.006
				−0.189	−0.186	−0.665
Constant	−0.807	−0.724	−1.04	0.031	0.033	−0.079
	(0.001)***	(0.006)***	(0.000)***	−0.323	−0.298	(0.082)*
Observations	2,999	2,999	2,301	2,991	2,991	2,296
Countries	114	114	87			
R^2	0.743	0.743	0.865	0.011	0.011	0.038

Source: World Bank staff.
Note: The data on the fraction of U.S. banks reporting tighter credit standards in any given quarter is from the U.S. Federal Reserve's "Senior Loan Officer Opinion Survey." ICRG = International Country Risk Guide. * significant at the 10% level; ** significant at the 5% level; *** significant at the 1% level.

Annex 3C: The impact of foreign bank presence on the transmission of monetary policy

To study how foreign bank presence affects the transmission of monetary policy, we specify a linear model of lending rates as a function of the money-market rate and control variables that capture the degree of financial deepening. The interaction term between money-market rate and control variables is added to measure how the financial deepening variables, including the degree of foreign bank presence, affect the sensitivity of lending rates to money-market rates. The model constrains the slope coefficients to be identical across countries but allows for a country-specific intercept. We use the error correction framework developed by Pesaran, Shin, and Smith (2000) to allow for more flexibility across countries, especially in terms of different short-run dynamics.

The data used to estimate the model consist of quarterly observations from 22 developing countries, whose selection was based on data availability.[19] We used quarterly observations from the first quarter of 1995 to the third quarter of 2007, with some missing observations. The data contain series of money-market interest rates, lending interest rates, GDP, M2 (broad money), domestic credit, and the fraction of total assets in the banking sector owned by foreign banks. The series came from the IMF's International Financial Statistics database, except for the foreign bank data, which were obtained from Bankscope and other official sources, and the nominal GDP series for Mexico, Russia, Uruguay, and República Bolivariana de Venezuela, which were downloaded from official sources in these countries.[20] Table 3C.1 presents

Table 3C.1 Lending rate estimates

Lending rates	Estimate 1	Estimate 2	Estimate 3	Estimate 4	Estimate 5
Money market	1.04 [0.02]***	1.02 [0.02]***	0.92 [0.02]***	0.91 [0.02]***	0.94 [0.02]***
M2/GDP	−0.05 [0.01]***			−0.05 [0.01]***	
Credit/GDP		−0.04 [0.01]***			−0.04 [0.01]***
Foreign banks			0.17 [0.54]	−0.24 [0.55]	−0.85 [0.52]
Money market × M2/GDP	0.0005 [0.0001]***			0 [0.0002]***	
Money market × credit/GDP		0.0005 [0.0002]**			0 [0.0002]***
Money market × foreign banks			−0.09 [0.02]***	−0.08 [0.02]***	−0.03 [0.02]
Average speed of adjustment	−0.21 [0.03]***	−0.21 [0.04]***	−0.27 [0.05]***	−0.25 [0.05]***	−0.25 [0.05]***
Number of observations	933	933	848	826	826

Source: World Bank staff.
Note: M2 = broad money. ** significant at the 5% level; *** significant at the 1% level.

pooled mean group estimates when the control variables include the ratio of M2 to GDP (M2/GDP), the ratio of domestic credit to GDP (credit/GDP), and the fraction of assets in the banking sector owned by foreign banks (foreign banks), all in logarithms. Because of the high collinearity between M2/GDP and credit/GDP, we did not include both regressors simultaneously.

From this table we conclude:

- As expected, money-market rates are highly significant and with coefficients close to 1, suggesting a large long-run pass-though.
- Economies with deeper financial systems, as measured by M2/GDP and credit/GDP, have lower lending rates.
- Economies with deeper financial systems, as measured by M2/GDP and credit/GDP, have higher sensitivity of lending rates to money-market rates (see the positive and significant coefficients in rows 5 and 6).
- The presence of foreign banks does not seem to affect the levels of lending rates.
- Foreign bank presence *reduces* the sensitivity of lending rates to money-market rates (see the significantly negative coefficients in the interaction term of row 7).
- The dynamics of the pass-through are stable: the average speed of adjustment is significant, and between −2 and 0.

Summarizing, the estimates shown in table 3C.1 suggest that deeper financial markets *increase* the pass-through of interest rates, but a higher foreign bank presence *reduces* the transmission of policy interest rates. This last result is consistent with the view that foreign banks are less sensitive to domestic monetary conditions because of their access to a large pool of funds beyond the control of the monetary authority.

Notes

1. Data on foreign bank claims on developing-country residents are from the BIS (consolidated banking statistics). They measure claims denominated in foreign currency as well as the local currency of the country in which the borrower is domiciled. The number of countries whose banks report foreign claims to the BIS has increased from 10 in 1964—Belgium, France, Germany, Italy, Luxembourg, the Netherlands, Sweden, Switzerland, the United Kingdom, and Japan—to 30 today, including all members of the Organisation for Economic Co-operation and Development

plus Brazil, Chile, Hong Kong (China), India, Panama, and Singapore.

2. By definition, FDI is "investment made to acquire lasting interest in enterprises operating outside of the economy of the investor," where lasting interest is defined as 10 percent or more of the ordinary shares or voting power of an incorporated firm or its equivalent for an unincorporated firm. FDI in the banking sector is proxied by FDI in financial sector data, which are collected from central banks of selected economies. The definition of the banking sector, however, may differ among countries. The FDI data are compiled for Argentina, Brazil, Colombia, Peru, and Mexico in Latin America; Bulgaria, Hungary, Kazakhstan, Poland, Romania, Russia, the Slovak Republic, and Turkey in Europe and Central Asia; Pakistan in South Asia; and China, Indonesia, Malaysia, Pakistan, the Philippines, Thailand, and Vietnam in East Asia. Cross-border M&A transactions in the banking sector reflect purchased domestic banks in 150 developing countries by nonresidents as recorded at the time of closure of the deals. M&A values may not be paid out in a single year and may also include the financing that is generated in the host country. The foreign bank database used in Claessens and others (2008) includes bank-specific information for all banks operating in 100 developing countries during 1995–2006. These data also include foreign banks, defined as banks domiciled in a developing country but 50 percent or more owned by foreign nationals in a given year.

3. This figure includes all transactions that led to at least 10 percent minority share holdings as well as expansion of existing foreign banks.

4. In the case of U.S. bank branches, section 25C of the Federal Reserve Act establishes that "a member bank shall not be required to repay any deposit made at a foreign branch of the bank if the branch cannot repay the deposit due to an act of war, insurrection, or civil strife or (2) an action by a foreign government or instrumentality (whether de jure or de facto) in the country in which the branch is located, unless the member bank has expressly agreed in writing to repay the deposit under those circumstances" (Cerutti, Dell'Ariccia, and Martinez Peria 2005).

5. Banks have traditionally been heavily regulated for a number of reasons including potential systemic risk and policy makers' desire to control and influence the supply and allocation of credit. A large literature exists on the degree and nature of such banking regulation in both developed and developing country; see Dinç (2003); Demirgüç-Kunt, Laeven, and Levine (2004); and Bertrand, Schoar, and Thesmar (2007). For more detail on barriers against foreign competition, see Berger (2007) and Berger and others (2008).

6. Limited foreign entry was permitted in 1992 and was expanded in 1994 with new bank regulations and the adoption of NAFTA. Following the Tequila crisis in late 1994, the government further relaxed foreign bank acquisitions and kept an ownership cap in only the three major domestic banks. In 1999 this cap was abolished, and in 2001 FDI in the Mexican banking sector surged with the acquisition of Banamex by Citigroup, a deal valued at $12.5 billion.

7. China has removed geographic and client restrictions and allowed foreign banks to establish locally incorporated

subsidiaries to provide full renminbi services to all clients, but it maintains a cap on foreign ownership of a domestic bank at 25 percent, with a limit of 20 percent on a single foreign shareholder.

8. Note that this argument refers to the medium-term impact of foreign bank entry. The short-term implication of financial sector liberalization, which often includes opening to foreign capital inflows, is a more complicated subject.

9. The literature has reached different conclusions regarding the efficiency of domestic versus foreign banks in developing countries. For example, Martinez Peria and Mody (2004) find that foreign banks charge lower spreads and have lower costs than domestic banks, while Claessens, Demirgüç-Kunt, and Huizinga (2001) report that for low-income countries, foreign banks had significantly higher net interest margins, overhead expenses, and profitability than domestic banks (these comparisons tended to be not significant, or reversed, for middle-income countries).

10. An overnight index swap is a fixed-rate/floating-rate swap, where the floating-rate leg is linked to a daily overnight reference rate during the term of the swap.

11. During a recession, when even borrowers representing otherwise acceptable credit risks might not be able to service their debt, banks tend to exert more effort in identifying above-average borrowers. In the current credit crunch, however, the pool of acceptable credit risks has dwindled so much that the marginal benefit of more intensive screening is not worth the extra expenditure of time and cost (Ruckes 2004). As a consequence of the decrease in information collection, banks are likely to reduce their credit offers. But as the economic outlook improves, and the average repayment probability of borrowers rises along with it, lenders will be willing to spend more on borrower screening because expected returns on that activity will also increase.

12. Blank and Buch (2007) report that cross-border lending not only responds to macroeconomic shocks but also contributes to their propagation, echoing the findings of Forbes and Chinn (2004), who show that bilateral bank lending was an important determinant of cross-country financial links and the transmission of market shocks in the late 1990s. In analyzing the determinants of the amount of bilateral cross-border assets and liabilities in OECD countries, Blank and Buch (2007) find that geographical distance has a negative effect on banks' cross-border assets, so that banks limit their exposure in unfamiliar markets where distance exacerbates difficulties in information collection (Agarwal and Hauswald 2006).

13. Developing countries contracted a total of $68 billion of syndicated loans in the fourth quarter of 2007, compared with $81 billion in the fourth quarter of 2006 and an impressive $126 billion in the third quarter of 2007. The figure declined to $56 billion in the first quarter of 2008, compared with $94 billion a year ago. There were 324 and 164 deals in the fourth quarter of 2007 and first quarter of 2008, respectively, compared with 418 in the third quarter of 2007.

14. The sample of countries is those with an average annual growth rate above 33 percent in the period 2003–06. These countries are Albania, Angola, Armenia, Azerbaijan, Belarus, Democratic Republic of Congo, Georgia, Ghana, Guinea, Guinea-Bissau, Islamic Republic of Iran, Kazakhstan, Kyrgyz Republic, Latvia, Liberia, Lithuania, Malawi, Mongolia, Montenegro, Romania, Russia, Serbia, Tajikistan, Tanzania, Ukraine, República Boliviana de Venezuela, and Zambia.

15. In analyzing the relationship between foreign bank presence and private credit growth, we estimate the following model with time and regional fixed effects using panel data for 51 countries over the period 1995–2005:

$$\Delta PCGDP_{i,t} = \alpha + \beta \, \text{foreign\_bank}_{i,t} + \gamma \, \text{controls}_{i,t} + \varepsilon_{i,t},$$

where the dependent variable is the first difference of private credit/GDP, foreign bank is the ratio of foreign bank assets to total banking assets and the control variables include lagged GDP growth, logarithm of GDP per capita, the ratio of stock market capitalization to GDP, inflation, ICRG composite rating, KOF index of globalization economic openness, creditor rights, number of foreign banks as a proportion of total banks, ratio of overseas borrowing by banking sector to GDP, and a banking crisis dummy. Regression results show that the relationship between foreign bank presence and private credit growth is positive and statistically significant.

16. Indeed, many developing countries initially placed little emphasis on prudential regulation, because they had inherited colonial-era financial systems dominated by established and reputable foreign banks subject to strict prudential control from home country authorities (Brownbridge and Kirkpatrick 2000).

17. These have been set out in *Minimum Standards for the Supervision of International Banking Groups and their Cross-Border Establishment* (1992); *The Supervision of Cross-Border Banking* (1996); and subsequent reports by the Working Group on Cross-Border Banking.

18. For burden-sharing issues arising in the context of the European banking system, see Srejber (2006).

19. The countries in the sample are Argentina, Bolivia, Brazil, Bulgaria, Chile, Colombia, Czech Republic, Estonia, Hungary, Latvia, Malaysia, Mauritius, Mexico, Moldova, Peru, Poland, Russia, Slovak Republic, Thailand, Ukraine, Uruguay, and República Boliviana de Venezuela. The panel is unbalanced.

20. The banking data come in annually. Quarterly observations were log-linearly interpolated. For the construction of the banking data, see Claessens and others (2008).

References

Agarwal, S., and R. Hauswald. 2006. "Distance and Information Asymmetries in Lending Decisions." Unpublished paper, American University, Washington, DC.

Arnold, Jens, Beata Javorcik, and Aaditya Mattoo. 2007. "Does Services Liberalization Benefit Manufacturing Firms? Evidence from the Czech Republic." Policy Research Working Paper 4109, World Bank, Washington, DC.

Arnone, Marco, Salim M. Darbar, and Alessandro Gambini. 2007. "Banking Supervision: Quality and Governance." Working Paper 07/82. International Monetary Fund, Washington, DC.

Barth, J., G. Caprio, and R. Levine. 2001. "Banking Systems around the Globe: Do Regulations and Ownership Affect Performance and Stability?" In *Prudential*

Supervision: What Works and What Doesn't, ed. R. Mishkin. Chicago: University of Chicago Press.

Barth, J., J. Marchetti, D. Nolle, and W. Sawangngoenyuang. 2008. "WTO Commitments vs. Reported Practices on Foreign Bank Entry and Regulation: A Cross-Country Analysis." Available at http://ssrn.com/abstract=1033268.

Baudino, Patrizia, Giacomo Caviglia, Ettore Dorrucci, and Georges Pineau. 2004. "Financial FDI to EU Accession Countries." European Central Bank, Frankfurt. Available at http://www.bis.org/publ/cgfs22ecb.pdf.

Beck, Thorsten, Asli Demirgüç-Kunt, and Vojislav Maksimovic. 2004. "Bank Competition and Access to Finance: International Evidence." *Journal of Money, Credit and Banking* 33: 627–48.

Berger, Allen N. 2007. "Obstacles to a Global Banking System: 'Old Europe' versus 'New Europe'." *Journal of Banking and Finance* 31(7): 1955–73.

Berger, Allen N., Leora F. Klapper, Maria Soledad Martinez Peria, and Rida Zaidi. 2008. "Bank Ownership Type and Banking Relationships." *Journal of Financial Intermediation* 17(1): 37–62.

Bertrand, Marianne, Antoinette Schoar, and David Thesmar. 2007. "Banking Deregulation and Industry Structure: Evidence from the French Banking Reforms of 1985." *Journal of Finance* 62 (2): 597–628.

BIS (Bank for International Settlements). 2004. "Foreign Direct Investment in the Financial Sector of Emerging Market Economies." Committee on the Global Financial System, Bank for International Settlements, Geneva.

Blank, Sven, and Claudia M. Buch. 2007. "International Bank Portfolios: Short- and Long-Run Responses to the Business Cycle." Available at http://ssrn.com/abstract=985070.

Brownbridge, M., and C. Kirkpatrick. 2000. "Financial Regulation in Developing Countries." *Journal of Development Studies* 37 (1): 1–24.

Bruno, Valentina, and Robert Hauswald. 2007. "The Real Effects of Foreign Banks." Unpublished paper, American University, Washington, DC.

Cerutti, Eugenio, Giovanni Dell'Ariccia, and Maria Soledad Martinez Peria. 2005. "How Banks Go Abroad: Branches or Subsidiaries?" World Bank Policy Research Working Paper No. 3753. Available at http://ssrn.com/abstract=844766

Claessens, Stijn, Asli Demirgüç-Kunt, and Harry Huizinga. 2001. "How Does Foreign Bank Entry Affect Domestic Banking Markets?" *Journal of Banking and Finance* 25: 891–911.

Claessens, Stijn, and Neeltje van Horen. 2008. "Location Decisions of Foreign Banks and Institutional Competitive Advantage." Available at http://ssrn.com/abstract=904332.

Claessens, Stijn, Neeltje van Horen, Tugba Gurcanlar, and Joaquin Mercado Sapiain. 2008. "Foreign Bank Presence in Developing Countries 1995–2006: Data and Trends." Available at http://ssrn.com/abstract=1107295.

Clarke, George R. G., Robert Cull, and Maria Soledad Martinez Peria. 2006. "Foreign Bank Participation and Access to Credit across Firms in Developing Countries." *Journal of Comparative Economics* 34: 774–95.

Coppel J., and M. Davies. 2003. "Foreign Participation in East Asia's Banking Sector." Contribution to the CGFS Working Group on FDI in the Financial Sector of Emerging Market Economies. Available at http://www.bis.org/publ/cgfs22cbpapers.htm.

Corsetti, Giancarlo, and Paolo Pesenti. 2005. "International Dimensions of Optimal Monetary Policy." *Journal of Monetary Economics* 52: 281–305.

Cull, Robert, and Maria Soledad Martinez Peria. 2007. "Foreign Bank Participation and Crises in Developing Countries." Policy Research Working Paper 4128. World Bank, Washington, DC. Available at http://ssrn.com/abstract=961096.

De la Torre, Augusto, Eduardo Levy-Yeyati, and Sergio L. Schmukler. 2002. "Argentina's Financial Crisis: Floating Money, Sinking Banking." World Bank, Washington, DC.

Demirgüç-Kunt, Asli, Luc Laeven, and Ross Levine. 2004. "Regulations, Market Structure, Institutions, and the Cost of Financial Intermediation." *Journal of Money, Credit and Banking* 36 (3): 593–622.

Detragiache, Enrica, Poonam Gupta, and Thierry Tressel. 2006. "Foreign Banks in Poor Countries: Theory and Evidence." IMF Working Paper 6/18. International Monetary Fund, Washington, DC.

Dinç, Sedar. 2003. "Government Ownership of Banks and Political Lending in Developing Countries." Unpublished paper, Ross School of Business, University of Michigan.

ECB (European Central Bank). 2008. "The Euro Area Bank Lending Survey." Frankfurt.

ECLAC (Economic Commission for Latin America and the Caribbean). 2002. *Foreign Investment in Latin America and the Caribbean*. May 2001 Report LC/G.2178-P. Santiago, Chile.

Financial Stability Forum. 2008. "Report of the Financial Stability Forum on Enhancing Market and Institutional Resilience." Bank for International Settlements, Basel, Switzerland. Available at http://www.fsforum.org/publications/FSF_Report_to_G7_11_April.pdf.

Forbes, Kristin J., and Menzie D. Chinn. 2004. "A Decomposition of Global Linkages in Financial Markets over Time." *Review of Economics and Statistics* 86 (3): 705–22.

Galindo, A., A. Micco, and C. Serra. 2003. "Better the Devil That You Know: Evidence on Entry Costs Faced by Foreign Banks." Working Paper 477, Inter-American Development Bank, Washington, DC.

Garber, Peter. 2000. "What You See vs. What You Get: Derivatives in International Capital Flows." In *Managing Financial and Corporate Distress: Lessons from Asia*, ed. Charles Adams, Robert E. Litan, and Michael Pomerleano. Washington, DC: Brookings Institution.

Gelos, R. G., and Jorge Roldos. 2004. "Consolidation and Market Structure in Emerging Market Banking Systems." *Emerging Markets Review* 5: 39–59.

Giannetti, Mariassunts, and Steven Ongena. 2005. "Financial Integration and Entrepreneurial Activity: Evidence from Foreign Bank Entry in Emerging Markets." Working Paper 91/2005, European Corporate Governance Institute, Brussels.

Goldberg, Linda. 2004. "Financial-Sector FDI and Host Countries: New and Old Lessons." Working Paper 10441, National Bureau of Economic Research, Cambridge, Mass.

Hagmayr, Bettina, Peter R. Haiss, and Kjell Sümegi. 2007. "Financial Sector Development and Economic Growth: Evidence for Southeastern Europe." Available at http://ssrn.com/abstract=968253.

International Swaps and Derivatives Association. 2007. Market Survey. http://www.isda.org/.

Levine, Ross. 2001. "International Financial Liberalization and Economic Growth." *Review of International Economics* 9 (4): 688–701.

Martinez Peria, Maria Soledad, and Ashoka Mody. 2004. "How Foreign Participation and Market Concentration Impact Bank Spreads: Evidence from Latin America." *Journal of Money, Credit and Banking* 36: 511–37.

Mian, A., 2004. "Distance Constraints: The Limits of Foreign Lending in Poor Economies." The *Journal of Finance* 61: 1465–1505.

Peek, J., and E. S. Rosengren. 2000. "Implications of the Globalization of the Banking Sector: The Latin American Experience." *Federal Reserve Bank of Boston New England Economic Review* (September/October): 45–62.

Pesaran, M. H., Y. Shin, and R. J. Smith. 2000. "Structural Analysis of Vector Error Correction Models with Exogenous I(1) Variables." *Journal of Econometrics* 97: 293–343.

Rajan, Raghuram G., and Zingales, Luigi. 1998. "Financial Dependence and Growth." *American Economic Review* 88 (3): 559–86.

Rose, Andrew K. 2006. "A Stable International Monetary System Emerges: Inflation Targeting Is Bretton Woods, Reversed." Working Paper 12711, National Bureau of Economic Research, Cambridge, Mass.

Ruckes, M. 2004. "Bank Competition and Credit Standards." *Review of Financial Studies* 17 (4): 1073–102.

Srejber, Eva. 2006. "Footing the Bill for Europe's Next Banking Crisis." *The Financial Regulator* 11(1): 29–35.

Sturm, Jan-Egbert, and Barry Williams. 2005. "What Determines Differences in Foreign Bank Efficiency? Australian Evidence." CESifo Working Paper No. 1587. http://ideas.repec.org/p/ces/ceswps/_1587.html

UNCTAD (U.N. Conference on Trade and Development). 2006. "Measuring Restrictions on FDI in Services in Developing Countries and Transition Economies." New York. http://www.unctad.org/Templates/Webflyer.asp?intItemID=1397&docID=7158.

UNIDO (United Nations Industrial Development Office). 2005. *Industrial Statistics*. Geneva.

U.S. Federal Reserve Board. 2008. "Senior Loan Officer Opinion Survey on Bank Lending Practices." Washington, DC (January).

Wooldridge, Philip D., Dietrich Domanski, and Anna Cobau. 2003. "Changing Links between Mature and Emerging Financial Markets." *BIS Quarterly Review* September: 45–57. Available at http://www.bis.org/publ/qtrpdf/r_qt0309e.pdf.

Appendix: Regional Outlooks

East Asia and Pacific

Recent developments

In 2007 the economies of East Asia and Pacific recorded robust growth of 10.5 percent, up from 9.7 percent in 2006 (table A.1). This pace was the highest in over a decade and came despite growing concerns about the potential impact of the slowdown in the U.S. economy, rising volatility in global financial markets, and soaring fuel and food prices. The key driving force for growth in many East Asian countries in 2007 was domestic demand; exports to markets other than the United States provided additional impetus for a number of countries. Consumer spending accelerated in most of the region's economies, while business investment was particularly strong in Indonesia (12.1 percent) and Vietnam (20.8 percent). Weakening U.S. demand for East Asian exports was offset to a large degree by continued strong momentum in developing-country and other high-income-country export markets. In particular, East Asia benefited from robust import demand among the oil exporters of the Middle East and North Africa and from the Europe and Central Asia region. Moreover, the sharp fall in the value of the dollar now favored increased shipments to Japan as well.

China continued to lead regional output gains with another robust double-digit growth

Table A.1 East Asia and Pacific forecast summary
annual percentage change unless indicated otherwise

Indicator	1991–2000[a]	2005	2006	2007	Forecast 2008	2009	2010
GDP at market prices (2000 $)[b]	8.4	9.1	9.7	10.5	8.6	8.5	8.4
GDP per capita (units in $)	7.1	8.2	8.9	9.6	7.7	7.7	7.6
PPP GDP[c]	—	9.3	10.0	10.8	8.7	8.6	8.5
Private consumption	7.3	8.5	9.3	9.9	8.0	7.4	6.7
Public consumption	9.0	10.2	8.4	9.4	9.6	8.6	7.7
Fixed investment	10.3	10.6	3.2	6.2	9.0	9.7	11.4
Exports, GNFS[d]	11.7	17.9	18.7	16.3	11.3	13.7	15.6
Imports, GNFS[d]	11.3	12.7	14.2	12.3	11.6	14.5	17.6
Net exports, contribution to growth	0.3	3.1	3.4	3.5	1.3	1.4	1.2
Current account bal/GDP (%)	0.1	5.7	8.4	9.9	8.6	8.4	8.0
GDP deflator (median, LCU)	6.6	5.5	6.2	5.5	2.1	3.6	3.4
Fiscal balance/GDP (%)	−0.7	−1.4	−0.7	−1.0	−1.2	−1.2	−1.2
Memorandum items: GDP							
East Asia excluding China	4.8	5.4	5.7	6.2	5.8	6.2	6.3
China	10.4	10.4	11.1	11.9	9.4	9.2	9.0
Indonesia	4.2	5.7	5.5	6.3	6.0	6.4	6.5
Thailand	4.5	4.5	5.1	4.8	5.0	5.4	5.5

Source: World Bank.
— Not available.
a. Growth rates over intervals are compound averages; growth contributions, ratios, and the GDP deflator are averages.
b. GDP is measured in constant 2000 $.
c. GDP is measured at PPP exchange rates.
d. Exports and imports of goods and nonfactor services.

performance of 11.9 percent, up from 11.1 percent in 2006. Growth in East Asia and Pacific countries excluding China registered 6.2 percent, up from 5.7 percent in 2006, supported by strong consumer spending and an unexpected upturn in investment. GDP gains averaged 6.6 percent, up from 6 percent in 2006, for oil-exporting countries in the region. Leading these countries was Vietnam, which gained access to the World Trade Organization in early 2007; since 2000 Vietnam has become the fastest-growing southeast Asian economy, thanks to investment growth, booming exports, and foreign direct investment (FDI). In the oil-importing countries of the region, GDP growth rose to 11.2 percent, from 10.4 percent in 2006, though output advances eased slightly in Thailand.

GDP growth was strong in Cambodia (9.6 percent) and in Vietnam (8.5 percent), driven by domestic consumption and booming private investment. The main drivers for Indonesia's economic growth in 2007 (6.3 percent) shifted during the year. External demand was the driving force in the first half of 2007, while investment and consumer demand played an important role in the second half. Malaysia's GDP grew 6.3 percent in 2007, up from 5.9 percent in 2006; the increase was supported mainly by domestic demand that offset slower export growth. The Philippines economy expanded by 7.3 percent, its highest growth in three decades, largely on higher public investment and private consumption (figure A.1).

The surge in commodity prices over the past six to nine months—especially for food—has pushed headline inflation higher and sparked concerns about adverse effects on the poor. Higher primary commodity prices have also generated a complicated pattern of national income gains and losses around the region.

Overall, worsening terms of trade are estimated to have cost East Asia income losses of approximately 0.9 percent of regional GDP per year on average over 2004–07. Within the region, net energy and non-energy primary commodity exporters such as Indonesia, Malaysia, and Vietnam are estimated to have received windfall terms-of-trade gains of 1–2 percent of GDP per year during 2004–07. However, significant net oil importers including Lao People's Democratic Republic, the Philippines, and Thailand are estimated to have experienced terms-of-trade losses of 1.5–2 percent of GDP in 2004–07, while China saw more moderate income losses of approximately 0.9 percent of GDP per year (figure A.2).

Higher food prices are expected to have relatively small effects on the level of national income even if they carry particularly adverse effects on the poor. But the effects of higher food prices, combined with those of additional increases in oil and metals prices, would cost the region an aggregate income loss of approximately 1 percent of GDP in 2008. Moreover, they could have a more negative effect if the global credit market crisis results in significantly lower growth in East Asia.

Figure A.1 Growth accelerates across most East Asia and Pacific countries in 2007

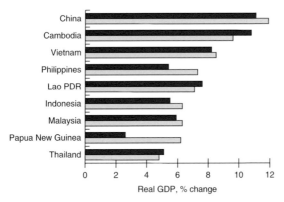

Source: World Bank.

Figure A.2 Income gains/losses due to commodity price changes

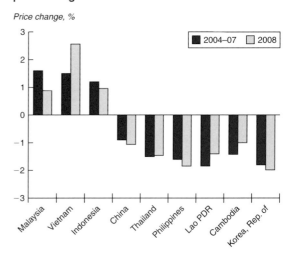

Source: World Bank.

Higher prices for fuel and other commodities, especially food, have contributed to rising inflation pressures in East Asia. In a few countries—China and Vietnam—inflation, particularly food inflation, is generally higher than in other emerging markets. Headline inflation exceeds 19 percent in Vietnam and nearly 8 percent in China. Food inflation in China and Vietnam was running above 20 percent and 30 percent, respectively, as of March 2008. In addition to higher imported food prices, specific factors in each country have contributed to higher prices. Examples are an outbreak of disease among pigs in China and bad weather in Vietnam.

Inflation had accelerated sharply in the Philippines and Thailand to rates above 8 percent and 6 percent, respectively, by April 2008 (figure A.3). For several countries in which inflation is in double digits, economies have experienced rapid monetary growth driven in part by strong, unsterilized capital inflows. In Vietnam monetary growth was running above 47 percent. In contrast, China has maintained its controlled appreciation of the yuan against the dollar and increased the pace of appreciation since October 2007. It has also been more successful in sterilizing capital inflows, and money and credit have grown at about the pace of nominal GDP, while reserves have accumulated sharply.

A range of policy responses has been designed to protect the poor through existing or new safety net programs, or through moderating the rise in food prices by one means or another. The instruments applied are generally fiscal measures such as taxes and subsidies or administrative measures. In general, administrative measures such as price controls may be helpful for managing expectations and could stabilize conditions for short periods, but they suffer from serious drawbacks in the way they affect incentives in the medium to longer terms. On the supply side, price controls typically discourage supply and lead to a reduction of both quantity and quality. On the demand side, capping prices in the face of changing market conditions prevents both the reduction in demand and the substitution to other similar products that would normally allow markets to rebalance. One concern is that administrative controls could be imposed across a broader range of countries should conditions in commodity markets deteriorate further.

The macroeconomic effects of U.S. and global financial volatility and associated financial sector losses in East Asia seem relatively limited. Most of the region's larger economies are running large current account surpluses and have sharply reduced their net external liabilities over the past decade. East Asia is a large net supplier of funds to the global financial system rather than a borrower. In 2007 net current account surpluses totaled close to 10 percent of regional GDP (World Bank 2008). Initial assessments by regulators, credit rating agencies, and investment banks suggested that emerging East Asian financial sector exposure to U.S. subprime-related assets was relatively limited.

Capital flows. Net private capital flows to East Asia and Pacific remained strong at $228 billion in 2007, up from $203 billion in 2006, while net official flows continued to be negative. The rise in private flows was largely attributable to an increase in net private debt flows ($18 billion), which was amplified by a moderate increase in net equity flows. The significant expansion in private debt flows mirrored a surge in cross-border loans by commercial banks, which picked up by $23 billion in 2007, with China accounting for $17 billion of that total. Note that net FDI inflows to the region remained robust at $117 billion, up from $105 billion the previous year, but the region's share of FDI among developing countries in aggregate fell from 29 percent in 2006 to 26 percent in 2007. Once again, China was the top FDI destination among developing countries, though its share continued to decline

Figure A.3 Trends in inflation for selected East Asian countries

Headline CPI indices, % change year over year

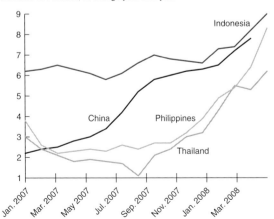

Source: National Agencies through Haver Economics.

Table A.2 Net capital flows to East Asia and Pacific
$ billions

Indicator	1999	2000	2001	2002	2003	2004	2005	2006	2007p
Current account balance	50.0	45.3	35.5	53.8	70.3	88.4	173.4	292.6	409.3
as % of GDP	3.2	2.7	2.0	2.7	3.1	3.4	5.7	8.4	9.9
Net equity flows	51.7	51.8	50.7	63.2	69.3	89.6	130.3	159.8	166.0
Net FDI inflows	50.4	45.2	48.9	59.4	56.8	70.3	104.2	105.0	117.4
Net portfolio equity inflows	1.3	6.6	1.8	3.8	12.5	19.3	26.1	54.8	48.6
Net debt flows	−11.7	−16.3	−8.1	−10.4	1.6	35.3	49.6	35.1	58.4
Official creditors	12.5	6.6	3.2	−7.9	−7.2	−5.3	−2.8	−7.6	−2.3
World Bank	2.4	1.8	0.9	−1.7	−1.5	−1.9	−0.6	−0.4	−1.1
IMF	1.9	1.2	−2.5	−2.7	−0.5	−1.6	−1.6	−8.5	0.0
Other official	8.2	3.5	4.8	−3.5	−5.2	−1.7	−0.6	1.3	−1.2
Private creditors	−24.2	−22.9	−11.3	−2.5	8.8	40.6	52.4	42.7	60.7
Net medium- and long-term debt flows	−10.9	−13.1	−13.0	−12.4	−9.7	8.0	7.2	15.0	28.8
Bonds	0.9	−0.7	0.4	0.1	1.8	9.7	7.8	5.5	6.5
Banks	−12.0	−11.3	−11.8	−10.2	−8.4	0.2	1.6	11.1	29.1
Other private	0.2	−1.0	−1.6	−2.3	−3.1	−1.9	−2.2	−1.6	−6.8
Net short-term debt flows	−13.3	−9.9	1.7	9.9	18.5	32.6	45.2	27.7	31.9
Balancing item[a]	−60.6	−71.8	−30.1	−18.6	−4.3	23.8	−134.6	−194.7	−137.2
Change in reserves (− = increase)	−29.3	−8.9	−47.9	−88.1	−136.8	−237.2	−218.7	−292.8	−496.5
Memorandum item									
Worker's remittances	15.7	16.7	20.1	29.5	35.4	39.1	46.6	52.8	58.0

Source: World Bank.
Note: p = projected.
a. Combination of errors and omissions and net acquisition of foreign assets (including FDI) by developing countries.

relative to other countries. It is also notable that net FDI outflows from China increased by almost $14 billion, mainly through cross-border acquisitions and investments in newly established overseas trade and economic zones (table A.2).

Medium-term outlook

The latest data from the region indicate that the momentum of output and trade remains strong and that the underlying trend rate of growth is not driven by year-to-year fluctuations in world demand, but rather by fundamentals like improvements in productivity, innovation, quality control, education, and skills, all of which are unlikely to be affected by the financial turmoil or by a slowing global market. Although risks have increased in the context of slowing global economies, medium-term economic prospects for the East Asia and Pacific region remain strong. GDP growth is expected to ease by almost 2 percentage points to 8.6 percent in 2008, the lowest since 2002. Growth should continue to moderate into 2009 and 2010, at a pace of 8.5 percent and 8.4 percent, respectively. Despite the softening trend, overall GDP growth is still significant and higher than in other developing regions. Lower export growth will be one of the main factors sending output gains lower. Export growth is expected to continue to temper into 2008 and early 2009 as

the decline of exports to the United States is compounded by a slowdown in the European Union and Japan. The contribution of net exports to GDP growth for the region softens from 3.5 points in 2007 to 1.2 points by 2010.

In China while the uncertain global outlook may slow exports, the country's growth is expected to remain robust, as domestic demand plays a significant and growing role in the economy, and Chinese exporters are able to seek alternative markets to the United States. GDP growth is projected at 9.4 percent for 2008, a substantial 2.5 percentage points lower than in 2007 (table A.3). As external demand is anticipated to pick up in 2009 and 2010, the pace at which China's growth slows should moderate to 9.2 percent and 9 percent, respectively. Growth in other East Asian countries is projected to slow to 5.8 percent in 2008 before picking up to 6.2 percent in 2009 and 6.3 percent in 2010.

Risks and uncertainties

The economic outlook for East Asian countries remains favorable, but this outlook is subject to a number of downside risks. Countries in the region are vulnerable to a continued acceleration in inflation tied to higher food and fuel prices, the possibility of a sharper-than-expected slowdown among the high-income countries, and a potential deterioration in global financial conditions.

Table A.3 East Asia and Pacific country forecasts

annual percentage change unless indicated otherwise

					Forecast		
Country/indicator	1991–2000[a]	2005	2006	2007	2008	2009	2010
Cambodia							
GDP at market prices (2000 $)[b]	—	13.5	10.8	9.6	7.5	7.0	7.0
Current account bal/GDP (%)	—	−10.9	−8.7	−10.8	−18.7	−15.8	−12.0
China							
GDP at market prices (2000 $)[b]	10.4	10.4	11.1	11.9	9.4	9.2	9.0
Current account bal/GDP (%)	1.5	7.1	9.6	11.7	10.2	9.9	9.5
Fiji							
GDP at market prices (2000 $)[b]	2.1	0.7	3.6	−3.9	2.0	2.0	2.0
Current account bal/GDP (%)	−3.7	−14.0	−25.0	−20.8	−25.4	−26.8	−26.8
Indonesia							
GDP at market prices (2000 $)[b]	4.2	5.7	5.5	6.3	6.0	6.4	6.5
Current account bal/GDP (%)	−0.4	0.1	3.0	2.7	1.4	1.1	0.8
Lao PDR							
GDP at market prices (2000 $)[b]	—	7.1	7.6	7.1	7.6	8.2	8.0
Current account bal/GDP (%)	—	−23.7	−14.4	−22.8	−26.7	−26.3	−26.3
Malaysia							
GDP at market prices (2000 $)[b]	7.1	5.0	5.9	6.3	5.6	6.0	6.2
Current account bal/GDP (%)	−0.4	15.2	16.9	14.3	15.8	14.9	14.3
Papua New Guinea							
GDP at market prices (2000 $)[b]	4.8	3.4	2.6	6.2	6.0	5.0	4.5
Current account bal/GDP (%)	2.3	3.6	3.8	7.5	16.8	15.3	13.0
Philippines							
GDP at market prices (2000 $)[b]	3.0	4.9	5.4	7.3	5.8	6.1	6.2
Current account bal/GDP (%)	−3.1	2.0	4.9	4.3	2.4	2.9	3.8
Thailand							
GDP at market prices (2000 $)[b]	4.5	4.5	5.1	4.8	5.0	5.4	5.5
Current account bal/GDP (%)	−1.2	−4.4	1.1	6.6	4.1	3.4	3.3
Vanuatu							
GDP at market prices (2000 $)[b]	4.1	6.5	7.2	5.0	3.8	3.5	2.5
Current account bal/GDP (%)	−8.2	−24.3	−22.1	−19.2	−30.9	−26.7	−21.9
Vietnam							
GDP at market prices (2000 $)[b]	7.6	8.4	8.2	8.5	8.2	8.5	8.5
Current account bal/GDP (%)	−5.1	−0.6	−0.4	−9.7	−6.3	−6.4	−7.6

Source: World Bank.

Notes: Growth and current account figures presented here are World Bank projections and may differ from targets contained in other Bank documents. American Samoa, the Federated States of Micronesia, Kiribati, the Marshall Islands, Myanmar, Mongolia, Northern Mariana Islands, Palau, the Democratic People's Republic of Korea, the Solomon Islands, Timor-Leste, and Tonga are not forecast owing to data limitations.　　— Not available.
a. Growth rates over intervals are compound averages; growth contributions, ratios, and the GDP deflator are averages.
b. GDP is measured in constant 2000 $.

Surging rice and commodity prices in the region are posing a risk of social unrest and higher production costs. Inflation is fueled by surging international food prices compounded by domestic shortfalls because of severe weather in the beginning of 2008. Combining the effects of higher food prices with those of additional increases in oil and metals prices, the region could experience an aggregate income loss of approximately 1 percent of GDP in 2008. A second downside risk is the depth and duration of any U.S. downturn, given the still dominant role that U.S. import demand plays in most economies of the region. A slowdown in the United States more severe than projected would exacerbate the slowdown in East Asian and Pacific exports and the moderate slowing of growth anticipated in the baseline. But the impact of a slowing U.S. economy will take time to flow through trade and financial channels.

Europe and Central Asia
Recent developments

In 2007 Europe and Central Asia[1] achieved a remarkable 6.8 percent GDP advance, down moderately from 7.3 percent in 2006, against a background of global financial turmoil, rapid changes in commodity prices, and incipient slowing of demand in the Euro Area. Growth was supported by robust domestic demand, whose contribution to regional growth peaked at 10.7 points in 2007. Private consumption and fixed capital formation grew by 8 percent and 15.8 percent, respectively, during 2007. At the same time, net exports asserted increasing drag on the region's growth, from minus 0.6 points of growth in 2002 to almost minus 4 points by 2007, reflecting buoyant import demand that fostered a larger regional current account shortfall—and increasing dependence on foreign financing. Both central and eastern European (CEE) and Commonwealth of Independent States (CIS) countries sustained double-digit growth in investment and imports, while private consumption growth exceeded 8 percent (table A.4).

GDP growth for the CEE economies, at 6.1 percent during 2007, remained sturdy, but the group's current account deficit spiked to a new high of 7.8 percent of GDP. CIS countries, many of which are commodity exporters taking advantage of surging prices, recorded their second-strongest growth in a decade at 8.6 percent, to which domestic demand contributed 16.4 percentage points. Commodity revenues have allowed strong

expansionary fiscal policies in CIS countries, pushing wage and credit growth up. Across the region, the growth situation has been diverse: while five countries enjoyed double-digit GDP advances, Hungary achieved a meager 1.3 percent gain (figure A.4). Moreover, quarterly data show diverging trends: for some countries growth continued, some showed a gradual easing, and others (Kazakhstan and the Baltic states) saw a sudden falloff in the final quarter of 2007.

Hungary has shown no sign of economic recovery since its fiscal austerity measures depressed domestic demand. It appears more fragile than it did earlier, given its worrisome levels of public and external debt (about 70 percent and 90 percent of GDP, respectively) in the current unfavorable external environment. Meanwhile, growth of three other Central European countries (the Czech Republic, Poland, and the Slovak Republic) accelerated into 2007. The Slovak Republic's 10.4 percent performance was especially notable. The Baltic States are cooling: the end of real estate booms in all countries has turned the direction of concern from overheating to "hard landing." The abrupt slowing of growth in Latvia, from 10.9 percent year over year in the third quarter of 2007 to 3.6 percent during

Table A.4 Europe and Central Asia forecast summary
annual percentage change unless indicated otherwise

Indicator	1991–2000[a]	2005	2006	2007	2008	2009	2010
					Forecast		
GDP at market prices (2000 $)[b]	−1.0	6.3	7.3	6.8	5.8	5.4	5.4
GDP per capita (units in $)	−1.1	6.3	7.2	6.8	5.8	5.4	5.3
PPP GDP[c]	−0.9	6.2	7.4	7.2	6.1	5.6	5.5
Private consumption	0.6	7.6	7.3	8.0	7.5	6.9	6.9
Public consumption	0.0	3.1	5.0	3.8	3.8	3.6	3.5
Fixed investment	−6.6	11.5	14.3	15.8	14.8	13.6	13.4
Exports, GNFS[d]	0.9	6.7	9.8	9.7	7.7	8.4	9.0
Imports, GNFS[d]	−1.6	10.4	14.4	16.8	13.2	13.0	13.4
Net exports, contribution to growth	0.9	−1.7	−2.4	−3.9	−3.6	−3.6	−3.9
Current account bal/GDP (%)	—	1.8	1.0	−0.9	0.1	−0.8	−1.4
GDP deflator (median, LCU)	118.5	5.9	8.3	7.2	7.2	7.9	5.0
Fiscal balance/GDP (%)	−5.1	2.0	2.3	1.9	1.7	0.6	0.6
Memorandum items: GDP							
Transition countries	2.1	5.9	6.5	5.5	4.8	4.6	4.8
Central and Eastern Europe	1.2	4.4	6.2	6.1	5.2	4.9	4.8
Commonwealth of Independent States	−4.2	6.8	8.3	8.6	7.2	6.5	6.0
Russia	−3.9	6.4	7.4	8.1	7.1	6.3	6.0
Turkey	3.7	8.4	6.9	4.5	4.0	4.3	5.0
Poland	3.8	3.6	6.1	6.5	5.7	5.1	5.0

Source: World Bank.
— Not available.
a. Growth rates over intervals are compound averages; growth contributions, ratios, and the GDP deflator are averages.
b. GDP is measured in constant 2000 $.
c. GDP is measured at PPP exchange rates.
d. Exports and imports of goods and nonfactor services.

Figure A.4 Real GDP growth rates for selected Europe and Central Asia countries

Percent

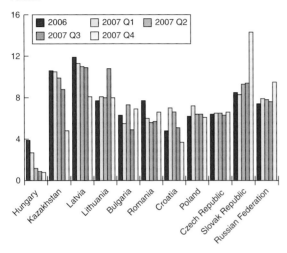

Source: World Bank.

the first quarter of 2008, shows that the risk is significantly biased toward the downside. Other economies tending toward overheating—Bulgaria and Romania—seem to have performed well during 2007, but they have become more vulnerable given difficulties in financing large current account deficits in an anxious global financial environment. After experiencing a volatile exchange rate in mid-2006, Turkey tightened its monetary policy, which dampened domestic demand. Growth dropped by more than 2 points and depressed import demand.

Still-strong export and investment growth supported 4.6 percent GDP gains in 2007.

Among CIS countries, the Russian Federation grew by a strong 8.1 percent during 2007; it retained that momentum into the first quarter of 2008, thanks in part to higher-than-expected oil prices, registering an 8 percent GDP advance year over year. Russia's budget surplus stood at 5.4 percent of GDP during 2007 and increased to 6.6 percent during the first quarter of 2008. The country's current account surplus rose to $37 billion in the quarter, up from $23 billion a year earlier. Net FDI inflows to Russia reached $52 billion in 2007. At the same time, the strength of domestic demand, rapid increases in liquidity, and hikes in food and fuel costs have seen inflation ramp up to 12.8 percent year over year in the first quarter—the highest rate in several years.

But Russia's oil production advanced only 2.3 percent in volume terms during 2007, compared with average growth of 9 percent earlier this decade; natural gas production declined 0.5 percent during the year. The current stagnancy in energy output may be attributable to an uncertain investment environment for foreign direct investment in energy, as well as high tax burdens on the sector: the overall tax burden on natural gas is 46 percent and is as much as 62 percent on crude petroleum.

A notable vulnerability facing the region is deteriorating current account deficits in many countries (figure A.5). With the exception of CIS

Figure A.5 Current account as a share of GDP in Europe and Central Asia, 2006–07

Percent

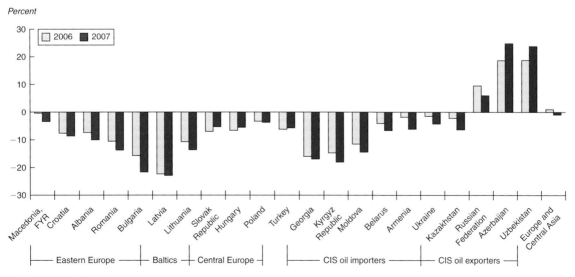

Source: World Bank.

Note: CIS = Commonwealth of Independent States.

hydrocarbon exporters, almost all economies showed deterioration in current account balances during 2007. The deficit has reached more than 10 percent of GDP in the Baltics, Bulgaria, Romania, Georgia, the Kyrgyz Republic, and Moldova, underscoring existing worries about unsustainable growth in several economies. Substantial inflow of remittances to the smaller countries of the CIS, however (which in 2006 accounted for 18.3 percent of GDP in Armenia, 6.4 percent in Georgia, 27.4 percent in the Kyrgyz Republic, and 36.2 percent in Moldova), have helped to finance demand for imported goods.

Net FDI flows to the region established a record in 2007 but are expected to decline in 2008 due to the global credit crunch, covering a smaller portion of current account deficits. Moreover, an increasing reliance on foreign bank borrowing suggests that should external finance dry up on the back of a sharp deterioration in international markets, households and businesses would be unable to roll over debts created by the current credit boom and would be forced to consolidate, with an ensuing—potentially substantial—drag on economic activity.

Contagion from high-income countries' financial and real-side troubles to the region would be passed through the trade link and external financing, so the impact on the countries of Europe and Central Asia will differ depending on the country's trading pattern and its reliance on external finance. The region's export growth is expected to be negatively affected particularly by an easing of import demand in the European Union in 2008. This effect is likely to be more pronounced in the CEE (where a large portion of exports is shipped to the Euro Area) than in the CIS (where export destinations within the group, such as Russia, and emerging markets, such as China, remain resilient and commodity prices are projected to remain at elevated levels).

International investor perceptions of the apparent increase in risk in several countries in the region have been reflected in widening spreads on credit default swaps and government bonds for these countries. Sovereign Emerging Markets Bond Index (EMBI) spreads widened across all countries since the start of the financial turmoil, peaked in March, and then declined slightly, but with much differentiation among them (figure A.6). Between mid-2007 and the end of April 2008, spreads increased for Russia (63 basis points, or bp),

Figure A.6 Spreads rising for selected Europe and Central Asia countries

Basis points

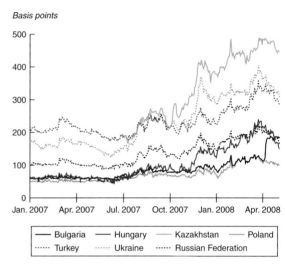

Source: Thomson/Datastream.

Bulgaria (93bp), Hungary (95bp), Turkey (110bp), Ukraine (169bp), and Kazakhstan (270bp), in contrast with Poland (42bp), which has recently displayed stronger fundamentals and less reliance on external financing.

Capital flows. After a big surge in 2006, net capital flows to the Europe and Central Asia region continued to increase in 2007—by $72 billion—reaching $404 billion and accounting for about 40 percent of total flows to developing countries. Net private capital flows reached $409 billion, representing a moderate increase of $44 billion from 2006. Repayments to official creditors continued to outstrip lending, although by a smaller magnitude ($5 billion) than in 2006 ($33 billion, mostly due to Russia's prepayment to Paris Club creditors).

Net FDI inflows to the region increased to $162 billion in 2007 from $125 billion in 2006, with Russia accounting for the largest share with $52 billion, followed by Turkey ($22 billion) and Poland ($18 billion). Despite a lack of improvement in Russia's investment climate, FDI continued to increase on the back of higher oil prices and growth potential in domestic consumption. FDI flows to Turkey continued to be driven by privatization and mergers and acquisitions, with half of the total targeted on the financial sector. Net portfolio equity inflows almost doubled to $21 billion in 2007, from $11 billion in 2006, with Russia

Indicator	1991–2000ᵃ	2005	2006	2007	2008	2009	2010
					Forecast		
GDP at market prices (2000 $)ᵇ	8.4	9.1	9.7	10.5	8.6	8.5	8.4
GDP per capita (units in $)	7.1	8.2	8.9	9.6	7.7	7.7	7.6
PPP GDPᶜ	—	9.3	10.0	10.8	8.7	8.6	8.5
Private consumption	7.3	8.5	9.3	9.9	8.0	7.4	6.7
Public consumption	9.0	10.2	8.4	9.4	9.6	8.6	7.7
Fixed investment	10.3	10.6	3.2	6.2	9.0	9.7	11.4
Exports, GNFSᵈ	11.7	17.9	18.7	16.3	11.3	13.7	15.6
Imports, GNFSᵈ	11.3	12.7	14.2	12.3	11.6	14.5	17.6
Net exports, contribution to growth	0.3	3.1	3.4	3.5	1.3	1.4	1.2
Current account bal/GDP (%)	0.1	5.7	8.4	9.9	8.6	8.4	8.0
GDP deflator (median, LCU)	6.6	5.5	6.2	5.5	2.1	3.6	3.4
Fiscal balance/GDP (%)	−0.7	−1.4	−0.7	−1.0	−1.2	−1.2	−1.2
Memorandum items: GDP							
East Asia excluding China	4.8	5.4	5.7	6.2	5.8	6.2	6.3
China	10.4	10.4	11.1	11.9	9.4	9.2	9.0
Indonesia	4.2	5.7	5.5	6.3	6.0	6.4	6.5
Thailand	4.5	4.5	5.1	4.8	5.0	5.4	5.5

Table A.5 Net capital flows to Europe and Central Asia
$ billions

Indicator	1999	2000	2001	2002	2003	2004	2005	2006	2007p
Current account balance	0.5	19.6	21.3	11.0	6.8	13.3	38.1	25.2	−27.3
as % of GDP	0.1	2.2	2.3	1.1	0.5	0.8	1.8	1.0	−0.9
Net equity flows	24.7	25.5	26.2	26.2	34.2	68.6	80.1	135.7	182.2
Net FDI inflows	23.1	24.8	26.6	26.1	34.9	63.5	72.2	124.6	161.6
Net portfolio equity inflows	1.6	0.7	−0.4	0.1	−0.7	5.1	7.9	11.1	20.7
Net debt flows	19.0	21.7	2.4	24.8	52.9	77.1	92.3	196.3	222.1
Official creditors	−0.4	0.1	2.2	2.7	−6.7	−10.0	−36.2	−33.0	−4.7
World Bank	1.9	2.1	2.1	1.0	−0.6	0.4	−0.7	0.3	−0.3
IMF	−3.1	−0.7	6.1	4.6	−2.0	−5.9	−9.8	−6.2	−4.0
Other official	0.8	−1.3	−6.0	−3.0	−4.0	−4.5	−25.6	−27.0	−0.4
Private creditors	19.4	21.6	0.2	22.1	59.5	87.1	128.4	229.3	226.8
Net medium- and long-term debt flows	18.9	13.3	6.2	17.9	29.1	68.8	103.0	173.8	166.8
Bonds	7.7	5.5	1.1	3.6	8.9	23.6	28.2	33.9	52.0
Banks	11.8	9.3	7.2	15.9	20.4	46.5	76.0	139.5	115.9
Other private	−0.7	−1.5	−2.2	−1.6	−0.2	−1.3	−1.2	0.4	−1.0
Net short-term debt flows	0.6	8.3	−6.0	4.2	30.4	18.3	25.5	55.5	60.0
Balancing item[a]	−38.3	−48.1	−37.8	−23.1	−33.5	−82.4	−117.3	−184.3	−134.7
Change in reserves (− = increase)	−5.9	−18.7	−12.1	−39.0	−60.3	−76.6	−93.2	−172.9	−242.3
Memorandum item									
Worker's remittances	11.9	13.1	12.7	14.0	16.7	21.3	29.6	35.4	38.6

Source: World Bank.
Note: p = projected.
a. Combination of errors and omissions and net acquisition of foreign assets (including FDI) by developing countries.

($15 billion) and Turkey ($5 billion) accounting for most of total (table A.5).

Net private debt flows to the region eased to $227 billion in 2007 from $229 billion in 2006, with a decrease in net cross-border bank lending to $116 billion from $140 billion in 2006. This compares with an increase of bank lending to developing countries of $215 billion in 2007, up from $172 billion in 2006. The current credit market crisis has had some negative impacts on the private debt flows to the region as a whole. Both gross international bond issuance and gross syndicated loan borrowing decreased in the fourth quarter of 2007 and first quarter of 2008. As external financing conditions deteriorated, some countries in the region experienced more negative effects than others. Some of these countries, for example, Bulgaria, the Kyrgyz Republic, Latvia, Lithuania, and Romania, have been financed largely by record capital inflows in recent years. In other countries, such as Hungary, Kazakhstan, Russia, and Ukraine, the banking sector had been borrowing large sums from external debt markets to finance domestic lending before the current turmoil. Continued credit woes and re-pricing of risks in the international markets may continue to

affect cross-border debt flows and the financing of domestic consumption and investment, and thus carry a negative impact on economic growth.

Current account balances deteriorated across the region in 2007, falling to deficit from surplus in 2006. But as capital and financial accounts still registered large surpluses, foreign reserves increased by $242 billion in 2007 (of which Russia accounted for over two-thirds with $169 billion).

The threat of inflation also looms alongside the global phenomenon of surging commodity prices. Monthly inflation reached double digits at the beginning of 2008 in nine of ten CIS countries, as well as in the Baltic States and FYR Macedonia. In Azerbaijan, Kazakhstan, the Kyrgyz Republic, and Ukraine, inflation breached 20 percent (year over year). Strong domestic demand and high global food and energy prices are common factors behind the widespread upturn in inflation. Among the CEE countries, other factors, such as increased taxes and duties, are contributing to inflation, while in the CIS, high food and energy import prices play a big role, as does the substantial pickup in wage growth. Moreover, the imported gas price from Russia to CIS members is being increased to catch up with the price of shipments to Europe.

Table A.6 Europe and Central Asia country forecasts

annual percentage change unless indicated otherwise

Country/indicator	1991–2000[a]	2005	2006	2007	Forecast 2008	Forecast 2009	Forecast 2010
Albania							
GDP at market prices (2000 $)[b]	1.4	5.5	5.0	6.0	5.8	6.2	6.2
Current account bal/GDP (%)	−5.6	−6.8	−7.4	−10.0	−11.9	−9.7	−8.6
Armenia							
GDP at market prices (2000 $)[b]	−3.8	13.9	13.3	13.7	10.0	8.1	7.3
Current account bal/GDP (%)	−12.0	−1.1	−1.8	−6.1	−8.6	−7.9	−7.2
Azerbaijan							
GDP at market prices (2000 $)[b]	−5.2	26.2	34.5	25.0	16.7	12.3	8.1
Current account bal/GDP (%)	−15.8	1.3	18.7	24.8	46.6	42.7	35.7
Belarus							
GDP at market prices (2000 $)[b]	−1.2	9.4	10.0	8.2	7.4	6.3	6.0
Current account bal/GDP (%)	—	1.4	−3.9	−6.6	−7.0	−9.0	−7.6
Bulgaria							
GDP at market prices (2000 $)[b]	−1.7	6.3	6.3	6.2	5.6	5.3	5.1
Current account bal/GDP (%)	−2.3	−12.1	−15.7	−21.6	−21.9	−19.0	−16.9
Croatia							
GDP at market prices (2000 $)[b]	−1.5	4.3	4.8	5.6	4.5	4.7	5.0
Current account bal/GDP (%)	1.0	−6.6	−7.6	−8.6	−9.6	−9.5	−9.0
Georgia							
GDP at market prices (2000 $)[b]	−9.3	9.6	9.4	12.4	9.8	8.9	8.0
Current account bal/GDP (%)	—	−11.9	−16.0	−16.9	−18.8	−15.7	−13.1
Hungary							
GDP at market prices (2000 $)[b]	0.8	4.1	3.9	1.3	2.3	3.3	3.5
Current account bal/GDP (%)	−5.4	−6.8	−6.6	−5.5	−4.3	−4.0	−3.7
Kazakhstan							
GDP at market prices (2000 $)[b]	−3.6	9.7	10.7	8.5	6.1	6.3	6.7
Current account bal/GDP (%)	−2.1	−1.8	−2.2	−6.3	−1.1	−2.7	−4.7
Kyrgyz Republic							
GDP at market prices (2000 $)[b]	−4.0	−0.2	3.1	8.2	6.6	6.2	5.8
Current account bal/GDP (%)	−10.6	−2.2	−14.7	−18.0	−18.5	−14.5	−11.6
Lithuania							
GDP at market prices (2000 $)[b]	−3.3	7.9	7.7	8.8	6.0	5.5	5.8
Current account bal/GDP (%)	−5.9	−7.1	−10.7	−13.6	−11.7	−11.2	−10.2
Latvia							
GDP at market prices (2000 $)[b]	−2.8	10.6	11.9	10.3	3.0	2.5	3.5
Current account bal/GDP (%)	−1.6	−12.4	−22.3	−22.9	−16.5	−11.3	−9.3
Moldova							
GDP at market prices (2000 $)[b]	−9.8	7.5	4.8	3.0	6.5	5.5	5.0
Current account bal/GDP (%)	—	−8.3	−11.5	−14.4	−17.3	−13.6	−10.5
Macedonia, FYR							
GDP at market prices (2000 $)[b]	−0.9	4.1	3.7	5.1	5.0	5.4	5.4
Current account bal/GDP (%)	—	−1.4	−0.4	−3.4	−8.6	−8.4	−8.3
Poland							
GDP at market prices (2000 $)[b]	3.8	3.6	6.1	6.5	5.7	5.1	5.0
Current account bal/GDP (%)	−3.5	−1.6	−3.3	−3.7	−5.5	−5.4	−5.4
Romania							
GDP at market prices (2000 $)[b]	−1.7	4.1	7.7	6.0	6.0	5.0	4.3
Current account bal/GDP (%)	−4.8	−8.5	−10.5	−13.7	−15.7	−14.5	−13.3
Russian Federation							
GDP at market prices (2000 $)[b]	−3.9	6.4	7.4	8.1	7.1	6.3	6.0
Current account bal/GDP (%)	—	10.9	9.6	6.0	6.8	4.6	2.9
Slovak Republic							
GDP at market prices (2000 $)[b]	0.3	6.6	8.5	10.4	7.3	6.0	5.3
Current account bal/GDP (%)	—	−8.5	−7.0	−5.3	−5.2	−4.7	−4.2
Turkey							
GDP at market prices (2000 $)[b]	3.7	8.4	6.9	4.5	4.0	4.3	5.0
Current account bal/GDP (%)	−1.1	−4.7	−6.2	−5.7	−7.3	−7.5	−6.8
Ukraine							
GDP at market prices (2000 $)[b]	−8.0	2.7	7.3	7.3	5.5	5.0	4.5
Current account bal/GDP (%)	—	2.9	−1.5	−4.2	−9.4	−9.5	−8.4
Uzbekistan							
GDP at market prices (2000 $)[b]	−0.2	7.0	7.2	9.5	7.7	7.5	6.8
Current account bal/GDP (%)	—	14.3	18.8	23.8	26.8	23.6	20.6

Source: World Bank.
Notes: Growth and current account figures presented here are World Bank projections and may differ from targets contained in other Bank documents. Bosnia and Herzegovina, Tajikistan, Turkmenistan, and the former Yugoslavia (Serbia/Montenegro) are not forecast owing to data limitations. — Not available.
a. Growth rates over intervals are compound averages; growth contributions, ratios, and the GDP deflator are averages.
b. GDP is measured in constant 2000 $.

Medium-term outlook

Despite the array of uncertainties and risks, the region's outlook seems likely to feature a gradual slowing from recent peaks, but performance is likely to become more diverse across countries. Improved fundamentals have made it more likely that Turkey will weather the financial-market storm and continue its growth after 2008 (table A.6). The cooling of growth in the Baltics may expose hidden problems in their banks, nonperforming loans, and other elements that might exacerbate the situation. Hungary sacrificed current growth for a more sustainable path in the future, and the change of the central bank's focus to inflation points to less monetary support for the economy; thus it is projected to recover only slowly. Other central European countries should remain healthy, as long as they continue their commitment to improve their fiscal positions, and increasingly reap the benefits of EU integration.

Current assumptions that high oil and commodity prices will persist should allow CIS oil exporters to maintain momentum through 2008, and neighboring countries will benefit from the exporters' import demand, especially from a thriving Russia.

Risks and uncertainties

The major risk facing Europe and Central Asia is the unfavorable and uncertain external financing environment. External financing requirements from the region will not abate, and current account positions are unlikely to turn around in 2008, largely because the slowdown in Western Europe offers fewer export opportunities, while Europe and Central Asia's import demand will not slow as much as its exports. In Russia, rising real incomes underpinned by mounting oil revenues imply a possible decrease in surplus position in 2008. Although higher inflation is a global phenomenon, the situation in the region is more subtle, and harder to contain; unlike other regions where inflation is mainly caused by high food and energy prices with second-round effects still unclear, the Europe and Central Asia region has already experienced strong real wage growth (due to tightening labor markets).

Should the global economy enter into a prolonged recession and commodity prices plunge, the pain will be acute for many CIS countries, In particular, economies are either reliant on certain types of commodity exports (Russia and Azerbaijan on oil, Ukraine on steel, and Armenia on metals), focused on only a few export destinations, or dependent on one particular importer for critical recourses (Belarus and Moldova on Russian energy).

Latin America and the Caribbean
Recent developments

GDP growth in Latin America and the Caribbean came in at 5.7 percent in 2007, up from 5.6 percent in 2006. The current growth spell marks the first time in nearly three decades that growth has exceeded 5 percent for two consecutive years, and the first time since the early 1970s that GDP gains have eclipsed 4 percent for four consecutive years. In 2007 the large regional economies, Argentina, Brazil, and Chile, achieved growth rates well above the 5 percent mark (8.7 percent, 5.4 percent, and 5.1 percent, respectively), while Mexican GDP expanded at a 3.3 percent pace. Smaller economies in Central America and the Caribbean also performed well during the year (table A.7).

This strong performance underscores the view that growth in the region has become more resilient and is better positioned to weather the unfolding slowdown in the United States. Although a favorable external environment has played a role in the improved regional performance, stronger domestic fundamentals have been just as important. Indeed, as figure A.7 highlights, capital formation has made a stronger contribution to growth during the most recent growth spell than during the two previous episodes in the mid-1980s and early 1990s. Higher investment activity has been underpinned by a number of factors, including improved macroeconomic stability. A major factor has been improved effectiveness of central banks in controlling inflation and in anchoring expectations to a stable, low level of inflation. In some countries, this development has been recently translated into lower real interest rates. In turn, the continued strong pace of new investments bodes well for future growth, mainly through faster improvements in productivity.

In fact, this positive spillover to productivity can already be detected in recent data: for a group of countries including Brazil, Chile, Colombia,

Table A.7 Latin America and the Caribbean forecast summary

annual percentage change unless indicated otherwise

Indicator	1991–2000[a]	2005	2006	2007	Forecast 2008	Forecast 2009	Forecast 2010
GDP at market prices (2000 $)[b]	3.4	4.7	5.6	5.7	4.5	4.3	4.2
GDP per capita (units in $)	1.7	3.4	4.2	4.3	3.2	3.0	2.9
PPP GDP[c]	4.3	4.6	5.5	5.7	4.5	4.3	4.3
Private consumption	3.4	6.7	6.2	6.1	5.2	4.7	4.5
Public consumption	1.5	2.9	3.4	3.9	2.9	2.9	2.8
Fixed investment	4.7	10.9	10.7	15.3	9.3	6.7	6.3
Exports, GNFS[d]	8.1	8.1	7.8	5.3	2.9	5.4	5.8
Imports, GNFS[d]	10.7	12.0	14.1	13.2	7.9	8.1	7.3
Net exports, contribution to growth	−0.3	−0.8	−1.5	−2.1	−1.5	−1.0	−0.8
Current account bal/GDP (%)	−2.9	1.5	1.7	0.5	0.3	−0.3	−0.7
GDP deflator (median, LCU)	10.8	5.7	10.2	9.3	8.8	4.1	3.8
Fiscal balance/GDP (%)	—	1.1	1.5	1.5	0.9	0.6	0.2
Memorandum items: GDP							
LAC excluding Argentina	3.2	4.0	5.1	5.2	4.1	4.1	4.2
Central America	3.6	3.0	5.0	3.7	2.8	3.6	3.7
Caribbean	3.6	6.5	8.8	6.0	4.7	4.6	4.9
Brazil	2.7	3.2	3.8	5.4	4.6	4.4	4.5
Mexico	3.5	2.8	4.8	3.3	2.7	3.5	3.6
Argentina	4.5	9.2	8.5	8.7	6.9	5.0	4.5

Source: World Bank.
— Not available.
a. Growth rates over intervals are compound averages; growth contributions, ratios, and the GDP deflator are averages.
b. GDP is measured in constant 2000 $.
c. GDP is measured at PPP exchange rates.
d. Exports and imports of goods and nonfactor services.

Panama, and Peru, growth rates in total factor productivity during 2001–06 ranged from 1.25 to 2.25 percent a year, well above historic averages. In another group of countries, however, including the Dominican Republic, El Salvador, Honduras,

Figure A.7 Contributions to GDP growth in Latin America and Caribbean, 1985 – 2007

Percentage points

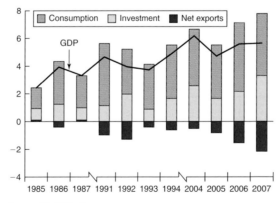

Source: World Bank.

and Mexico, productivity growth has been sluggish or even negative.

Financial stability has played a key role in supporting growth in recent years and is likely to help mitigate a portion of the contagion effects of the U.S. slowdown in 2008–09. In contrast with previous episodes of financial market instability in high-income countries, increases in sovereign bond spreads for Latin American countries have been fairly muted during the current credit squeeze (figure A.8). This regional performance masks divergent behavior of two groups of countries. A first group, comprised of Argentina, Bolivia, the Dominican Republic, Ecuador, and República Bolivariana de Venezuela, has experienced a sharper rise in the spread, showing a convergence toward the junk bond market. A second group, including Colombia, El Salvador, Panama, Peru, and Uruguay, has shown reduced spread movements and seems to be joining the solid investment-grade group of Brazil, Chile, and Mexico.

Additionally, capital inflows have not reversed but remained buoyant, suggesting the region's financial markets may be providing diversification benefits for investors. Moreover, stocks of international

Figure A.8 Spreads in Latin America and the Caribbean little affected, contrasted with U.S. high-yield bonds

Basis points

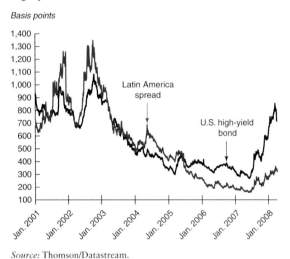

Source: Thomson/Datastream.

reserves are large, and foreign debt continues to decline, limiting the region's vulnerability to terms-of-trade shocks and to a sudden stop in capital flows.

In contrast with this positive backdrop, a number of concerns are emerging. The surge in domestic demand has reduced excess capacity in many of the region's economies and, together with rising food and energy prices, has resulted in increasing inflation. Central banks have responded promptly in several countries: Brazil has suspended the easing of its monetary policy; Chile, Colombia, and Peru have raised their policy rates; and Mexico is holding its rates at a high level. Elsewhere, inflation problems have caused social and political unrest, as in the case of Haiti, or have been addressed with the use of unorthodox policy measures, such as widespread price controls in Argentina and República Bolivariana de Venezuela.

Between 2006 and 2007, the region's current account surplus decreased from 1.7 percent of GDP to 0.5 percent. Surpluses have narrowed in Argentina, Brazil, Peru, and República Bolivariana de Venezuela, while deficits have widened in Colombia and Mexico. Part of the narrowing of the region's current account surplus is tied to shrinking goods surpluses, a consequence of imports growing at a markedly faster rate than exports. But lower growth in remittance inflows also contributed. Declining activity in the U.S. con-

struction sector, where a large share of migrant workers is employed, explains the slowing of remittance incomes.

And though contagion from the U.S. credit freeze-up has not sharply affected bond spreads in the region, broader financial markets have shown some weakness. Equity markets have recorded losses during the first quarter of 2008.

Capital flows. Net debt flows to the region rebounded to $59.1 billion in 2007 after plummeting in 2006. Though gross bank lending increased only slightly to $27 billion from $19 billion in 2006, the proportion of bank lending to the region denominated in domestic currency increased dramatically, led by Brazil and Mexico, where the rise reflected a single transaction in each case. Net bond flows recovered from negative levels in 2006 to $8 billion in 2007, while principal repayments declined by $20 billion in 2007, following record-high repayments in 2006 resulting from sovereign debt buybacks by Brazil, Colombia, Mexico, and República Bolivariana de Venezuela totaling almost $30 billion. Short-term debt flows to the region—debt instruments with original maturity of less than one year (mostly bank loans and trade credit)—rebounded from −$3.3 billion to $29.4 billion (table A.8).

Similarly, the net equity flows (FDI and portfolio equity) surged to $135 billion in 2007, from $81.9 billion in 2006, partially reversing a longer-term trend. Net FDI inflows to the region, in particular, increased by $37 billion in 2007, raising the region's share of total FDI flows to developing countries from 19 percent in 2006 to 24 percent; strong gains came in Brazil ($16 billion), Chile ($6 billion), and Mexico ($5 billion). Despite the rebound, the region's share in total FDI to developing countries is still only half of what it was in the late 1990s. The more recent pickup in inflows to Latin America stems from investment in the manufacturing sector and higher overall retained earnings, whereas in 2000 the bulk of FDI inflows entailed privatization in the service sector.

Medium-term outlook

On the heels of very strong growth in the past four years, the pace of economic activity in Latin America and the Caribbean is likely to be less brisk over the coming years. Regional growth is expected to ease from 5.7 percent in 2007 to

Table A.8 Net capital flows to Latin America and the Caribbean
$ billions

Indicator	1999	2000	2001	2002	2003	2004	2005	2006	2007p
Current account balance	−55.8	−48.0	−53.3	−15.8	7.9	20.1	35.8	46.4	15.8
as % of GDP	−3.2	−3.2	−2.8	−0.9	0.4	1.0	1.5	1.7	0.5
Net equity flows	84.3	78.9	74.6	54.5	45.6	64.0	82.9	81.9	135.3
Net FDI inflows	87.9	79.5	72.1	53.0	42.3	64.6	70.4	70.5	107.2
Net portfolio equity inflows	−3.6	−0.6	2.5	1.4	3.3	−0.6	12.5	11.4	28.1
Net debt flows	11.5	−5.1	12.6	−6.3	16.2	−2.5	−2.0	−23.4	59.1
Official creditors	1.6	−11.1	20.4	12.5	4.9	−10.1	−31.0	−20.0	−4.8
World Bank	2.1	2.0	1.3	−0.6	−0.4	−1.0	−0.7	−3.4	−0.7
IMF	−0.9	−10.7	15.6	11.9	5.6	−6.3	−27.6	−12.1	−0.2
Other official	0.4	−2.3	3.6	1.2	−0.3	−2.8	−2.7	−4.5	−3.9
Private creditors	9.9	6.0	−7.9	−18.7	11.3	7.5	29.0	−3.3	63.9
Net M-L term debt flows	15.1	6.9	6.8	−8.5	9.0	0.6	14.5	−0.1	34.5
Bonds	15.7	7.1	2.8	−0.8	11.0	−0.3	16.0	−19.0	8.1
Banks	−1.4	0.6	5.6	−6.0	−1.4	0.8	−1.4	19.6	27.0
Other private	0.8	−0.8	−1.7	−1.7	−0.6	0.0	−0.1	−0.6	−0.6
Net short-term debt flows	−5.2	−0.9	−14.6	−10.3	2.3	7.0	14.5	−3.3	29.4
Balancing item[a]	−47.8	−23.5	−31.9	−31.6	−36.9	−57.3	−86.4	−47.4	−81.6
Change in reserves (− = increase)	7.7	−2.4	−2.0	−0.8	−32.7	−24.3	−30.2	−57.6	−128.6
Memorandum item									
Worker's remittances	17.6	20.0	24.2	27.9	35.2	41.5	48.3	56.9	59.9

Source: World Bank.
Note: p = projected.
a. Combination of errors and omissions and net acquisition of foreign assets (including FDI) by developing countries.

4.5 percent in 2008 with further moderation to 4.3 percent in 2009 and 4.2 percent by 2010. A large portion of the slowdown in growth is attributable to an expected deceleration in Argentina—from 8.7 percent in 2007 to 4.5 percent by 2010—and an even sharper easing in República Bolivariana de Venezuela—from 8.4 percent in 2007 to 3 percent. Excluding these countries, the regional slowdown is much less pronounced: growth is likely to moderate from 4.9 percent in 2007 to 4.3 percent in 2010, with a dip to 4 percent in 2008 resulting from weakness in the United States. On balance, despite slower growth in the coming three years, and the contraction in regional output in 2002, real GDP for the decade is on track to be the second-strongest in the last forty years.

With gradual moderation in regional GDP growth and easing of commodity price gains from current record rates by late 2008, the region's current account surplus of the last five years is expected to diminish further in 2008. Looking further ahead, the surplus is likely to shift to a deficit from 0.3 percent of GDP in 2008 to −0.3 percent by 2010. The widening of the aggregate deficit position obscures a great deal of country heterogeneity, with current account improvements in many smaller countries being offset by deterioration among large commodity exporters.

There are several subregional themes to the overall picture of strong but moderating economic growth performance (see tables A.7 and A.8).[2] Growth among energy exporters is likely to slow considerably in 2008—to 4.4 percent from 5.8 percent in 2007—and to moderate further to 3.9 percent by 2010. The main drivers of this slowdown are declining oil prices beginning in late 2008 and signs of potential overheating—manifested in accelerating inflation—that are likely to lead to a deterioration in current account balances and thus a curtailment of spending. In the case of Argentina and República Bolivariana de Venezuela, which account for 38 percent of regional energy exporters' GDP, these factors will be compounded by mounting capacity constraints and even sharper reductions in public spending. Excluding these countries, the moderation in growth is much less pronounced: the pace of output expansion is likely to decline from 4.1 percent in 2007 to 3.8 percent in 2010.

Metal exporters are likely to experience a similar falloff in growth, easing from 5.7 percent in 2007 to 4.7 percent by 2010. Most of the reduction in the pace of economic activity is anticipated to take place in 2008, when growth slows to 4.8 percent. And growth among agriculture exporters (excluding Argentina) is also likely to slow, from 6 percent in 2007 to 4 percent in 2008, with further deceleration to 3.9 percent by 2010. If Argentina is included in the group, the slowdown is much more pronounced: growth falls from 8.1 percent in 2007 to 4.4 percent in 2010.

Growth among small energy importers (excluding Brazil and Chile) is likely to fall off significantly, from 7.4 percent in 2007 to 5.1 percent in 2008, and then ease further to 4.8 percent by 2010. This slowing is largely due to a return to more sustainable growth rates in the Dominican Republic, Panama, Peru, and Uruguay, all of which have enjoyed record or near-record growth during 2007. Despite the slowing of overall growth, the negative contribution of net exports to GDP will ease, reflecting expected moderation in oil prices.

Growth in Brazil is likely to slow in 2008 to 4.6 percent, losing another tenth of a percentage point by 2010. Increasing inflation pressures—the growth in consumer prices is expected to be above 4 percent per year in the forecast period—have caused the central bank to hike the SELIC policy rate in April 2008 and are likely to give pause to future easing of the monetary stance. Furthermore, reduction in global demand will moderate export growth. In Mexico growth is likely to rebound from a relatively weak 2.7 percent in 2008 to 3.5 percent in 2009 and to 3.6 percent in 2010. The deceleration of 2008 is largely the result of a sharp contraction in export growth caused by slowing demand in the United States, already evident in a decline in the monthly manufacturing index compiled by the Mexican Institute of Financial Executives. At the same time, and despite an expected slowing of the inflow of workers' remittances, domestic demand is likely to fall off only slightly, as evidenced by recent increases in the Mexican consumer confidence index (table A.9).

Risks and uncertainties

Despite strong recent performance and improved resilience, there are a number of risks to sustained future growth. Many countries in the region have been riding a wave of high commodity prices, which has buttressed current account surplus positions—and in the case of Chile, has turned a potential deficit into a surplus of 18 percent of GDP (figure A.9). As commodity prices weaken, the surpluses of oil, metal, and agriculture exporters are likely to diminish substantially. In the near to medium term, the combination of falling international interest rates

Figure A.9 Commodity price surge has carried quite different effects across Latin America and the Caribbean

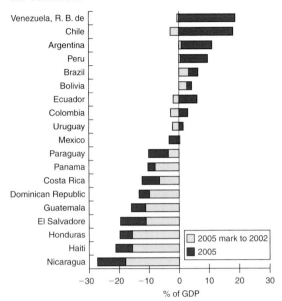

Source: World Bank.

and high food and energy prices also poses a challenge to monetary policy, which has to cope simultaneously with inflationary pressures and appreciating currency. Finally, high food prices create distributive tensions within countries; these are particularly acute for many energy and food importers in Central America and the Caribbean. Resorting to unorthodox measures to mitigate the impacts of the high prices on the consumers presents yet another risk. A preferred mechanism, although not available to all countries, would be to expand the existing cash transfer systems to compensate the most vulnerable.

While many exporters in the region have capitalized on the benefits of high commodity prices, the region has been less successful in exploiting the opportunities of the changing global trade landscape. As shown in figure A.10, the region has not taken advantage of China's rising share in global imports, a factor that is likely to be particularly important in the next several years as import demand in the high-income countries wanes and global trade growth comes to slow substantially. This observation highlights one of the region's remaining vulnerabilities, namely, its low level of integration with the rest of the developing world. This is especially significant for countries such as Mexico whose trade dependency on the United

Table A.9 Latin America and the Caribbean country forecasts
annual percentage change unless indicated otherwise

Country/indicator	1991–2000[a]	2005	2006	2007	Forecast 2008	Forecast 2009	Forecast 2010
Argentina							
GDP at market prices (2000 $)[b]	4.5	9.2	8.5	8.7	6.9	5.0	4.5
Current account bal/GDP (%)	−3.1	2.8	3.5	2.8	2.2	1.2	0.6
Antigua and Barbuda							
GDP at market prices (2000 $)[b]	3.3	5.3	11.5	7.0	5.3	5.4	5.6
Current account bal/GDP (%)	−6.0	−8.8	−15.2	−15.1	−16.5	−16.4	−14.9
Belize							
GDP at market prices (2000 $)[b]	5.9	3.1	5.6	3.0	2.8	2.8	2.9
Current account bal/GDP (%)	−7.3	−14.5	−1.9	−3.3	−3.1	−5.3	−5.8
Bolivia							
GDP at market prices (2000 $)[b]	3.8	4.1	4.5	4.2	4.1	4.1	4.2
Current account bal/GDP (%)	−6.1	6.6	11.4	10.6	15.2	12.7	11.0
Brazil							
GDP at market prices (2000 $)[b]	2.7	3.2	3.8	5.4	4.6	4.4	4.5
Current account bal/GDP (%)	−2.1	1.8	1.5	0.3	−0.4	−1.0	−0.6
Chile							
GDP at market prices (2000 $)[b]	6.4	5.7	4.0	5.1	4.6	5.0	5.2
Current account bal/GDP (%)	−2.7	1.2	5.5	4.3	2.8	1.8	0.9
Colombia							
GDP at market prices (2000 $)[b]	2.5	4.7	6.8	7.5	5.4	5.0	4.8
Current account bal/GDP (%)	−1.9	0.7	−2.3	−3.1	−1.4	−1.4	−3.1
Costa Rica							
GDP at market prices (2000 $)[b]	5.2	5.9	8.2	6.7	4.0	4.8	5.0
Current account bal/GDP (%)	−3.6	−4.8	−4.8	−5.5	−6.6	−6.4	−5.3
Dominica							
GDP at market prices (2000 $)[b]	1.8	3.1	4.1	3.2	3.1	3.0	6.5
Current account bal/GDP (%)	−14.6	−32.6	−23.1	−20.7	−26.1	−29.1	−23.1
Dominican Republic							
GDP at market prices (2000 $)[b]	6.0	9.3	10.7	8.5	5.2	4.5	4.8
Current account bal/GDP (%)	−3.2	−1.9	−2.5	−3.8	−6.8	−5.5	−4.9
Ecuador							
GDP at market prices (2000 $)[b]	1.8	4.7	4.1	1.9	2.5	2.6	2.5
Current account bal/GDP (%)	−2.3	0.8	3.6	2.2	6.1	5.0	3.6
El Salvador							
GDP at market prices (2000 $)[b]	4.6	2.8	4.2	4.2	2.0	2.5	2.8
Current account bal/GDP (%)	−2.0	−5.4	−4.7	−6.0	−8.4	−7.5	−7.3
Guatemala							
GDP at market prices (2000 $)[b]	4.1	3.2	5.0	5.7	2.8	3.5	3.4
Current account bal/GDP (%)	−4.6	−4.5	−4.4	−5.2	−7.7	−7.1	−6.3
Guyana							
GDP at market prices (2000 $)[b]	4.9	−1.9	4.7	5.5	3.7	3.5	3.4
Current account bal/GDP (%)	−15.1	−12.0	−11.2	−4.9	−5.5	−2.0	−1.9
Honduras							
GDP at market prices (2000 $)[b]	3.3	6.1	6.3	6.3	3.1	4.4	4.7
Current account bal/GDP (%)	−7.7	−1.6	−5.2	−10.9	−15.5	−12.8	−12.0
Haiti							
GDP at market prices (2000 $)[b]	−1.3	1.8	2.3	3.5	3.8	4.0	4.0
Current account bal/GDP (%)	−1.7	−6.4	−7.6	−1.8	−11.3	−12.4	−13.1
Jamaica							
GDP at market prices (2000 $)[b]	1.9	1.8	2.5	1.2	1.4	2.4	2.6
Current account bal/GDP (%)	−2.7	−11.4	−10.9	−11.7	−14.0	−16.0	−15.7
Mexico							
GDP at market prices (2000 $)[b]	3.5	2.8	4.8	3.3	2.7	3.5	3.6
Current account bal/GDP (%)	−3.7	−0.7	−0.3	−0.8	−0.8	−1.0	−1.3
Nicaragua							
GDP at market prices (2000 $)[b]	3.4	3.1	3.7	3.5	2.2	2.7	3.0
Current account bal/GDP (%)	−28.7	−15.8	−16.4	−17.7	−20.5	−20.5	−17.7

(Continues)

Table A.9 (*Continued*)

Country/indicator	1991–2000ᵃ	2005	2006	2007	Forecast 2008	2009	2010
Panama							
GDP at market prices (2000 $)ᵇ	5.1	6.9	8.1	11.2	7.8	6.7	6.5
Current account bal/GDP (%)	−4.8	−4.9	−2.2	−5.4	−6.6	−7.6	−8.3
Peru							
GDP at market prices (2000 $)ᵇ	4.0	6.7	7.6	9.0	7.0	6.4	5.9
Current account bal/GDP (%)	−5.5	1.6	3.2	1.4	0.7	−0.5	−1.9
Paraguay							
GDP at market prices (2000 $)ᵇ	1.8	2.7	4.0	6.0	4.2	3.8	3.7
Current account bal/GDP (%)	−2.2	0.5	−1.9	−3.1	−2.9	−2.5	−2.1
St. Lucia							
GDP at market prices (2000 $)ᵇ	3.1	5.8	5.7	4.0	4.4	4.8	5.0
Current account bal/GDP (%)	−11.4	−22.5	−23.4	−21.4	−22.4	−23.1	−22.9
St. Vincent and the Grenadines							
GDP at market prices (2000 $)ᵇ	3.1	1.5	4.5	5.5	6.3	5.9	5.8
Current account bal/GDP (%)	−18.8	−24.3	−25.9	−24.8	−25.2	−21.8	−17.3
Uruguay							
GDP at market prices (2000 $)ᵇ	3.0	6.8	7.0	7.4	4.6	4.1	3.8
Current account bal/GDP (%)	−1.5	0.1	−2.3	−0.7	−1.9	−2.2	−2.3
Venezuela, RB							
GDP at market prices (2000 $)ᵇ	2.1	10.3	10.3	8.4	5.0	3.4	3.0
Current account bal/GDP (%)	2.6	18.0	14.0	7.5	8.1	6.2	4.3

Source: World Bank.
Notes: Growth and current account figures presented here are World Bank projections and may differ from targets contained in Bank documents. Barbados, Cuba, Grenada, and Suriname are not forecast owing to data limitations.
a. Growth rates over intervals are compound averages; growth contributions, ratios, and the GDP deflator are averages.
b. GDP is measured in constant 2000 $.

Figure A.10 Exporters in Latin America and the Caribbean have not capitalized on growing demand from China

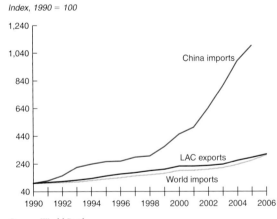

Index, 1990 = 100

Source: World Bank.

States is very high. Notwithstanding the negative aspects of this lack of market diversification, the region is still benefiting from growth in China through higher foreign investments and terms-of-trade gains.

An additional danger to continued strong growth lies in the signs of potential overheating, which is manifested in rising inflation in many countries in the region. The median GDP deflator for the region, already high at 9.9 percent in 2006, increased to an estimated 10 percent in 2007. Although a significant portion of that inflation has been imported, strong growth, rising remittance inflows, and less restrictive monetary positions (particularly in Argentina and República Bolivariana de Venezuela) have played a large role in building inflationary pressures. Such pressure may undermine the possibility of a countercyclical monetary policy, while constraining the margin for maneuver of fiscal policy. For many countries the structural government balance has not improved in line with the nominal balance. Indeed some governments may find themselves in a difficult situation when revenues from beneficial terms of trade abruptly disappear.

Middle East and North Africa
Recent developments
Growth in the developing countries of the Middle East and North Africa region found impetus in 2007 from both oil exporters and the more

diversified economies of the region, which faced a generally favorable external environment during the first half of the year.[3] The region appears (to date) to have weathered the financial fallout stemming from the U.S. subprime mortgage and related turmoil, with little escalation in sovereign bond spreads and a recovery in equity markets following the initial shocks in summer 2007. GDP growth attained a 12-year high during 2007 of 5.7 percent, up from 5.4 percent in 2006, with gains among oil exporters ramping up sharply to 5.8 percent from 4.7 percent in 2006, offsetting a step-down among the diversified economies (due wholly to drought in Morocco) to 5.5 percent from a robust 6.2 percent during 2006 (figure A.11).

The region's growth advances have had significant spillovers for job creation, one of the greatest development challenges facing the region. The countries are at the absolute crest of a labor force growth surge, with labor force growth averaging 3.4 percent a year between 2002 and 2007. Yet in the midst of this burgeoning labor force, unemployment dropped from more than 15 percent in 2000 to 11 percent in 2007. Most of the region's new jobs have come from the private sector. This is a tremendously important development for a region in which job creation, especially for an increasingly educated population, has become the litmus test for economic performance.

The regional current account surplus eased moderately during the year from $79 billion in 2006 to $69 billion (or from 11.7 to 9.1 percent of GDP) as goods exports, remittances, and tourism

receipts broadly underpinned revenue flows. Oil export revenues picked up by 6.7 percent to $130 billion, on the back of a 10.6 percent hike in the average global oil price to $71.10 per barrel. Production difficulties in Algeria and Iran, as well as restraints implied by quotas set by the Organization of Petroleum-Exporting Countries (OPEC), constrained export volumes and revenue growth from stronger performance. Goods exports from the diversified economies registered rapid nominal gains of 20 percent on strong demand from Europe, the United States (which had recently signed free trade agreements with several countries in the region), and emerging markets.

FDI inflows to developing countries in the region continued at a rapid 11 percent pace, amounting to a record $30.5 billion (largely originating in the economies of the Gulf Cooperation Council [GCC]) coming to support growth and provide financing for a larger number of countries in 2007. Inflation picked up across most countries in the region, however, tied to sharp escalation in food and fuel prices, and will continue to present a difficult challenge for policy makers. On balance 2007 was an exceptional year for growth, but the external environment and economic activity could potentially take a turn for the worse moving into 2008 (table A.10).

The diversified economies. For the diversified, or resource-poor, labor-abundant economies, output growth slipped to 5.5 percent in 2007. With the exception of Morocco, however, GDP accelerated or equaled its 2006 pace in all other economies. Inflation continued to increase, rising from 5.3 percent in 2005 to 6.7 percent in 2007. This development occurred across the board but was more severe in the Arab Republic of Egypt, (9.9 percent), where food and fuels prices, as well as strong liquidity conditions, contributed. The group's industrial production picked up to a GDP-weighted 4.6 percent in 2007, with favorable performances in Tunisia (10 percent), Morocco (5 percent), Egypt (4 percent) and Jordan (4 percent). Fiscal balances deteriorated only moderately, coming to stand at deficit of 6 percent of GDP in 2007. And the groups' current account balance fell to modest deficit ($7.5 billion), with Egypt and Morocco registering small surplus positions. Aside from the GCC countries, the diversified group has been the prime focus of interest for FDI, with

Figure A.11 Real GDP takes a step up, 1990–2007

Percentage change

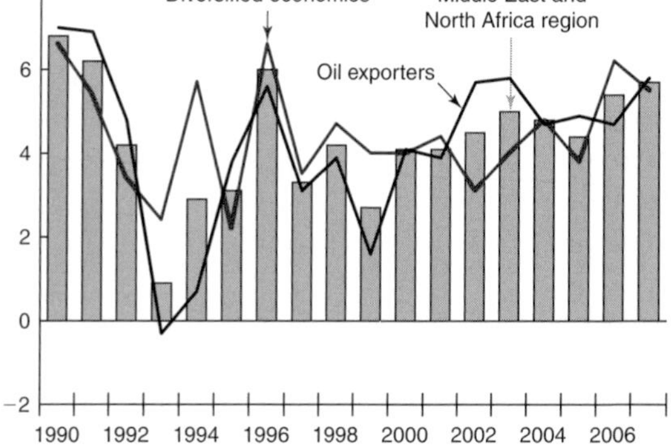

Source: World Bank.

Table A.10 Middle East and North Africa forecast summary

annual percentage change unless indicated otherwise

Indicator	1999–2000[a]	2005	2006	2007	Forecast 2008	Forecast 2009	Forecast 2010
GDP at market prices (2000 $)[b]	3.8	4.4	5.4	5.7	5.5	5.3	5.1
GDP per capita (units in $)	1.6	2.7	3.6	3.8	3.7	3.5	3.4
PPP GDP[c]	4.7	4.4	5.5	5.9	5.5	5.3	5.0
Private consumption	3.8	3.7	4.9	4.6	5.0	6.8	5.5
Public consumption	4.3	7.4	4.8	6.9	7.4	4.4	5.2
Fixed investment	3.3	2.6	14.4	22.5	14.6	9.1	9.2
Exports, GNFS[d]	4.4	11.1	4.9	3.8	−0.3	4.5	6.0
Imports, GNFS[d]	1.6	9.5	6.5	14.1	6.6	8.8	8.8
Net exports, contribution to growth	0.7	0.3	−0.6	−3.5	−2.5	−1.9	−1.6
Current account balance GDP (%)	−0.5	11.1	11.7	9.1	12.8	9.6	6.4
GDP deflator (median, LCU)	7.4	11.5	8.6	5.5	11.6	5.3	4.7
Fiscal balance/GDP (%)	3.5	3.7	2.5	−0.2	−1.2	−1.7	−1.8
Memorandum items: GDP							
MENA geographic region[e]	3.4	5.4	5.2	4.9	5.8	5.3	5.1
Resource poor, labor abundant[f]	4.2	3.8	6.2	5.5	6.2	6.1	5.9
Resource rich, labor abundant[g]	3.3	4.8	4.5	5.7	4.9	4.6	4.3
Resource rich, labor importing[h]	3.0	7.0	4.9	4.0	6.3	5.3	5.0
Egypt, Arab Rep. of	4.3	4.4	6.8	7.1	7.0	6.8	6.5
Iran, Islamic Rep. of	3.7	4.6	5.9	7.6	5.7	5.2	4.5
Algeria	1.7	5.1	1.8	3.0	3.5	3.5	4.0

Source: World Bank
a. Growth rates over intervals are compound averages; growth contributions, ratios, and the GDP deflator are averages.
b. GDP is measured in constant 2000 $.
c. GDP is measured at PPP exchange rates.
d. Exports and imports of goods and nonfactor services.
e. Geographic region includes high-income countries: Bahrain, Kuwait, and Saudi Arabia.
f. Egypt, Jordan, Lebanon, Morocco, and Tunisia.
g. Algeria, the Islamic Republic of Iran, Syria, and the Republic of Yemen.
h. Bahrain, Kuwait, Oman, and Saudi Arabia.

inflows equal to 10.5 percent of GDP in 2007, down slightly from the 10.9 percent results of 2006.

Output gains for the diversified group were driven by strong growth in domestic demand, particularly investment. Of the 5.5 percent GDP growth in 2007, absorption accounted for some 8.6 points of growth, offset by a 3.1 point negative contribution from net exports. Though export volumes registered a strong 12.6 percent gain in the year, imports grew still faster at 17 percent. GDP in Egypt jumped 7.1 percent in 2007, with growth broadly based, as non-oil-manufacturing and retail trade accounted for half of overall output gains. Reforms in Morocco and Tunisia, as well as in Egypt, are making headway in improving the business climate and increasing the competitiveness of the export sector. Egypt, Jordan, Morocco, and Tunisia signed a free trade agreement (the Agadir Agreement) to help promote trade within the region. For the diversified group, 2007 also

marked a watershed for several countries in finance. Fitch Agency raised Egypt's issuer default rating to a positive outlook. And Morocco was awarded investment-grade status for its sovereign bonds and quickly raised €500 million ($685 million) at a low, 55 basis point spread above comparable European securities.

The developing oil exporters. Because of capacity constraints or management of crude oil output to keep production in line with OPEC quotas, cuts in production amounted to 4.3 percent for all resource-rich economies in the region in 2007 (including the high-income exporters). Reductions in output ranged from 11.7 percent in the Republic of Yemen to 8.4 percent in Kuwait to 4.9 percent in Saudi Arabia to 0.7 percent in Algeria. These reductions carried important implications for growth, through public sector revenues and spending, as well as through management and disposition of the fiscal surplus.

Growth among the developing oil exporters— or resource-rich, labor-abundant economies—of the region stepped up from 4.7 percent in 2006 to 5.8 percent in 2007. Output gains in Algeria were constrained by a fall in hydrocarbon output, with GDP advancing just 1.8 percent in 2006 and 3 percent in 2007. Following a massive 40 percent surge in oil and gas output in 2004, production tailed off to decline by 2007, but non-hydrocarbon activity expanded by a strong 6 percent in 2007. A major government investment initiative has started belatedly and is slated to expend more than $22 billion over the next years on housing, transport, and agriculture. This initiative is now boosting job growth in construction and related sectors and underpinning strong household spending. In the Islamic Republic of Iran, growth stepped up to 7.6 percent from 5.9 percent in 2006. The main driver was major fiscal expansion over 2006 and 2007, seen in the movement from a budget surplus in 2005 to a budget deficit equal to 11.9 percent of GDP by the end of 2007.

Exports of merchandise from the region amounted to $285 billion in 2007, of which $130 billion came from oil and related products. This represents a 9.6 percent advance on 2006, with oil gaining 6.7 percent and non-oil exports growing at a robust 15 percent. Higher oil prices account for the full upswing in export receipts in the year, while a pickup in shipments of manufactured goods helped underpin export gains for the diversified group. Adding services exports (largely tourism at $20 billion) and remittances receipts ($29 billion) to goods exports, current account revenues as a share of GDP moved up to a record 45.1 percent for the diversified economies in 2007, from 28 percent in 2000 (figure A.12). In contrast, revenues for the oil-exporting countries diminished relative to GDP, reflecting declines in hydrocarbon output and other production difficulties.

Egypt and Morocco have enjoyed the strongest growth in tourism revenues over the past years, in part as investment in improved tourism infrastructure is increasingly in place (much tied to FDI from the Gulf countries) and as economic growth in Europe gained firmer footing. Egypt's efforts to diversify its tourism base, appealing to residents of the GCC, as well as to new markets in Central Europe and the former Soviet Union, have paid handsome dividends. During Egypt's fiscal 2007, tourist arrivals grew by 12.6 percent, with earnings

Figure A.12 Current account revenues as share of GDP, 2000–07

Percent

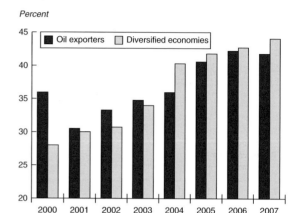

Sources: World Bank, IMF and National Agencies.

up 14 percent to $8.2 billion (6.5 percent of GDP). In Morocco tourism receipts advanced 22 percent in 2007, to reach $7.2 billion (almost 10 percent of GDP).

Gross remittance inflows to recipient countries in the Middle East and North Africa increased 9 percent in 2007 to $28.5 billion. This increase comes on the heels of an 11 percent jump during 2006. Morocco has maintained its first place in "league standings," with remittances advancing 25 percent to $6.7 billion in 2007, in part reflecting the continuation of stronger economic activity in the Euro Area. Egypt stands as the second-largest recipient, with remittances amounting to $6.3 billion in 2007, also up 25 percent over 2006 levels.

Capital flows. Net debt flows to the region rebounded to $8.4 billion in 2007, following negative levels in 2006. Both bank and bond flows to the region increased, with bank loans showing strong gains in 2007, reaching $5.4 billion from −$0.9 billion in 2006. Net equity flows (FDI and portfolio equity) picked up fairly sharply in the year to $32.6 billion, growth of 10.5 percent following the large-scale gains of 2006. FDI flows to the region increased to $31 billion in 2007 from $27 billion the previous year. While resource-related investment in the region is on the rise—particularly in Algeria, investment in other sectors such as banking, manufacturing, real estate, tourism, and transportation is also increasing. In addition to European countries, the main investors in the region

Table A.11 Net capital flows to Middle East and North Africa
$ billions

Indicator	1999	2000	2001	2002	2003	2004	2005	2006	2007p
Current account balance	3.1	22.4	12.1	7.8	23.7	39.1	64.6	79.3	69.3
as % of GDP	0.8	5.8	3.0	1.9	5.3	7.7	11.1	11.7	9.1
Net equity flows	3.5	5.1	4.2	4.4	8.4	8.0	17.0	29.5	32.6
Net FDI inflows	2.8	4.8	4.2	4.9	8.2	7.1	14.4	27.5	30.5
Net portfolio equity inflows	0.7	0.2	0.0	−0.6	0.2	0.9	2.6	2.0	2.1
Net debt flows	−3.0	−3.8	−0.3	1.3	0.3	4.0	−1.1	−12.5	8.4
Official creditors	−2.5	−2.7	−1.1	−2.5	−2.4	−4.0	−3.7	−11.6	1.3
World Bank	0.2	−0.3	−0.1	−0.3	−0.3	−0.6	0.0	−0.8	1.0
IMF	0.0	−0.2	−0.1	−0.3	−0.6	−0.5	−0.7	−0.2	−0.1
Other official	−2.8	−2.2	−0.9	−1.9	−1.6	−2.9	−3.0	−10.6	0.4
Private creditors	−0.5	−1.1	0.8	3.8	2.8	8.0	2.6	−0.9	7.1
Net medium- and long-term debt flows	−1.5	0.8	3.8	4.5	0.2	2.6	2.5	−1.5	6.2
Bonds	1.4	1.2	4.4	5.0	0.7	3.3	2.3	0.6	2.7
Banks	−1.8	0.2	−0.4	−0.5	−1.2	−0.6	1.2	−0.9	5.4
Other private	−1.1	−0.6	−0.2	0.0	0.7	−0.1	−1.0	−1.2	−1.9
Net short-term debt flows	1.0	−1.9	−3.0	−0.7	2.5	5.4	0.1	0.6	0.9
Balancing item[a]	−4.7	−18.8	−6.6	−1.5	−10.4	−36.8	−59.2	−59.3	−66.9
Change in reserves (− = increase)	1.2	−4.8	−9.5	−12.0	−22.0	−14.3	−21.3	−37.0	−43.4
Memorandum item									
Worker's remittances	11.8	12.1	14.3	14.9	19.9	22.6	23.6	26.1	28.5

Source: World Bank.

Note: p = projected.

a. Combination of errors and omissions and net acquisition of foreign assets (including FDI) by developing countries.

also include Gulf countries as well as a few developing Asian economies (China, India and Malaysia). Egypt continues to receive the largest FDI flows within the region with $7.5 billion in 2007, mainly in the oil sector as well as in manufacturing, real estate, and tourism. But the amount was lower than the $10 billion Egypt received in 2006, which FDI was supported by resource-related investments and privatization in the banking sector (table A.11).

Medium-term outlook

A number of factors are likely to shape the profile for growth for the developing economies of the Middle East and North Africa region. In the external environment, demand from the United States primarily but also from Europe and Japan, is expected to slow markedly in 2008. Yet, this development is likely to be accompanied by continued rapid escalation in global oil prices to average $108/bbl in 2008, diminishing to a still-high $99/bbl by 2010. This is tied to strong demand in emerging markets, shortfalls in non-OPEC supply and restraint exercised by OPEC itself. Growth in the region is viewed to ease gradually from a peak of 5.7 percent in 2007 to 5.1 percent by 2010, largely as hydrocarbon output- and non-oil GDP

gains among the oil exporters, particularly the Islamic Republic of Iran, diminish. At the same time, oil export revenues will be boosted by higher global prices, carrying the current account balance for oil-dominant economies to $132 billion in 2008 from $77 billion during 2007, increasing sharply to 21.3 percent of GDP from 15.6 percent, before easing to 10.5 percent by 2010.

The Islamic Republic of Iran's GDP growth is expected to fall from the strong 7.6 percent pace of 2007 to 5.7 percent in 2008, and to 4.5 percent by 2010, despite continued strong fiscal expansion. Most of the surge in spending will lead to exceptionally rapid import gains, and not to increased domestic production, while advances in export volumes are anticipated to be meager. Continued work to supplement hydrocarbon output in Algeria, with implementation of the government's infrastructure plan, should underpin investment and consumption and carry GDP growth back to a 4 percent range (table A.12).

For the diversified group, rebounds in Morocco to 5.5 percent growth from the depths of drought and in Lebanon to 3.5 percent, are key to the 2008 outlook, tending to offset modest easing across the remainder of the group tied to increasingly adverse conditions in the external

Table A.12 Middle East and North Africa country forecasts
annual percentage change unless indicated otherwise

Country/indicator	1991–2000[a]	2005	2006	2007	Forecast 2008	2009	2010
Algeria							
GDP at market prices (2000 $)[b]	1.7	5.1	1.8	3.0	3.5	3.5	4.0
Current account bal/GDP (%)	3.2	20.4	23.1	19.4	25.7	22.0	18.1
Egypt, Arab Rep.							
GDP at market prices (2000 $)[b]	4.3	4.4	6.8	7.1	7.0	6.8	6.5
Current account bal/GDP (%)	0.9	2.3	2.6	−0.3	0.6	1.3	1.5
Iran, Islamic Rep.							
GDP at market prices (2000 $)[b]	3.7	4.6	5.9	7.6	5.7	5.2	4.5
Current account bal/GDP (%)	1.2	19.8	19.5	19.7	25.1	17.7	10.5
Jordan							
GDP at market prices (2000 $)[b]	5.1	7.1	6.3	6.3	5.8	6.0	6.0
Current account bal/GDP (%)	−4.3	−18.2	−14.7	−19.5	−30.2	−24.4	−18.9
Lebanon							
GDP at market prices (2000 $)[b]	7.2	1.0	0.0	1.0	3.5	4.5	5.0
Current account bal/GDP (%)	—	−12.2	−5.5	−5.2	−11.4	−10.5	−9.0
Morocco							
GDP at market prices (2000 $)[b]	2.2	2.4	8.0	2.3	5.5	4.5	4.5
Current account bal/GDP (%)	−1.4	2.0	3.1	−3.2	−8.5	−5.6	−2.5
Oman							
GDP at market prices (2000 $)[b]	4.6	5.6	7.0	6.9	5.0	4.8	5.0
Current account bal/GDP (%)	−3.7	13.9	12.1	3.7	11.7	9.5	6.2
Syrian Arab Republic							
GDP at market prices (2000 $)[b]	5.1	4.5	5.1	3.9	4.0	4.8	4.6
Current account bal/GDP (%)	1.0	1.0	2.7	−0.7	3.0	1.1	−0.9
Tunisia							
GDP at market prices (2000 $)[b]	4.7	4.0	5.3	6.3	5.8	6.2	6.0
Current account bal/GDP (%)	−4.3	−1.1	−2.1	−2.0	−3.4	−1.5	0.3
Yemen, Rep.							
GDP at market prices (2000 $)[b]	5.5	5.6	3.2	3.1	4.2	4.0	4.0
Current account bal/GDP (%)	−4.3	3.7	1.0	−5.1	−2.7	−3.9	−5.4

Source: World Bank
Notes: Growth and current account figures presented here are World Bank projections and may differ from targets contained in other Bank documents. Djibouti, Iraq, Libya, and the West Bank and Gaza are not forecast owing to data limitations.
a. Growth rates over intervals are compound averages; growth contributions, ratios, and the GDP deflator are averages.
b. GDP is measured in constant 2000 $.

environment—and supporting a fillip in growth to 6.2 percent in the year. Beyond 2008, GDP advances are anticipated to average 6 percent, as investment-led growth appears increasingly well established in Egypt, and activity there should remain within a 6.5-to-7 percent range in the next years. Growth in Jordan and Tunisia near 6 percent is also likely, grounded in services exports and increasingly in investment and construction funded by FDI. And a stronger profile of growth emerges in Lebanon as economic conditions gradually improve.

Risks and uncertainties
Rising food prices represent a growing vulnerability and risk for the region, especially in the context of poorly targeted safety nets. The sharp rise in both oil and food prices have spotlighted the region's heavy subsidization of prices within the domestic market, which particularly threatens fiscal positions for resource-poor economies.

The Middle East and North Africa region is particularly vulnerable to a food price crisis, given the poverty within the region. At the aggregate, the region suffers from low levels of poverty, with only 1.5 percent of the population living on less than $1 a day (World Bank 2007). However, there is tremendous disparity across countries in the region and within countries in the region. While there is virtually no poverty in some of the oil-exporting nations of the GCC, in the Republic of Yemen, more than a third of the population lives below the poverty line. Within countries, poverty exists in deep pockets, most often in rural areas. In addition, the degree of poverty vulnerability is very high in the region, with large numbers of people living just barely above the poverty line. For example, only 3 percent of Egyptians live below $1 a day, but some 43 percent live on less than $2 a day; in the Republic of Yemen, 10 percent of the population lives on less than $1 a day, but a full 45 percent of the population lives on less than $2 a day. Overall, while less than 2 percent of the region's population lives on less than $1 a day, some 20 percent lives on less than $2 a day. With such deep clustering of large proportions of the population around the poverty line, rising global food prices represent a serious risk to wide-scale poverty in the Middle East and North Africa.

Markets for manufactures and services may suffer a more pronounced slowdown linked to the ripple effects of financial difficulties already present in the United States and the Euro Area. Moreover, should a significant credit crunch occur, slowing growth across developed as well as developing countries, demand for crude oil and refined petroleum products could decline quite abruptly, leading to a sharp falloff in price, with attendant effects for revenues and growth.

For the region's oil exporters, management of the hydrocarbon windfalls of the last years remains a continuing challenge. And with oil prices anticipated to remain at quite elevated levels through 2010, the risk of overheating domestic demand, with potentially inflationary consequences, looms as an overarching threat. Judicious use of oil stabilization funds to counter such trends and to offer a cushion for future growth should be a priority, as should prudent disposition of surplus funds across asset classes. Moreover, domestic reform efforts may stand at some risk against the background of abundant liquidity and rapid growth. On the other hand, should oil prices take a sudden and sustained downturn, economies may find adjustment to be a difficult transition.

South Asia
Recent developments

GDP growth in the South Asia region registered 8.2 percent in 2007, moderating from a 25-year high of 9 percent in 2006.[4] Slackening of growth was evident across all countries of the region, except Afghanistan and Bhutan. Regional growth reflected continued—albeit softening—strength in domestic activity, dampened by tighter credit conditions. An easing in demand from key export markets contributed to waning export growth and a widening in the regional current account deficit. Into the first half of 2008, surging food prices, higher petroleum prices, and an overall deterioration in the external environment linked to the subprime crisis in the United States, are straining regional government coffers and external positions. Early indicators for 2008 point to a sharper slowdown in growth and a challenging adjustment path ahead, aggravated by widespread subsidies for food and fuels, large investment demands, and rising inflationary pressures.

GDP growth in India eased to a still strong 8.7 percent in 2007, from 9.7 percent in 2006, and is projected to slow further to 7 percent in 2008, as monetary tightening in 2007 led to a softening in domestic demand. Though slowing, consumption has maintained a strong tone resulting from healthy wage growth and large remittance inflows, with the latter primarily fueled by increased demand for migrant work in the oil-exporting countries of the Middle East. Buoyant capital inflows, high capacity utilization, and reinvestment of corporate profits served to underpin investment growth in 2007. The more restrictive monetary policy helped prevent an acceleration in inflation in 2007 but contributed to an appreciation of the rupee (on a trade-weighted basis, and particularly against the dollar), leading to a loss in competitiveness for India's exporters. Combined with rising import prices and a largely resilient domestic demand, this led to deterioration in the country's current account deficit. Starting in 2008, inflationary pressures began to build. There are growing signs of a cooling economy, with a deceleration in industrial production to 3 percent in April 2008, year over year (table A.13).

In Pakistan, output growth also slowed during 2007, moderating half a percentage point to 6.4 percent. Heightened political uncertainty in the lead-up to elections in early 2008 undermined overall confidence and led to weaker investment and private consumption outlays. Output was also disrupted by growing power shortages. And, in part because of high fuel costs, Pakistan's current account deficit deteriorated substantially in 2007

Table A.13 South Asia forecast summary
annual percentage change unless indicated otherwise

Indicator	1991–2000[a]	2005	2006	2007	Forecast 2008	2009	2010
GDP at market prices (2000 $)[b]	5.2	8.7	9.0	8.2	6.6	7.2	7.6
GDP per capita (units in $)	3.1	7.0	7.3	6.7	5.2	5.7	6.2
PPP GDP[c]	6.4	8.8	9.2	8.3	6.7	7.2	7.7
Private consumption	4.0	7.2	6.3	6.0	5.1	5.7	6.4
Public consumption	3.9	8.8	10.1	5.7	8.1	8.5	8.4
Fixed investment	5.5	23.5	14.6	15.1	9.2	10.0	10.6
Exports, GNFS[d]	9.0	19.1	17.6	6.1	5.6	9.2	10.6
Imports, GNFS[d]	7.9	21.7	22.5	6.3	5.8	9.4	11.4
Net exports, contribution to growth	−0.1	−1.0	−1.7	−0.3	−0.3	−0.5	−0.7
Current account bal/GDP (%)	−1.6	−1.2	−1.5	−1.9	−3.4	−3.1	−2.9
GDP deflator (median, LCU)	8.0	5.0	6.6	7.0	9.2	10.1	7.8
Fiscal balance/GDP (%)	−7.7	−6.5	−6.7	−6.5	−6.5	−6.5	−6.2
Memorandum items: GDP							
South Asia excluding India	4.4	6.7	6.7	6.3	5.2	5.8	6.1
India	5.5	9.2	9.7	8.7	7.0	7.5	8.0
Pakistan	3.9	7.7	6.9	6.4	5.0	5.5	6.0
Bangladesh	4.8	6.0	6.6	6.4	5.7	6.5	6.6

Source: World Bank.
a. Growth rates over intervals are compound averages; growth contributions, ratios, and the GDP deflator are averages.
b. GDP is measured in constant 2000 $.
c. GDP is measured at PPP exchange rates.
d. Exports and imports of goods and nonfactor services.

and has continued to further deteriorate into 2008. To cover the widening current account deficit, about $3.4 billion in foreign exchange reserves have been drawn down since July 2007, bringing the merchandise import cover below three months, as of May 2, 2008—an unsustainable trend. The fiscal deficit has also widened substantially. This deficit primarily reflects a rise in government borrowing on the domestic market, as foreign lending has largely halted, the privatization program has stalled, and Pakistan's spreads on international markets have risen. Surging food and fuel prices are contributing to rising inflationary pressures. Consumer price inflation was up 17.2 percent year over year in April 2008, from 14.1 percent in March; that is the fastest pace in at least 25 years.

GDP growth in Sri Lanka dropped to 6.8 percent in 2007, from 7.4 percent in 2006. The deceleration is attributable in large measure to ongoing civil strife, continued inflationary pressures that squeezed household incomes, and a falloff in growth from the sharp recovery posted in the wake of the December 2004 tsunami. Inflation accelerated sharply since 2006, rising to an average of over 15 percent during 2007, and to nearly 24 percent in March 2008. Rising food prices in

combination with strong credit growth—tied to both large fiscal deficits and negative real interest rates (to aid budget financing)—have fueled inflationary pressures. However, this macroeconomic stimulus has not yet resulted in a deteriorating current account. Sri Lanka's trade deficit narrowed in 2007, given strong export growth and a deceleration in import growth.

In Bangladesh, growth slowed from 6.6 percent in 2006 to 6.4 percent in 2007. This moderation mainly reflects a falloff in export growth, which was partly offset by a firming in domestic demand, particularly private consumption. Growth decelerated in the interim, following the losses from two consecutive natural disasters in the second half of the year—severe flooding in July and a devastating cyclone in November—which resulted in the deaths of 4,400 people and displaced an estimated 8.7 million people. The impact from these disasters will be captured in the 2008 growth figures (fiscal 2007–08). Damage from the disasters is estimated at $2.7 billion, or the equivalent of about 3.7 percent of GDP. Despite these sharp negative impacts to growth, domestic demand is being supported by strong, record-high remittance inflows. Remittance inflows have cushioned the impact of surging import prices but have not prevented a narrowing of the current account surplus and a projected shift to deficit in 2008. Further, a concerted drive against corruption and tax evasion, combined with a crimping of purchasing power caused by rising inflationary pressures, has dampened economic activity.

In Nepal, GDP growth decelerated to 2.5 percent in 2007, from 2.8 percent in 2006, amid election-related disturbances (including frequent blockades and strikes) that disrupted economic activity, labor unrest, power shortages, and high inflation. Early indicators are for a firming of growth in 2008 on the strength of the recuperated agricultural sector and high tourism growth, as well as improved confidence following the peaceful April 2008 elections.

The Maldives experienced a slowing of growth to 6.6 percent in 2007, retreating from the double-digit rebound that occurred in 2006 following the tsunami-related disruptions of 2005. Growth was supported by a revival in tourism but was partly offset by a particularly low fish catch, resulting in a sharp decline for the fisheries industry. Given that the small island economy is dependent on imports, rising international price pressures were quickly transmitted into higher domestic inflation.

In contrast with developments in the rest of South Asia, growth in Afghanistan and Bhutan accelerated during the year, tied in part to special circumstances. In Afghanistan, GDP growth increased to an estimated 14 percent, up from 6 percent in 2006, buoyed by recovery in agricultural output following the 2006 drought. Security, however, continued to deteriorate throughout 2007 and early 2008, with a sharp rise in incidents. Associated deaths have reached the highest levels since 2001. The Tala hydroelectric power project in Bhutan, which led to a sharp rise in power exports to India and boosted government revenues, supported a vigorous expansion in GDP to an estimated 17 percent gain in 2007, more than double the 8 percent advance of 2006. Growth has also been bolstered by vibrant tourism activity, as well as by improved confidence. Bhutan held its first multiparty election in March 2008, which generated a high turnout and marked the advent of a democratic, constitutional monarchy in the country.

By early 2008 surging food prices had become a serious concern in South Asia, where food

Figure A.13 Food consumption as a share of total consumption across South Asian countries

Percent

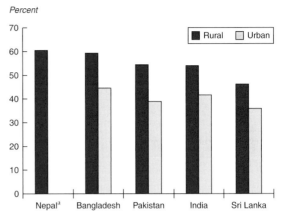

Sources: U.N. Food and Agriculture Organization and World Bank.
Note: Unweighted average for Germany, United Kingdom and United States is 17 percent. Ranked by rural data.
a. Urban data is not available for Nepal.

insecurity is relatively high and food represents close to 50 percent of total consumption in most countries (figure A.13).[5] The extreme poor spend even a greater proportion of their budgets on food. The rapidly rising gap between food prices and wages indicates a sharp reduction in the purchasing power of the poor. The situation has become increasingly acute across the region—especially in Afghanistan and Bangladesh. Among other factors, rice producers, such as China, India, and Vietnam have introduced export restrictions to keep stocks for domestic use and to prevent sharp domestic price increases; these policies have contributed to the increase in international grain prices. Food supply difficulties are prevalent across the region, affecting Afghanistan, where fighting continues; Bangladesh, where the November 2007 cyclone affected an estimated 8.7 million people and reduced the 2007 paddy production; and Nepal, which is experiencing sustained political instability despite the successful postwar elections. India is self-sufficient, but grain stocks are low and crop production has been in decline. Bhutan and the Maldives are also vulnerable, as they import over 30 percent of their grains. In Pakistan, the U.N. World Food Programme estimates that nearly half of the country's 160 million people are at risk of running short of food due to rising grain prices. The poverty impact of the surge in food prices could be high and in some areas could wipe out years of gains in poverty reduction.

High international commodity prices, especially oil prices, combined with increasingly sluggish external demand, contributed to deterioration in the region's current account deficit, despite sustained strong inflows of worker remittances. The current account deficit of the region widened from $17 billion in 2006 to $27 billion in 2007. Foreign reserves increased by a record $100 billion in 2007 compared with an increase of $40 billion in 2006; most of the increase resulted from a $96 billion increase in India's reserves.

Capital Flows. The turmoil in international financial markets, which commenced in the second half of 2007 and has continued through the first months of 2008, has affected the region primarily through a falloff in portfolio flows and weakness in equity markets. The latter has been most pronounced in India, particularly during the first quarter of 2008. In contrast, Pakistan's bourse rose by close to 10 percent in the quarter, with a short-term improvement in confidence in the wake of elections. Net portfolio equity inflows to the region more than tripled, from $10 billion in 2006 to $35 billion in 2007, almost all of which ($34 billion) went to India where the stock market enjoyed a boom. Given the volatile nature of portfolio equity flows, the large inflows also pose risks, especially

amid increased risk aversion and volatility as credit market turmoil continues and global growth prospects weaken for 2008. The sell-off in the Indian stock market in the first quarter of 2008, stemming from concerns over a possible U.S. recession, was a warning sign.

In contrast with strong equity flows, net FDI registered a small increase of $6 billion, reaching $29 billion in 2007, with three-fourths of the total going to India. This compared with a more than doubling of net FDI inflows in 2006 to $23 billion from $10 billion in 2005. Net private debt flows to the region increased to $33 billion in 2007 from $12 billion in 2006, led by a large increase in net inflows of cross-border bank lending to $25 billion in 2007, from $5 billion in 2006. In aggregate, net capital flows to South Asia jumped to $102 billion in 2007, from $50 billion in 2006. The increase resulted entirely from a rise in net private flows to $98 billion in 2007 from $46 billion in 2006; net official flows remained at an inflow of $4 billion (table A.14).

Medium-term outlook

South Asia appears poised for a significant slowdown in GDP growth to 6.6 percent in 2008, from 8.2 percent in 2007 (table A.14). Private consumption and investment are expected to decelerate

Table A.14 Net capital flows to South Asia
$ billions

Indicator	1999	2000	2001	2002	2003	2004	2005	2006	2007p
Current account balance	−5.3	−6.3	2.2	11.4	12.5	−1.0	−12.2	−16.9	−26.8
as % of GDP	−0.9	−1.1	0.4	1.8	1.6	−0.1	−1.2	−1.5	−1.9
Net equity flows	5.5	6.7	8.8	7.8	13.4	16.6	22.4	33.3	64.2
Net FDI inflows	3.1	4.4	6.1	6.7	5.4	7.6	10.0	22.9	28.9
Net portfolio equity inflows	2.4	2.4	2.7	1.0	8.0	9.0	12.4	10.4	35.4
Net debt flows	0.5	3.5	−0.7	−0.4	0.3	8.6	5.8	16.8	37.7
Official creditors	2.5	0.5	2.2	−2.4	−1.8	1.0	3.1	4.3	4.3
World Bank	1.0	0.7	1.5	−1.0	−0.2	2.0	2.2	1.7	1.9
IMF	−0.1	−0.3	0.3	0.1	−0.1	−0.3	0.0	−0.1	−0.1
Other official	1.6	0.0	0.4	−1.5	−1.6	−0.7	0.9	2.7	2.6
Private creditors	−2.0	3.0	−2.8	2.0	2.0	7.6	2.7	12.5	33.4
Net medium- and long-term debt flows	−2.1	3.9	−1.9	0.2	1.3	4.9	1.1	8.9	29.4
Bonds	−1.2	5.4	−0.4	−0.7	−3.1	4.1	−2.9	4.3	4.2
Banks	−0.5	−2.0	−1.1	1.0	4.4	1.1	4.1	4.6	25.2
Other private	−0.4	0.5	−0.3	−0.1	0.0	−0.3	−0.1	0.0	0.0
Net short-term debt flows	0.1	−0.9	−0.9	1.8	0.7	2.6	1.6	3.6	4.0
Balancing item[a]	4.3	0.8	−0.1	8.2	8.8	3.1	−9.6	7.3	26.0
Change in reserves (− = increase)	−5.0	−4.7	−10.2	−27.0	−35.0	−27.2	−6.3	−40.5	−101.2
Memorandum item									
Worker's remittances	15.1	17.2	19.2	24.1	30.4	28.7	33.1	39.8	43.8

Source: World Bank.

Note: p = projected.

a. Combination of errors and omissions and net acquisition of foreign assets (including FDI) by developing countries.

because of tighter international and domestic credit conditions in combination with weakened external demand. Rising inflationary pressures, particularly for food, will reduce the purchasing power of the urban poor. A moderation in domestic growth will contribute to a slowdown in import volume, including capital goods imports. This, however, will be insufficient to prevent further widening of the region's current account deficit—given a falloff in export growth and continued high international commodity prices. High grain, oilseed, and energy prices, in particular, will represent the greatest challenge for regional policy makers. The challenge is to protect the poor, while keeping fiscal positions manageable and preventing second-round inflationary spirals. Ongoing volatility in international financial markets and decreased risk appetite among international investors are expected to lead to lower capital inflows.

Effects on South Asia's external demand stemming from turbulent financial markets and potential recession in the United States are expected to be relatively small compared with other developing regions. Of note, the importance of the United States and Western European trade partners for South Asia has declined over the last decade, while China and oil-exporting economies have come to represent a larger portion of their markets (figure A.14). And while South Asia's integration with the global economy advanced rapidly in recent years—with openness (measured by exports and imports of goods and services as a share of GDP)

increasing by more than 15 percentage points since 2000 to 47 percent by 2007—it remains the least integrated of developing regions. From this perspective, the impact of the slowdown in external demand should be somewhat less pronounced than in other regions.

For South Asia's poor, one of the more direct impacts from the deterioration in the external environment could come through the international remittances channel. In a number of countries, such as Bangladesh and India, remittances have risen rapidly in recent years, posting record levels. A falloff in growth in countries where migrants are employed, combined with the sharp depreciation of the dollar, could lead to lower remittance inflows in local currency terms. This could in turn lead to weaker consumer demand. For the poor, whose incomes are already being squeezed by higher food and fuel prices, lower remittance inflows could make the situation still more difficult. For most South Asian countries, remittances represent a major source of hard currency, and for some countries, the inflows significantly offset deficits on trade. In Nepal, remittances inflows were equivalent to 15.1 percent of GDP in 2006, while in Sri Lanka and Bangladesh they represented close to 9 percent and 7.3 percent, respectively (figure A.15). Data on the countries of origin for remittances is sparse, but important sources include the Arabian Gulf economies outside of the region and India within the region, in particular for Nepal. Nepal's economy is strongly linked to India's, and shifts in growth in India could have a major impact there.

Figure A.14 Shifts in South Asia's export partner composition

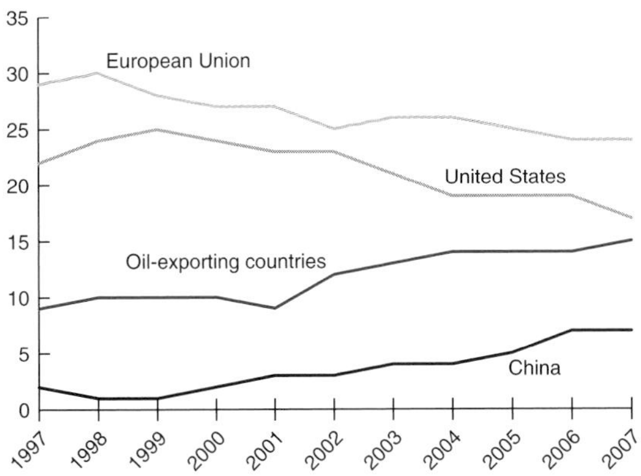

Total merchandise exports, %

Figure A.15 Worker remittances as a share of GDP in South Asian countries, 2006

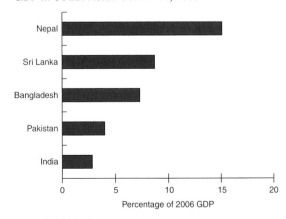

Sources: International Monetary Fund and World Bank.

Source: World Bank.

Growth for the region in the latter years of the forecast, in 2009 and 2010, is projected to pick up incrementally to 7.2 percent and 7.6 percent, respectively, well above the 5.2 percent average of the 1990s (table A.15). The projected weakening in world demand in 2008 is expected to lead to a softening of oil and non-oil commodity prices, manifested more clearly in 2009, allowing some easing of monetary conditions, which should contribute to a firming in domestic demand. Easing monetary policy should provide a fillip to regional investment, which in turn is expected to be supported by anticipated recovery in external demand in 2009 and 2010. Similarly, private consumption growth is expected to be underpinned by easing credit conditions and rising incomes, and as a reduction in inflation pressures raises disposable incomes. In line with the pickup in domestic demand, import growth is projected to revive, in part because of South Asia's high capital requirements. Hence, despite rising external demand and export growth, the current account deficit is expected to show only modest improvement as a proportion of GDP.

Risks and uncertainties

The degree and duration of the growth slowdown in the United States, and the extent of its impact on other countries, could represent downside risks to prospects for South Asia. A disorderly adjustment, including a hard landing of the dollar, would bring about a sharper deterioration in external demand and larger financial market repercussions, as well as further upward pressure on international commodity prices. Volatile and declining equity prices in the region, particularly in India—just as ownership of stocks and other financial assets is beginning to take hold among the burgeoning middle class—could hamper both consumer and business outlays, while depressing overall confidence levels in the economy.

A number of South Asian economies have been able to reduce their fiscal deficits in recent years, though these deficits remain large in some cases. As food and fuel prices are widely subsidized, the growing gap between domestic and international prices could lead to significant fiscal deterioration, aside from creating problems in incentives. In Pakistan, high subsidies that have kept wheat prices relatively low have led to smuggling. More broadly, slower growth outcomes will compress government revenues and make further consolidation more difficult, providing policy makers with less maneuverability to stave off potential effects of deterioration in the external

Table A.15 South Asia country forecasts
annual percentage change unless indicated otherwise

Country/indicator	1991–2000[a]	2005	2006	2007	2008	2009	2010
Bangladesh							
GDP at market prices (2000 $)[b]	4.8	6.0	6.6	6.4	5.7	6.5	6.6
Current account bal/GDP (%)	−0.4	−0.3	1.5	1.0	−0.5	−0.6	−0.7
India							
GDP at market prices (2000 $)[b]	5.5	9.2	9.7	8.7	7.0	7.5	8.0
Current account bal/GDP (%)	−1.2	−1.0	−1.1	−1.5	−2.9	−2.6	−2.6
Nepal							
GDP at market prices (2000 $)[b]	5.0	3.1	2.8	2.5	3.5	4.5	5.0
Current account bal/GDP (%)	−6.4	2.0	2.2	0.5	1.2	0.6	−0.3
Pakistan							
GDP at market prices (2000 $)[b]	3.9	7.7	6.9	6.4	5.0	5.5	6.0
Current account bal/GDP (%)	−3.7	−3.4	−5.5	−6.1	−8.9	−8.1	−7.6
Sri Lanka							
GDP at market prices (2000 $)[b]	5.2	6.0	7.4	6.8	5.0	5.6	5.6
Current account bal/GDP (%)	−4.6	−3.1	−5.1	−4.2	−4.6	−4.4	−4.1

Source: World Bank.
Notes: Growth and current account figures presented here are World Bank projections and may differ from targets contained in other Bank documents. Afghanistan, Bhutan, and the Maldives are not forecast owing to data limitations.
a. Growth rates over intervals are compound averages; growth contributions, ratios, and the GDP deflator are averages.
b. GDP is measured in constant 2000 $.

environment. Given tight domestic supplies, a poor crop year could sustain or reignite inflationary pressures and put remote regions at particular risk.

Sub-Saharan Africa
Recent developments

Growth outturns for Sub-Saharan Africa in 2007 were stronger than first estimates suggested, with GDP picking up to 6.1 percent. Growth in South Africa surprised to the upside, and gains for oil-importing countries outside South Africa were also stronger than first thought. One of the more heartening characteristics of recent growth in the region is that it is broad-based, with one in three countries growing by more than 6 percent. And growth has accelerated not only in resource-rich countries but also in countries that are resource poor, whether coastal or landlocked (figure A.16). Subsequently, per capita GDP growth has increased markedly for most countries, carrying the aggregate rate for the region to a robust 4.1 percent in 2007.

Stronger growth in South Africa was the main reason for the upward revision in regional growth. The region's largest economy expanded 5.1 percent during 2007, marginally down from 5.4 percent the previous year, with output boosted by robust private consumption and a higher contribution to growth from investment. GDP gains accelerated to 5.3 percent in the fourth quarter (year over year), from 4.8 percent the previous

Figure A.16 Growth across selected Sub-Saharan Africa subregions

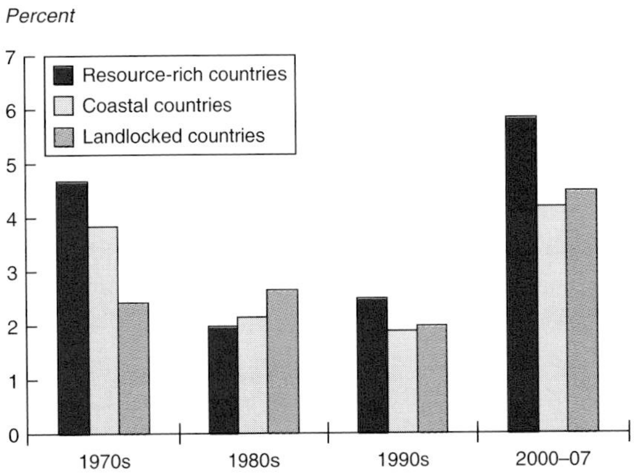

Percent

Source: World Bank.

quarter, boosted by higher output in agriculture and a marked acceleration in manufacturing growth.

Angola was the star performer of the region during 2007, expanding an impressive 22.9 percent, for a fourth consecutive year of double-digit growth. This helped to propel growth among oil exporters in Sub-Saharan Africa to 8.0 percent in 2007, up from 6.7 percent in 2006 (table A.16). In Nigeria economic expansion remained near 6 percent, as the oil sector continued to contract, while growth in the non-oil sectors picked up slightly. Notably, robust advances in telecommunications and financial services led strong growth in the services industries. The banking sector has also benefited from the consolidation and recapitalization program initiated in 2006 and is in turn fostering growth in the private sector through increased financial intermediation.

In the Central African Economic and Monetary Community, growth accelerated to 3.3 percent, as most governments in the group markedly increased public investment outlays. Growth was particularly robust in Gabon, where GDP exceeded 5 percent growth in 2007; notwithstanding relatively flat oil output, Gabon enjoyed strong expansion in manganese and forestry output. Oil production was also disappointing in the Republic of Congo and Equatorial Guinea due to technical difficulties. Growth in the Western African Economic and Monetary Union (WAEMU) inched up to 3.2 percent in 2007, from 3.0 percent in 2006, as output gains edged up in Senegal. The union's largest economy, Côte d'Ivoire, experienced disappointing outturns, caused by subpar performance in the industry and services sectors. Surging energy prices have taken a toll on WAEMU economies, and lower agricultural output has also acted as a deterrent to faster economic expansion.

In East Africa improved weather conditions yielded higher agriculture output and stronger growth in the related industry and services sectors. In Kenya economic performance improved in 2007, driven by robust expansion across the board, including in agriculture, by a rebound in tea and horticulture output, building and construction, and manufacturing and financial services. In Tanzania a combination of stronger growth in agriculture and mining, tourism, and manufacturing is anticipated to support growth. And in Uganda, GDP gains should be underpinned

Table A.16 Sub-Saharan Africa forecast summary
annual percentage change unless indicated otherwise

Indicator	1991–2000[a]	2005	2006	2007	Forecast 2008	Forecast 2009	Forecast 2010
GDP at market prices (2000 $)[b]	2.3	5.7	5.8	6.1	6.3	5.6	5.9
GDP per capita (units in $)	−0.4	3.2	3.3	4.1	4.3	3.6	3.9
PPP GDP[c]	3.4	6.1	6.2	6.6	6.7	5.7	6.0
Private consumption	1.2	5.4	6.5	6.8	5.4	5.3	5.4
Public consumption	2.6	5.5	5.3	6.3	6.4	5.9	5.9
Fixed investment	3.7	15.3	18.0	17.5	14.4	11.9	10.7
Exports, GNFS[d]	4.7	6.0	5.1	6.0	7.8	6.6	6.3
Imports, GNFS[d]	4.4	12.7	13.3	11.6	10.8	10.3	9.6
Net exports, contribution to growth	0.2	−2.4	−3.2	−2.6	−1.9	−2.2	−2.1
Current account bal/GDP (%)	−2.1	1.6	0.6	−1.7	−0.3	−2.5	−3.9
GDP deflator (median, LCU)	10.1	7.4	7.0	7.4	7.8	5.8	4.8
Fiscal balance/GDP (%)	−4.2	0.9	2.2	0.7	1.3	0.6	−0.3
Memorandum items: GDP							
Sub-Saharan Africa excluding South Africa	2.6	6.2	6.1	6.8	7.6	6.3	6.5
Oil exporters	2.2	7.5	6.7	8.0	9.8	6.9	7.1
CFA countries	2.6	4.2	2.6	3.2	4.5	5.0	5.1
South Africa	1.8	5.0	5.4	5.1	4.2	4.4	4.8
Nigeria	2.8	6.9	6.0	6.1	7.9	7.2	6.6
Kenya	1.9	5.8	6.1	6.3	5.0	5.7	5.9

Source: World Bank.
a. Growth rates over intervals are compound averages; growth contributions, ratios, and the GDP deflator are averages.
b. GDP is measured in constant 2000 $.
c. GDP is measured at PPP exchange rates.
d. Exports and imports of goods and nonfactor services.

by improved electricity supply and improved stability in northern Uganda, with the private sector one of the main pillars of growth.

Notably, consumer price inflation has accelerated markedly in the first months of 2008 in a number of countries in the region, driven by significantly higher food price inflation and increased transportation and electricity costs in some cases. Inflationary pressures are increasing in tandem in all subregions, the result of external shocks and drought rather than lax macroeconomic policies.

Capital flows. Net capital flows to Sub-Saharan Africa were up sharply in 2007, increasing to an estimated $58 billion, from $38 billion in 2006. Net private capital flows to the region reached $56.6 billion in 2007, the highest level on record. The rise was mostly due to a surge in FDI and private debt flows. Net FDI inflows climbed from $17 billion to $25.3 billion, largely due to a single transaction, the $5.5 billion purchase of a 20 percent equity stake in the South African commercial bank, Standard Bank, by the Industrial and Commercial Bank of China (ICBC). Net medium- and

long-term bank lending increased by $13.6 billion, while net short-term borrowing decreased by $6.5 billion. Net bond flows rose by $5.7 billion in 2007, after falling by $1.2 billion in 2006. The rebound reflects a combination of more issuance and lower principal repayments. Meanwhile, net portfolio equity inflows to the region dropped by $4.9 billion, with South Africa accounting for much of the decline. For South Africa, the marked decline in portfolio equity inflows likely reflects the confluence of two factors: increased risk aversion by foreign investors following the global credit turmoil; and reduced holdings of South African equities by nonresident portfolio investors while building up debt securities.

The year also saw the expansion of an African sovereign issuer base. Ghana became the first heavily indebted poor country (HIPC) to issue an external bond, with a $750 million Eurobond issue in September 2007. The bond issue was oversubscribed several times, despite being launched in the midst of the turmoil in international financial markets. Gabon issued its inaugural sovereign bond in December 2007 when it launched a $1 billion 10-year Eurobond with a yield of 8.25 percent

Table A.17 Net capital flows to Sub-Saharan Africa

$ billions

Indicator	1999	2000	2001	2002	2003	2004	2005	2006	2007p
Current account balance	−10.2	3.3	−5.0	−6.3	−4.2	4.4	9.8	4.4	−14.4
as % of GDP	−3.1	0.9	−1.5	−1.8	−1.0	0.8	1.6	0.6	−1.7
Net equity flows	18.7	11.0	14.2	10.1	15.1	19.2	24.7	32.2	35.5
Net FDI inflows	9.7	6.8	15.1	10.5	14.4	12.5	17.3	17.1	25.3
Net portfolio equity inflows	9.0	4.2	−0.9	−0.4	0.7	6.7	7.4	15.1	10.2
Net debt flows	−0.9	−0.1	−2.1	−0.4	1.4	6.5	6.6	5.3	22.6
Official creditors	0.4	0.7	−0.1	2.6	1.5	2.2	−1.1	−2.6	1.5
World Bank	1.1	1.5	1.8	2.2	2.2	2.5	2.4	1.9	2.2
IMF	0.0	0.1	0.1	0.5	−0.1	−0.1	−0.4	−0.1	−0.2
Other official	−0.7	−0.8	−2.0	0.0	−0.7	−0.2	−3.1	−4.5	−0.5
Private creditors	−1.3	−0.8	−2.0	−2.9	0.0	4.4	7.7	7.9	21.1
Net medium- and long-term debt flows	−0.7	0.3	0.0	−1.1	0.9	2.8	4.9	−2.2	17.5
Bonds	1.2	1.0	1.9	1.5	0.4	0.6	1.3	0.1	5.8
Banks	−1.7	−0.7	−1.6	−1.9	1.2	2.4	3.8	−1.5	12.1
Other private	−0.2	0.0	−0.3	−0.7	−0.7	−0.3	−0.2	−0.8	−0.4
Net short-term debt flows	−0.6	−1.1	−2.1	−1.8	−1.0	1.6	2.8	10.1	3.6
Balancing item[a]	−6.4	−7.9	−6.7	−3.3	−8.3	−8.0	−20.2	−9.2	−23.3
Change in reserves (− = increase)	−1.2	−6.3	−0.4	−0.2	−4.0	−22.2	−20.9	−32.6	−20.4
Memorandum item									
Worker's remittances	4.4	4.6	4.7	5.0	6.0	8.0	9.3	10.3	10.8

Source: World Bank.

Note: p = projected.

a. Combination of errors and omissions and net acquisition of foreign assets (including FDI) by developing countries.

that was used to prepay its Paris Club creditors (table A.17).

Medium-term outlook

Regional GDP continues to be driven by domestic demand (investment and private consumption), a growth profile that should help Sub-Saharan Africa to weather the marked slowdown anticipated among the high-income economies—barring a collapse in commodity prices. A key ingredient that contributed to robust expansion over the last several years remains: increased productivity linked to the surge in investment and supported by high commodity prices, increasing trade openness, and improved macroeconomic stability. But risks are tilted well to the downside, as weaker global expansion could translate into deterioration in current account positions, reducing available funds for improvements in productive capacity. GDP gains are expected to pick up to 6.3 percent in 2008, from 6.1 percent in 2007, on the back of growth acceleration in oil-producing countries, notably Cameroon, Republic of Congo, and Nigeria, which will bring growth in oil-exporting countries to close to 10 percent.

The improved regional performance comes despite expected easing of growth in South Africa to 4.2 percent. Weaker private consumption and lower export growth are likely to cause easing on the demand side, while on the supply side capacity constraints in the electricity sector will limit growth in mining and manufacturing. Moreover, manufacturing will be confronted with opposing forces, with a weaker rand increasing the export competitiveness of manufactured products, while electricity shortages and higher electricity tariffs will erode these gains. Large public investment in infrastructure in preparation for the 2010 FIFA World Cup will mitigate the slowdown to a degree. But slower growth and the electricity crisis in the regional powerhouse may spill over to neighboring countries.

GDP advances in WAEMU are viewed to move up to 4 percent in 2008. A rebound in energy production is expected to push growth in Côte d'Ivoire to 2.8 percent, while stronger growth in phosphates, construction, and services will push growth in Senegal to 5.1 percent (table A.18).

East African countries are expected to see a growth slowdown largely attributable to weaker gains in the agriculture sector after a strong rebound in agricultural output in 2007 and the prospect of drought conditions in 2008. Drought conditions and rising import bills for food and especially for energy will erode real incomes throughout the region, undermining growth in

Table A.18 Sub-Saharan Africa country forecasts
annual percentage change unless indicated otherwise

Country/indicator	1991–2000[a]	2005	2006	2007	Forecast 2008	Forecast 2009	Forecast 2010
Angola							
GDP at market prices (2000 $)[b]	0.8	20.6	18.6	22.9	25.4	6.7	10.2
Current account bal/GDP (%)	−6.1	17.3	22.3	14.6	20.7	10.0	4.0
Benin							
GDP at market prices (2000 $)[b]	4.8	3.9	3.8	4.1	5.1	5.3	5.7
Current account bal/GDP (%)	−6.8	−6.3	−9.6	−7.6	−6.2	−6.0	−6.2
Botswana							
GDP at market prices (2000 $)[b]	6.2	−0.8	4.2	5.5	5.0	5.3	5.2
Current account bal/GDP (%)	8.1	16.8	21.5	21.3	11.9	11.0	7.5
Burkina Faso							
GDP at market prices (2000 $)[b]	4.0	7.1	5.5	4.0	4.3	5.5	5.3
Current account bal/GDP (%)	−5.6	−13.3	−13.4	−14.2	−15.3	−14.0	−13.1
Burundi							
GDP at market prices (2000 $)[b]	−1.7	0.9	5.1	3.4	4.4	4.9	5.1
Current account bal/GDP (%)	−3.4	−21.7	−34.0	−32.7	−29.9	−28.4	−27.7
Cape Verde							
GDP at market prices (2000 $)[b]	5.8	6.5	10.8	6.3	7.1	6.9	6.4
Current account bal/GDP (%)	−8.3	−8.5	−9.2	−14.5	−16.2	−15.4	−16.7
Cameroon							
GDP at market prices (2000 $)[b]	1.4	2.3	3.2	3.5	4.2	4.6	4.9
Current account bal/GDP (%)	−3.0	−2.4	−0.5	−1.1	−0.4	−1.4	−2.3
Central African Republic							
GDP at market prices (2000 $)[b]	1.6	2.2	4.1	4.0	4.3	4.6	4.7
Current account bal/GDP (%)	−4.3	−7.1	−6.3	−6.1	−7.1	−7.1	−7.6
Chad							
GDP at market prices (2000 $)[b]	2.3	8.4	0.5	−1.0	1.9	3.3	3.0
Current account bal/GDP (%)	−5.5	−6.6	−7.4	−6.8	−0.6	−0.7	−2.9
Comoros							
GDP at market prices (2000 $)[b]	1.1	4.2	1.3	1.8	2.5	2.7	2.7
Current account bal/GDP (%)	−6.8	−4.9	−5.9	−5.1	−5.2	−5.5	−5.8
Congo, Dem. Rep.							
GDP at market prices (2000 $)[b]	−5.6	6.5	5.6	6.3	6.7	7.2	7.3
Current account bal/GDP (%)	2.0	−10.0	−9.6	−10.7	−13.4	−13.0	−12.3
Congo, Rep.							
GDP at market prices (2000 $)[b]	1.5	9.2	6.2	−1.1	8.0	9.0	10.0
Current account bal/GDP (%)	−16.5	17.7	12.3	6.0	16.6	16.6	17.6
Côte d'Ivoire							
GDP at market prices (2000 $)[b]	2.3	1.8	0.9	1.5	2.8	4.2	4.9
Current account bal/GDP (%)	−4.0	0.2	3.0	−0.6	0.3	−1.4	−2.4
Equatorial Guinea							
GDP at market prices (2000 $)[b]	18.4	6.5	−5.6	11.0	9.0	3.3	3.0
Current account bal/GDP (%)	−40.6	6.8	6.8	3.9	7.6	3.6	2.3
Eritrea							
GDP at market prices (2000 $)[b]	—	4.8	−1.0	1.3	1.2	2.2	2.2
Current account bal/GDP (%)	—	−26.1	−30.6	−30.4	−28.0	−23.0	−19.5
Ethiopia							
GDP at market prices (2000 $)[b]	2.3	10.2	10.9	11.1	7.5	7.4	7.6
Current account bal/GDP (%)	−0.8	−8.5	−12.8	−10.6	−12.3	−11.5	−10.5
Gabon							
GDP at market prices (2000 $)[b]	2.4	3.0	1.2	5.3	4.9	5.5	3.9
Current account bal/GDP (%)	5.7	18.5	17.2	12.5	18.6	15.1	11.6
Gambia, The							
GDP at market prices (2000 $)[b]	3.3	5.0	6.4	6.1	5.3	5.8	5.8
Current account bal/GDP (%)	−1.6	−10.9	−10.9	−10.8	−11.9	−9.8	−7.9
Ghana							
GDP at market prices (2000 $)[b]	4.3	5.9	6.2	6.3	5.8	6.4	6.1
Current account bal/GDP (%)	−6.6	−8.9	−8.7	−9.7	−13.2	−12.0	−12.6

(Continues)

Table A.18 (*Continued*)

Country/indicator	1999–2000[a]	2005	2006	2007	Forecast 2008	2009	2010
Guinea							
GDP at market prices (2000 $)[b]	3.9	3.3	2.2	1.8	4.1	4.6	4.9
Current account bal/GDP (%)	−5.7	−5.0	−6.1	−10.4	−14.0	−13.7	−12.9
Guinea-Bissau							
GDP at market prices (2000 $)[b]	1.5	3.5	2.7	2.7	2.9	3.3	3.4
Current account bal/GDP (%)	−24.0	−7.2	−18.2	−14.2	−6.5	−5.0	−4.9
Kenya							
GDP at market prices (2000 $)[b]	1.9	5.8	6.1	6.3	5.0	5.7	5.9
Current account bal/GDP (%)	−1.6	−1.4	−2.7	−4.5	−8.2	−7.7	−8.8
Lesotho							
GDP at market prices (2000 $)[b]	3.4	1.2	7.1	4.9	5.1	4.9	4.8
Current account bal/GDP (%)	−13.3	−21.8	−22.3	−27.2	−31.7	−26.0	−21.2
Madagascar							
GDP at market prices (2000 $)[b]	1.7	4.6	4.9	5.6	6.3	6.9	8.4
Current account bal/GDP (%)	−7.8	−12.4	−9.7	−17.6	−25.6	−19.7	−12.6
Malawi							
GDP at market prices (2000 $)[b]	3.4	2.3	7.9	7.2	6.9	7.2	6.9
Current account bal/GDP (%)	−8.5	−14.2	−12.9	−15.1	−16.4	−16.3	−15.7
Mali							
GDP at market prices (2000 $)[b]	4.0	6.1	5.3	5.1	5.2	5.1	4.5
Current account bal/GDP (%)	−8.9	−8.3	−6.5	−7.3	−7.4	−5.9	−5.5
Mauritania							
GDP at market prices (2000 $)[b]	2.9	5.4	11.4	0.9	4.1	5.9	6.1
Current account bal/GDP (%)	−0.3	−48.6	−3.0	−6.5	−7.3	−6.5	−9.3
Mauritius							
GDP at market prices (2000 $)[b]	5.3	2.3	5.0	5.6	4.7	5.1	4.9
Current account bal/GDP (%)	−1.6	−5.2	−10.1	−11.7	−15.4	−14.6	−13.0
Mozambique							
GDP at market prices (2000 $)[b]	5.2	8.4	8.5	7.4	7.2	6.7	6.6
Current account bal/GDP (%)	−18.2	−11.0	−16.0	−16.8	−19.2	−19.0	−18.9
Namibia							
GDP at market prices (2000 $)[b]	4.2	5.3	4.2	4.0	4.4	4.3	4.5
Current account bal/GDP (%)	3.1	1.7	2.7	3.4	−1.1	−3.9	−5.2
Niger							
GDP at market prices (2000 $)[b]	1.8	7.2	5.2	3.2	4.1	4.6	4.9
Current account bal/GDP (%)	−6.9	−12.0	−11.6	−15.4	−14.8	−15.7	−16.7
Nigeria							
GDP at market prices (2000 $)[b]	2.8	6.9	6.0	6.1	7.9	7.2	6.6
Current account bal/GDP (%)	−0.8	24.5	20.1	11.5	14.2	8.5	4.0
Rwanda							
GDP at market prices (2000 $)[b]	0.2	7.1	5.5	6.1	6.2	5.0	5.1
Current account bal/GDP (%)	−3.5	−16.8	−17.4	−18.0	−21.0	−19.3	−19.3
Senegal							
GDP at market prices (2000 $)[b]	2.9	5.1	2.3	4.6	5.1	5.5	5.7
Current account bal/GDP (%)	−6.0	−6.8	−10.5	−10.7	−11.2	−11.7	−12.9
Seychelles							
GDP at market prices (2000 $)[b]	4.6	−2.3	5.3	5.5	4.8	4.1	4.1
Current account bal/GDP (%)	−7.4	−30.2	−25.2	−36.4	−47.9	−43.9	−38.7
Sierra Leone							
GDP at market prices (2000 $)[b]	−4.7	7.5	7.5	6.8	6.6	6.7	6.9
Current account bal/GDP (%)	−9.0	−12.0	−8.5	−11.0	−10.6	−10.6	−11.3
South Africa							
GDP at market prices (2000 $)[b]	1.8	5.0	5.4	5.1	4.2	4.4	4.8
Current account bal/GDP (%)	−0.2	−4.0	−6.5	−7.3	−8.9	−8.3	−7.5
Sudan							
GDP at market prices (2000 $)[b]	5.7	8.3	9.3	11.1	10.3	9.7	8.1
Current account bal/GDP (%)	−6.7	−9.4	−13.5	−10.3	−8.3	−7.8	−9.1

(*Continues*)

Table A.18 (*Continued*)

Country/indicator	1991–2000[a]	2005	2006	2007	Forecast 2008	2009	2010
Swaziland							
GDP at market prices (2000 $)[b]	3.1	2.4	2.8	2.2	1.9	1.8	1.9
Current account bal/GDP (%)	−2.4	−3.3	−2.3	1.2	−1.8	−2.2	−2.9
Tanzania							
GDP at market prices (2000 $)[b]	2.9	7.4	6.7	7.1	6.9	7.3	7.1
Current account bal/GDP (%)	−12.5	−7.1	−13.6	−14.5	−14.9	−14.3	−13.5
Togo							
GDP at market prices (2000 $)[b]	2.2	2.8	4.1	2.3	2.8	3.1	3.3
Current account bal/GDP (%)	−8.5	−12.3	−9.4	−10.8	−11.5	−11.4	−11.3
Uganda							
GDP at market prices (2000 $)[b]	6.8	6.6	5.4	5.9	6.0	6.3	6.9
Current account bal/GDP (%)	−7.0	−4.4	−9.2	−9.7	−12.2	−12.4	−12.3
Zambia							
GDP at market prices (2000 $)[b]	0.7	5.2	6.2	5.9	6.3	6.1	5.9
Current account bal/GDP (%)	−10.5	−8.5	−2.5	−5.3	−6.0	−6.3	−7.7
Zimbabwe							
GDP at market prices (2000 $)[b]	0.9	−6.5	−4.2	−6.3	−4.9	−2.1	−2.1
Current account bal/GDP (%)	−7.5	28.9	32.3	55.3	79.5	34.2	35.8

Source: World Bank.
Notes: Growth and current account figures presented here are World Bank projections and may differ from targets contained in other Bank documents. Liberia, Somalia, and São Tomé and Principe are not forecast owing to data limitations. — Not available.
a. Growth rates over intervals are compound averages; growth contributions, ratios, and the GDP deflator are averages.
b. GDP is measured in constant 2000 $.

private consumption spending. And postelection anxieties in Kenya are expected to take a toll on economic growth, above all on tourism and business investment. Political tensions in Kenya are likely to have a limited impact on the landlocked countries in the region, as transport disruptions—which already created supply shortages and resulted in higher prices for imported goods—proved to be short-lived.

Inflation will accelerate in a large number of Sub-Saharan African countries in 2008, fueled by surges in food prices, linked to sharp increases in internationally traded food prices, as well as higher domestic prices stemming from drought conditions in some regions. Stubbornly high crude oil prices are also playing a significant role in fueling inflation, although the second-round inflationary impacts are less clear at this stage, as indicated by relatively subdued core inflation. Inflationary pressures are expected to subside in 2009 along with food and fuel prices, which will still remain at elevated levels by historical standards.

Risks and uncertainties
Risks for Sub-Saharan Africa's growth lie mainly to the downside and include a sharper-than-expected slowdown in the global economy, with negative consequences for export growth and investment on the real side and weaker commodity prices on the nominal side; increased volatility in the international financial system, and increased risk aversion among international investors.

This last risk is particularly relevant for South Africa, which runs a significant current account deficit, traditionally financed by portfolio investment. In recent years 85 percent of South Africa's current account deficit was financed by portfolio investments, but that plummeted to 38 percent during the final quarter of 2007 (figure A.17). Unwillingness to continue providing short-term flows could put pressure on the rand, as has happened in the past, in turn pushing inflation up and prompting the Reserve Bank to hike interest rates. Additional risks to the growth outturn stem from a worsening electricity crisis in several countries in the region, including South Africa; this crisis threatens to undermine output in the manufacturing and mining sectors in particular. Though political turmoil and social tensions have abated in many countries ridden by instability in the past, the risk of relapse or even ignition of new skirmishes persists, as proven by recent clashes in Kenya and the uncertain election outcome in Zimbabwe. These tensions could carry economic

Figure A.17 Foreign portfolio flows coverage of South Africa's current account deficit

Portfolio flows, % of GDP   *Current account, % of GDP*

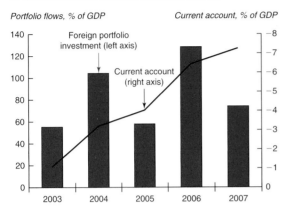

Source: Reserve Bank of South Africa.

spillover effects for landlocked neighbors and trading partners.

Finally, surging food prices are a heavy burden on the urban poor and have already led to violent street protests in several countries in Africa, including Burkina Faso, Cameroon, Côte d'Ivoire, and Senegal. In response, some governments have reduced or removed import tariffs on staple imports and cut taxes on basic products, actions that increase the risk that other government spending needed to support growth will have to be reduced.

Notes

1. The Europe and Central Asia region comprises 23 developing countries. It can be further divided into CEE, CIS and Turkey. CEE stands for Central and Eastern Europe, comprising Albania, Bulgaria, Croatia, Hungary, Latvia, Lithuania, the former Yugoslav Republic of Macedonia, Poland, Romania, and the Slovak Republic. CIS is the Commonwealth of Independent States, including Armenia, Azerbaijan, Belarus, Georgia, Kazakhstan, the Kyrgyz Republic, Moldova, the Russian Federation, Ukraine, and Uzbekistan. According to the World Bank's July 2007 definition, the Czech Republic and Estonia are now high-income countries and are thus not included in the calculation of aggregates for the region or CEE. They may, however, appear in the discussion to facilitate understanding and comparison within the region.

2. The following subregions include these countries (notice that countries can belong to more than one subregion): energy exporters (Argentina, Bolivia, Colombia, the Dominican Republic, Ecuador, Mexico, Panama, and República Bolivariana de Venezuela); metal exporters (Antigua and Barbuda, Bolivia, Brazil, Chile, the Dominican Republic, Guyana, Jamaica, and Peru); agriculture exporters (Argentina, Belize, Dominica, Ecuador, Guatemala, Guyana, Honduras, Nicaragua, Panama, Paraguay, St. Lucia, St. Vincent and the Grenadines, and Uruguay); energy importers (Antigua and Barbuda, Belize, Dominica, Dominican Republic, El Salvador, Guatemala, Guyana, Honduras, Jamaica, Nicaragua, Panama, Paraguay, Peru, St. Lucia, and Uruguay).

3. For the purposes of *Global Development Finance 2008*, the low- and middle-income countries of the broader Middle East and North Africa region are included in aggregates and discussed in analysis. Developing oil exporters in the region include Algeria, the Islamic Republic of Iran, Oman, Syria, and the Republic of Yemen. A more diversified set of economies is comprised of the Arab Republic of Egypt, Jordan, Lebanon, Morocco, and Tunisia. Due to data limitations and uncertainties, Djibouti, Iraq and the West Bank and Gaza are not covered among the middle-income countries of the region. High-income countries, not considered directly in this analysis, include Bahrain, Kuwait, Qatar, Saudi Arabia, and the United Arab Emirates.

4. Annual national income and product account data for the region are reported in calendar years, although official country data are originally reported by fiscal year. This is done to simplify presentation across countries and with other regions, as fiscal years vary across the South Asian countries (primarily linked to the harvest year) and as most countries elsewhere report calendar year national income and product account data.

5. The share of undernourished in the total population of the South Asia region is estimated at close to 22 percent (2001–03), compared with a third of the population in Sub-Saharan Africa, and shares as low as about 6 percent in Europe and Central Asia. *Source:* United Nations Food and Agriculture Organization.

References

World Bank. 2007. *World Development Indicators*. Washington, DC: World Bank.

———. 2008. East Asia: Testing Times Ahead. East Asia and Pacific regional update, World Bank, Washington, DC. Available at siteresources.worldbank.org/.../Resources/550192-1207007015255/EAPUpdate_Apr08_fullreport.pdf.

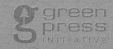